ADOPTION AND DISRUPTION

Rates, Risks, and Responses

MODERN APPLICATIONS OF SOCIAL WORK

An Aldine de Gruyter Series of Texts and Monographs

James K. Whittaker, Series Editor

Richard P. Barth and Marianne Berry, *Adoption and Disruption: Rates, Risks, and Responses*. 1988

Heather B. Weiss and Francine H. Jacobs (Eds.), *Evaluating Family Programs*. 1988

James Garbarino, Patrick E. Brookhouser, and Karen J. Authier, *Special Children, Special Risks: The Maltreatment of Children with Disabilities*. 1987

Roberta R. Greene, *Social Work with the Aged and Their Families*. 1986

James Garbarino, Cynthia J. Schellenbach, and Janet Sebes, *Troubled Youth, Troubled Families*. 1986

Robert M. Moroney, *Shared Responsibility*. 1986

Harry H. Vorrath and Larry K. Brendtro, *Positive Peer Culture*, Second Edition, 1985

Ralph E. Anderson and Irl Carter, *Human Behavior in the Social Environment*. Third Edition, 1984

Anthony M. Graziano and Kevin C. Mooney, *Children and Behavior Therapy*. 1984

Larry K. Brendtro and Arlin E. Ness, *Re-Educating Troubled Youth*. 1983

James K. Whittaker and James Garbarino, *Social Support Networks*. 1983

James Garbarino, *Children and Families in the Social Environment*. 1982

Norman A. Polansky, *Integrated Ego Psychology*. 1982

George Thorman, *Helping Troubled Families*. 1982

Steven P. Schinke (Ed.), *Behavioral Methods in Social Welfare*. 1981

James K. Whittaker, *Social Treatment: An Approach to Interpersonal Helping*. 1974

Thomas, Edwin J. (Ed.), Behavior Modification Procedure: A Sourcebook. 1974

James K. Whittaker and Albert E. Trieschman, *Children Away from Home: A Sourcebook of Residential Treatment*. 1972

Albert E. Trieschman, James K. Whittaker, and Larry K. Brendtro, *The Other 23 Hours*. 1969

ADOPTION AND DISRUPTION
Rates, Risks, and Responses

Richard P. Barth

Marianne Berry

ALDINE DE GRUYTER
New York

About the Authors

Richard P. Barth, a fost-adopt father, is Associate Professor, Associate Director of the Family Welfare Research Group, and Chairman of the School Social Work Program, in the School of Social Welfare at the University of California, Berkeley. He is Book Review Editor for the journal, *Children and Youth Services Review,* and Consulting Editor for the *Journal of Adolescent Research.* He is the author of "Social and Cognitive Treatment of Children and Adolescents."

Marianne Berry is a doctoral candidate in Social Welfare at the University of California, Berkeley. She is a Fellow of the American Association of University Women. She was previously a child welfare worker in Dallas, Texas, and has published extensively on the adoption of special-needs children, outcomes of children under permanency planning, and parent training in child welfare services.

ALDINE DE GRUYTER
A Division of Walter de Gruyter, Inc.
200 Saw Mill River Road
Hawthorne, New York 10532

Library of Congress Cataloging-in-Publication Data

Barth, Richard P., 1952-
    Adoption and disruption: rates, risks, and responses / Richard P. Barth, Marianne Berry.
        p. cm.—(Modern applications of social work)
    Bibliography: p.
    Includes index.
    ISBN 0-202-36049-0.   ISBN 0-202-36054-7 (pbk.)
    1. Older child adoption—United States.   I. Berry, Marianne.
II. Title.   III. Series.
HV875.55.B37 1988
362.7'34'0973—dc19   88-17640
                                                                               CIP

Printed in the United States of America
10 9 8 7 6 5 4 3 2 1

Dedicated with love to Nancy who graciously lends her strength, insight, and love for ventures like this book and to James and Catrina who are my most eye-opening and precious adventure. [RPB]

———

Dedicated with love to Barry, for his patience; to Jo, for her enthusiasm; and to Nandy, for his support. [MB]

CONTENTS

FOREWORD

James K. Whittaker

Speaking to his colleagues in mainstream child development research, Urie Bronfenbrenner (1979, 19–20) cautioned against the study of "development-out-of-context" aptly labeling it (and, by implication, much of then current developmental research) as "The science of the strange behavior of children in strange situations with strange adults for the briefest possible periods of time." His paradigm for study of the "ecology of human development" provided a much needed set of conceptual lenses for examining various levels of environment as they influenced and interacted with individual characteristics during the life course. Indeed, this splendid book by Barth and Berry is very much the sort of "development-in-context" investigation that Bronfenbrenner's argument calls for.

Painting on a smaller canvas and using their own empirical research as a base, the authors illuminate the multiple facets of older, special-needs adoption. Central to their many analyses are fundamental questions for child welfare policy and practice: For which children and which families, under what conditions are adoptive placements least likely to disrupt? What services or interventions delivered at what points in the adoption process might meliorate the effects of known risk factors? What, overall, is the value of adoption in society's genuine though, sometimes, antagonistic impulse to protect individual children while preserving family life?

The authors move easily and often between the worlds of policy, practice, and research in child and family welfare. Their own research delineates—better than any other to date—the particular factors associated with successful and unsuccessful older, special-needs adoptions. They take great pains to separate what we know and what we need to know in adoption research: future investigators in this area are considerably in their debt. But these same authors do not hide behind the general disclaimer, "more research needed" and offer several *potentially* fruitful suggestions for improving present adoptions practice with special needs children. I found particularly intriguing their notion of intensive adoption preservation services and specific parental stratagems for handling problematic child behavior postplacement: clinicians as well as researchers will find much of value here. At quite another level, their message concerns one particular aspect of what society's investment ought to be in improving and supporting the capacity of families to socialize their children: it is therefore, fundamentally, a book about the allocation of national resources for the future of our children and for our society.

PREFACE

Older child adoption has been around for more than a century but has received relatively little in the way of book-length treatments. Its time is due. Child welfare's permanency planning revolution is becoming institutionalized and concerned professionals are again reviewing all elements of the service system for abused and neglected children. Permanency planning legislation arose in much part because of grave concerns about growing numbers of children in foster care. Facilitating older child adoption was a major focus of that legislation. Yet, attention to this concern has been washed over by some initial success in reducing foster care use and by a more recent tidal wave of child abuse reports which are riveting the nation's attention on questions about who should and can be served in the child welfare system.

In this book we will focus a critical amount of attention on children who are in the child welfare system but have the chance to leave by joining adoptive families. Our investigations of older child adoptions and disruptions during the last 4 years, have increasingly convinced us that adoption is far more than an answer to the question of how to reduce the foster care census. Indeed, adoption is only a partial answer to that narrow question. Older child adoption is a far better, but not perfect, answer to the larger question of how to improve the lives of children in foster care. We add additional evidence to an argument we began elsewhere (Barth & Berry, 1986) that whereas foster care provides children and youth with protection and many developmental benefits that they would not receive at home, it is still no match for older child adoption. In these pages, we put dollars and sense into our argument and build a strong case for intensive adoption preservation services.

We planned the book to be sure that, as busy as our readers are, they will want to read more than the last few paragraphs of the last chapter to obtain our full story. Research on older child adoption is complex and linking it to practice and policy is challenging. Each chapter has summary material which is not merely repeated in the concluding chapter. The first three chapters address issues that are larger than the question of how many and what types of adoptions disrupt. The evolution of older child adoption calls for a greater effort and we attempted to provide a policy and historical framework for the study in Chapter 1, begin to build a case for preserving older child adoptions by offering a rough hewn but unique analysis of the value of adoption in Chapter 2, and articulate the tasks of the adjustment to adoption in Chapter 3.

Part II, beginning with Chapter 4, reviews prior adoption research and informs the reader of the design of our study. Chapter 5 describes the findings from the first part of the research and offers estimates of disruption rates and a disruption prediction model. Chapters 6 through 9 present more specific findings from our interviews with adoptive parents and social workers involved with 120 high-risk placements—about half of which disrupted. These chapters review features of placement preparation, child, family, and postplacement service characteristics related to disrupted or stable placements. Chapter 10 offers a summary statistical model.

Part III concludes with implications of the study. These are not summary chapters in the pure sense of repeating what has been said in the conclusions of each of the prior chapters. We admit to repetition of several key themes, but have used these chapters to allow us to venture additional ideas that follow from our study and that might be useful to practitioners, administrators, and policymakers. In Chapter 11, that adventure results in a description of the path from preplacement to disruption—an endeavor that draws on many case histories. In Chapter 12 we offer a range of suggestions for practice that include guidelines on referral and treatment for families in adoption crises as well as other practical matters related to information sharing, discussing disruption with adoptive applicants, and facilitating peer support for adopting families. In the concluding chapter, we cost out the price of a disruption to the agency and contrast that cost with intensive adoption preservation services. We also argue for changes in policy and practice about postplacement visits, subsidies, and single-parent transracial adoptions. In all, we provide ample evidence that disruptions are relatively infrequent, somewhat preventable, and very worth preventing. Despite this occasional outcome, older child adoption may represent the best value of any program now existing for our society's at-risk children.

Chapters 4 through 10 and many of the conclusions that follow, are based on a 2-year study conducted by Children's Garden and the University of California, Berkeley, School of Social Welfare for the Children's Bureau, Administration for Children, Youth, and Families, Office of Human Development Services, U. S. Department of Health and Human Services, Grant #90-PD10075. Regina Kahn Goodfield was Principal Investigator, Mary Lou Carson was Clinical Consultant, Richard P. Barth was Research Consultant, Rogers Yoshikami was Project Coordinator, and Marianne Berry was Research Associate in that study. Penelope Maza and Soledad Arenas Sambrano were the Project Officers at ACYF. Charles Gershenson was instrumental in obtaining support for our efforts to double our sample of families who experienced disruptions. The dedication and skill of Ginny Goodfield, Mary Lou Carson, Rogers Yoshikami, and the Children's Garden staff in overseeing the study were extraordinary. We also learned a great amount from them about older child adoption.

The authors thank Peter Breen, Jim Brown, Barbara Bull, Al Colon, Barry Feinberg, Rebecca Dominy, Charles Gershenson, Joan Hart, Joan Hirose, Serena Jones, B. J. Kane, Carole Sorenson, Cindy Tapp, and David Webber for a wide range of invaluable contributions to the research. The project could not have been completed without the extensive cooperation of many adoptive parents and administrators, staff, and social workers in host agencies who gave their precious time to be interviewed. We cannot name all the important contributors to the study but want to acknowledge the social workers who were liaisons between their agencies and the project. We are deeply indebted for the considerable efforts of: Joan Alderson, Ron Anderson, Susan Archibald, Rina Baker, Doe Cherry, Mary Eldridge, David Foster, Nancy Hold, Berthalee Kuderna, Sherry Marx, Ruth Miller, Pat Montgomery, Millie Munding, Don Pilcher, Tim Prince, Brian Quinn, Patti Rahiser, Pat Reynolds, Connie Rinne, Tom Sansone, Elizabeth Sasek, Verena Schumacher, and Halcea Valdez.

We are also indebted to Dean Harry Specht and the staff of the School of Social Welfare, and the Committee on Research of the University of California at Berkeley for their support. We warmly acknowledge friends and colleagues with whom we discussed adoptions, data analysis, and theory: among them, Helen Ahn, Mary Lou Carson, Ginny Goodfield, Jo Knox, Bessie Richmond, Lonnie Snowden, and Michael Pesce. Nancy Dickinson, Sid Frankel, and Brian Simmons read and helped us improve earlier drafts of several chapters. Shelley Leavitt at Behavioral Sciences Institute provided case material on intensive adoption preservation. We also thank Jim Whittaker for his support and guidance. Sharon Ikami deserves glowing praise for her work preparing this manuscript. Despite the demands of that job she somehow managed to be a wonderful friend and source of encouragement. The love of our birth families: Gary Piccione, Marilyn Piccione, Gary Barth, and Paul Piccione (RB) and Richard Berry, Rae Ann Berry, David Berry, and Mandy Berry (MB) sustained us often.

We were frequently stirred by the spirit of concern and self-examination shown by the social workers we interviewed. Their interest in expanding available knowledge augurs well for the future of adoption—we hope this book justifies their efforts. The parents who gave of their precious time to meet with us also inspired us. Whether their placements lasted or disrupted, they showed commitment, courage, and creativity. Although most of our interviews were long and done in the evenings, we routinely left invigorated. Adoption disruption is a painful subject—one carved out the solid hope of having a consistently happy family. Our study and others conclude that most adoptions approximate this hope—disruptions are haunting but rare. We cringe to consider that the book's focus on difficult and disrupted adoptions will wrongly persuade the reader that older child adoptions are generally exhausting and regrettable. Whereas virtually all parents live, at times, with fatigue and doubt, we do not hold that this is categorically greater for parents who adopt older children—that depends on many issues which we address. We have written this book to clarify the value of older child adoptions and to sustain and multiply that value for children and their families.

Richard P. Barth

Marianne Berry

I

Older Child Adoption Now

1

Overview of Older Child Adoption and Disruption

Child welfare has experienced sweeping policy and practice changes in recent years. Although just a link in the continuous evolution of services for children in need of protection, these changes are dramatic. One significant result of these changes has been a shift in the function, form, and importance of adoption. Older child adoption has become arguably the most essential component of successful child welfare services.

The Adoption Assistance and Child Welfare Act of 1980 (P.L. 96-272) mandated that child welfare agencies implement preplacement preventive services, programs to reunify placed children with their biological families, subsidized adoption, and periodic case reviews of children in care. This legislation, focusing on permanency and planning, was in part a reaction to indications that children were spending unnecessarily long periods in foster care, with no real plan for reunification with their families. The legislation was also a legal assertion of the child's right to a permanent home—a condition that child welfare professionals have long agreed is important to a child's development (Slingerland, 1916).

In describing the rationale for the new legislation, Senator Alan Cranston explained that "Our efforts from now on will be to reduce the foster care load by supporting programs that promise to restore children to their families, that prevent unnecessary foster care, or that promise the opportunity for adoption" (Congressional Record – Senate, June 13, 1980). The impact of permanency planning legislation since 1980 has been a decrease in the number of children in foster care, and an increase in the number of children legally freed from their parents for adoption (United States Department of Health and Human Services, 1984). In 1982 there were over 50,000 children legally free from their parents and waiting to be placed (Maza, 1983). Approximately 17,000 of these children had the specific permanent plan of adoption (Maximus, 1984). That year, approximately 14,400 older children were placed for adoption in the United States (Maximus, 1984). The

3

availability and placement of older children for adoption has greatly changed the historic purpose and scope of adoptions.

The child welfare "system" is actually a fragile weave of programs. The outcomes of efforts to prevent out-of-home placements, to reunify families, and to provide long-term care all depend on the quality of programs from which they receive children and to which they send them. Each program must work if the other programs are to do what they intend. Adoption is one such cornerstone. If older children in the child welfare system do not get adopted and stay adopted, then the rationale for moving quickly to terminate parental rights (after a determination that children cannot return home) is weakened. Indeed, the pressure to leave or return children to unsafe birth families is intensified when permanent adoptive homes are unavailable. Many agencies will not free children until a stable home is all but guaranteed. Without confidence in the benefits of terminating parental rights, judges lose the tenuous conviction to do so, time limits on foster care lose their significance, and mandates for speedy permanency planning become moot. To argue that successful services to promote older child adoption are the hub of effective child welfare services may be excessive. Still, they are critical. Special-needs adoption has been identified as a major contributor to reduced long-term foster care in studies of pilot permanency planning projects (e.g., Fein, Maluccio, Hamilton, & Ward, 1983; Lahti *et al.*, 1978; TenBroeck, 1981).

Yet these adoptions are risky. Older child adoption does not guarantee a blissful state of permanence. Adoptions that do disrupt and lead to a return to foster care are an affront to social workers, adoptive and birth families, and to children. Just as successful adoptions have substantial value and are cause for great satisfaction, rumors of climbing adoption disruption rates shake the faith and foundation of child welfare service providers. Before further describing disruption and its contributors, the current status of older child adoption is reviewed.

HISTORY OF OLDER CHILD ADOPTION

Moses is the best known adopted child. His placement was not trouble free, but was, at least, permanent. The earliest adoption laws are found in the Code of Hammurabi: "If a man takes a child in his name, adopts and raises him as a son, the grown-up man may not be demanded back" (cited in Sorosky, Baran, & Pannor, 1978). Franz Boas (1888) described older child adoption among the Central Eskimos: "if for any reason a man is unable to provide for his family or if a woman cannot do her household work, the children are adopted by a relative, or a friend, who considers them as his own children" (p. 580). These adoptions were considered permanent and the adopted child was considered a member of the family with all rights and privileges. No mention is made of adoption breakdowns or children seeking to return to their birth families. Birth families could, however, reclaim mistreated children.

In the United States, the process of older child adoption dates back, at least, to Charles Loring Brace (1859). Foster care and adoptions were intertwined in the late 19th century. The middle class leaders of child care agencies expected to save both souls and money by placing poor children in good homes (Clement, 1979). Foster placements were also based on the belief that they were preferable to institutional care, which trained children to be dependent and not self-sufficient. Placing agencies were concerned less with the individual problems of the child than they were with the social and moral problems he or she might eventually pose in the larger community. Many children were placed out by agencies after their birth families relinquished the child to the agency and gave up all rights to visit or correspond with the youngster. The most common reason for placement was not protection but poverty.

Although foster care placements were permanent, it was difficult to do what was often necessary for the safety of the child: remove him or her on the mere suspicion of ill treatment. At that time, as such, this basis for placement disruption was quite limited. As late as the middle of the 20th century, children were often not removed from placements characterized by abuse and neglect (Witmer et al., 1963). (From that perspective, adoption disruptions signal heightened attention to the rights of placed children.) When placements did fail they more often involved older children (K.E. Nelson, 1986). Brace (1872) estimated a 2% failure rate (he counted as failures only children who committed crimes or were put in almshouses and did not count the many placements that ended as a result of the child's voluntary departure by running away) for children placed under the age of 15 and 4% for those placed after age 15. Brace came to recommend that family placement be restricted to children under 14. The policy of older child adoption lost popularity after recognition of the error of placing children who were not voluntarily relinquished by their birth parents. For many decades thereafter, adoption was primarily limited to infant adoptions.

Legislation for adoption practices began in the United States in the 1850s (Whitmore, 1876). Statutes varied on several accounts but all reflected concern that adoption promote the welfare of the child. Concern that the adopted child's welfare could not be adequately protected without the oversight of public agencies arose later but is most clearly reflected in the report of the Wisconsin Children's Code Commission (cited in Breckinridge, 1934).

Adoption proceedings are, for the adoptable child, next to birth itself, the most important single transaction in his life. It is imperative, therefore that the child at this time have the benefit of the most thorough and careful work in the procedure that is to determine his whole future. Essential to this is the need that the court shall have for its guidance full and complete facts about the child and the adopting parents. This can be secured only through skillful investigation by completely trained persons.

Regulations requiring social investigations of prospective adoptive parents and trial placement periods in prospective adoptive homes were written between 1923 and 1933 (Heisterman, 1935). A few states also required visits by agents of the state child welfare department. The mandates of the visits were rarely clarified, although most contained some language similar to that found in Wisconsin code: "when the court is satisfied that the home of the petitioner and the child are suited to each other" [Wisconsin General Laws 1932 (Ter. ed.), C.210, Sec. 5A]. In some states, like Massachusetts, agents working for an institution that was expressly engaged in child care services could place children and have the waiting period and visits waived.

The earliest laws regarding the annulment (or disruption) of adoption were also established in the 1920s (Heisterman, 1935). Annulments were conditional on the adopted child manifesting feeble-mindedness, insanity, epilepsy, or venereal disease from conditions that existed prior to the adoption and then unknown to the adopting parent. In a few states, the adoption could be revoked on the grounds that such an action would promote the welfare of the child or on the basis of proof of bad character of the adoptive parent or parental neglect of the adopted child.

Older child adoption never fully ceased, but was not again heralded until 1949, when Children's Home Society began a "new type of child care program in North Carolina to provide ways and means of placing older children, in institutions, in family homes for adoption" (Weeks, 1953, p. i). This effort was partly in response to waiting lists in orphanages. Weeks (1953) reports that of the first 10 placements "only three of the children placed so far proved unable to adjust to adoptive homes;" this is perhaps not the first description of an adoption disruption rate, but seems to be the first recorded in the United States. Weeks' appraisal that the 30% disruption rate is no cause for concern—given the advantages that the other seven adopted children enjoyed—is noteworthy.

FORMS OF ADOPTION

Adoption is possible today through a variety of means and can involve different types of agencies and auspices, each with unique procedures and requirements. Although this book almost exclusively concerns older child adoptions, an overview of adoptions places older child and special-needs adoptions in the larger sphere of child welfare services, and clarifies how current adoption guidelines may contribute to disruption.

Adoption creates or expands a family through the legal severance of biological ties of a child to his birth parents and the establishment of new ties to an adoptive family. Until recently, formal adoption was viewed as a means to providing infertile couples with the ability to raise a family. The decrease in healthy infants available for adoption, coupled with the increase in older children freed for adoption as a result of permanency planning legislation, has resulted in the increased rate of older child adoptions.

Regardless of the type of child in question, adoptions follow some general guidelines based on the premise that every child has a right to a family, and that the child's needs are paramount (Child Welfare League of America, 1973). Arising from this fundamental right are other agency principles: that efforts should be made to find a family similar to the child's racial, ethnic, cultural and religious background; that finality of adoption be made as soon as possible (after a sufficient trial of the placement's viability); that every party have options and assistance in weighing these options; that confidentiality be ensured as far as possible; and that agency services be available before and after placement.

Generally, adoptions are grouped into four categories: relinquishment, independent, intercountry, and stepparent. Relinquishment adoptions are those adoptions following the legal severance of parental rights to the child. Independent adoptions occur when the parent(s) places the child directly with the adoptive family of their choice without an agency serving as an intermediary. Intercountry adoptions involve the adoption of foreign-born children by United States. Stepparent adoptions involve the children of one's spouse. These adoptions differ from most other adoptions, and are most like foster child adoptions, by involving the adoption of a child already in the home. Independent, stepparent, and intercountry adoptions are seldom reported to disrupt, but without comprehensive adoption statistics their precise level of stability is unknown. Disruption rates usually refer only to relinquishment adoptions which presumably have the highest rates.

In most states, stepparent adoptions are the most prevalent type of adoption. Of the three remaining types of adoptions, relinquishment and independent adoptions are about equally numerous. In California, relinquishment adoptions represented 48% of nonstepparent adoptions in the 1985–1986 fiscal year, whereas independent adoptions comprised 43%, (State of California Statistical Services Branch, 1987). Nationally, almost 9000 foreign-born children were adopted in the United States in 1985–1986 (INS, 1987)—this is roughly 10% of placements.

Permanency planning legislation hoped to increase the number of relinquishment adoptions, and the percentage of this type of adoption has increased. In California since 1981–1982; relinquishment adoptions increased from 1991 to 2489 in 1985–1986, independent adoptions also increased from 1823 to 2220 (see Fig. 1.1). Relinquishment adoptions do seem to be increasing, but adoption statistics, especially at the national level, inspire little confidence (Maza, 1984).

Independent adoptions held steady at about 20% of all adoptions in the 1960s and 1970s (Meezan, Katz, & Russo, 1978) but as seen above, have increased recently. Independent adoptions are usually more expensive, but facilitate choice for both adoptive and birth parents. A few states still outlaw independent adoptions.

THE RECENT EVOLUTION OF
OLDER CHILD ADOPTIONS

When adoptions were focused on finding infants for infertile couples, healthy babies were prime candidates for adoptions, and older children or children with special needs were not considered adoptable. The increase in older children moving out of foster care over the last decade has changed this practice, and more and more older children are considered adoptable. We do not know the exact effect of premanency planning practice on all adoptions because national data on older child adoptions since 1975 is scarce. Data from individual states offer some impressions of the range of practices and results. California places about 4000 children for adoption every year. Colorado (State of Colorado, 1985) placed 4150 children in 1981 and 3531 children in 1982. Alaska (State of Alaska, 1985) made 853 adoptive placements in 1983, and 85% of these involved children aged 1 or over. Mississippi (Mississippi State Department of Public Welfare, 1986) placed only 175 children in 1984, and 87% of these were aged 2 or over at the time of placement. Alabama made 4450 placements in 1981, 3268 in 1982, and 3469 in 1983 (State of Alabama, 1985). New York (New York State Department of Social Services, 1986) made 2626 adoptive placements in 1983; 90% were of children aged 3 or over. Older child adoptions are a large proportion of all publicly supervised adoptions.

These adoptions are often informally classified by some characteristic of the parents or child. For example, foster adoption refers to the adoption of a child by his/her foster family. Older child adoptions involve the adoption of children aged 3 or over. Special-needs adoptions typically involve children older than 3, minority children, handicapped children, emotionally or intellectually impaired children, or groups of siblings of three or more (State of California Department of Social Services, 1984). Views differ on whether minority children who are younger than 3 and not otherwise handicapped should be considered special needs. The North American Center on

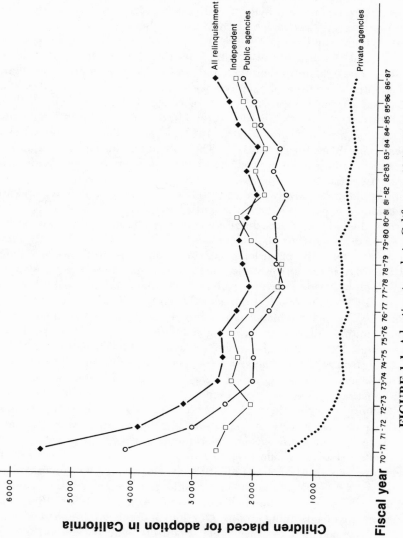

FIGURE 1.1: Adoption trends in California, 1970–1987.

Children placed for adoption in California

6000

5000

4000

3000

2000

1000

All relinquishment

Independent

Public agencies

Private agencies

Fiscal year   70-71 71-72 72-73 73-74 74-75 75-76 76-77 77-78 78-79 79-80 80-81 81-82 82-83 83-84 84-85 85-86 86-87

Adoption offers a more limited definition of special-needs children: black children over 10, white children over 13, emotionally disturbed or mentally retarded children of all ages, physically handicapped children, or sibling groups of three or more (Shyne & Schroeder, 1978). These are also called "hard-to-place" children or "children who wait" due to the typical placement history of these children.

Transracial or transcultural adoptions involve the adoption of a child by parents of a race different than the child, and are mostly found among older child adoptions. Transracial adoptive placements are currently used only in exceptional circumstances as a result of concerns that the child will be denied exposure to his or her own cultural heritage and preparation to cope with racism—a position espoused in 1972 and maintained by the National Association of Black Social Workers. The bulk of transracial placements are by foster parents who have privileged legal status for adopting children in their own home.

Sibling adoptions involve placing siblings together in one home and are most common in older child adoptions. Unlike transracial placements, there is a great diversity of practice regarding sibling adoptions due to opposing views about the extent to which this is best for the children. Some professionals value the provision of continuity and support between siblings (Ward, 1978; Carney, 1976), while others propose that breaking maladaptive patterns of behavior between siblings may offer them greater benefit (Jewett, 1978). Almost all professionals agree that the use of sibling placements depends on many factors. The placement of large sibling groups (three or more children) is encouraged in some literature (Ward, 1978), while others document the instability of such adoptions (Kadushin & Seidl, 1971). Regardless, finding adoptive parents willing to accept two or more children at once may lengthen the child's wait for a home—a disservice which must be weighed in every case.

In California, during the 1981–1982 fiscal year, 77% of all relinquishment adoptive placements were of special-needs children. Special needs adoptions were 84% of public agency placements and 56% of private agency placements (State of California Department of Social Services, 1984a). Specifically, one-third of the 1981–1982 placements in California involved children aged 4 or over. One-half of the children placed were racially mixed or of minority race, while one-half were white. Almost one-fifth (18%) of all placements involved sibling groups. One-fourth of the children had a health condition that affected the placement (State of California Department of Social Services, 1984b). Special-needs adoptions are thus increasing and are the key to child welfare's plans to increase permanency for children.

All of these categories of special needs identify characteristics of the child or family that make placement of the child more difficult than in traditional infant adoptions. They may create the need for a special type of adoptive home and may lengthen the child's wait for adoption. With the increased wait comes the double-edged sword of increased time for preparation and the increased delay and uncertainty of permanence for the child. This study will examine both effects on the outcome of the placement.

With the trend in adoptions shifting from infants to older special-needs children has come a shift in the philosophy and purpose of adoption. The recent legislation toward permanency planning recognizes the importance of permanent homes for children. "The primary purpose of adoption is to provide a permanent family for children who cannot be cared for by their own biological parents. Therefore, the child's welfare, her needs, and her interests are the basic determinants of good adoption practice" (Kadushin, 1984, pp. 3–4). With this shift to an emphasis on the child's needs and right to permanence, practitioners are recognizing that no child who needs a permanent home should be considered unadoptable (Cole, 1984), and efforts are made to find a permanent home for every child that needs one. These efforts are very gradually becoming more successful with evolving adjustments in many aspects of the adoption process: especially, eligibility, matching, recruitment, and postplacement services.

Adoptive Parent Eligibility

Often, couples considering adoption first apply to a private agency to adopt an infant, and learn that infants are scarce, competition among applicants is high, and the waiting period is counted in years. Competition and waiting for an older child with special needs are not nearly as forbidding, and parents often consider this option. In a study prior to permanency planning (Chambers, 1970), over one-half of the sample of adoptive applicants were willing to adopt a child with at least one major physical handicap. Applicants were questioned concerning only one handicap at a time, however, and today's adoptive children often have multiple special needs. Only 10% of the applicants were willing to adopt a child over 5 years old.

Once the applicants have decided to adopt a special-needs child, the agency (optimally) tries to find the child they can best parent. Adoption agencies have a general set of guidelines for selecting parents for adoptive children. The recent emphasis on special-needs adoptions has placed the importance on finding a home for the child, not a child for a home (Kadushin, 1984). While the interests of the parents are certainly considered, the needs of the child are paramount. Increasingly, professionals are stressing the need for creativity and flexibility in the assessment and acceptance of adoptive parents. Some of the general guidelines follow below.

AGE OF PARENTS.   Older parents may want older children. With the greater length of time couples are waiting to begin having children, and the long waiting lists for infant adoption, a couple could be approaching 40 before they are aware of their infertility, or of the long delays in adoptions. Social workers indicate that "older" parents are most suitable for adopting developmentally disabled children (Coyne & Brown, 1986). The traditional 40-year-old age limit for adoptive parents also excludes older people that may have already raised some children, and want to complete their families. A recent letter in *Ebony* described a couple who adopted an older child upon retirement. The mean age of 927 parents adopting older children in this study from 1980 to 1984 was around 40 years old, with a range from 22 to 74, indicating that, among public agencies, anyway, the age limit is relaxed.

RELIGION.   While most professionals agree that the child be allowed spiritual and ethical development, religious matching is increasingly disfavored (Child Welfare League of America, 1978). In California, only 24% of older child placements from 1980 to 1984 matched the child and parents on religion. Concern about religious matching has declined to the point that data on religion is no longer collected, so it is unknown how many of these matches were intentional. A few agencies still require that the child and parent be of the same religion. As recently as 1974, there were 35 states which had such "religious protection" statutes (Gollub, 1974).

INFERTILITY AND CHILDLESSNESS.   Families with and without children adopt older children. We have moved far forward of the days when a note from a physician indicating infertility was required by the agency. Among this sample of California older child adoptions, 73% of adoptive families had other children (natural, foster, and other) in the home at the time of placement. Many adoption workers are still concerned, however, that some adoptive families are making a career of adoption, and refuse to place a fourth, fifth, or sixth child with a willing family. In order to best serve waiting parents, a few agencies still require that the adoptive couple be infertile, and that no other biological children be present in the home.

SUFFICIENT AND STEADY INCOME.   Income requirements no longer narrow the parent pool to upper- and middle-class parents. The availability of subsidies illustrates the recognition that low income should not be a barrier to adoption. Middle-income families are viewed as most desirable in some reports of social worker preference (Coyne & Brown, 1986), but many workers find more affluent families appealing. In this study, the reported annual earned family incomes of the 927 adoptive families ranged from $0 to $170,569, with a mean income of $27,039. Of families adopting older children in California between 1980 and 1984, 54% were to receive subsidies. The concern among legislators and administrators about "paying people to be parents" has not been vanquished, however, and federal law requires a search for a family that does not need a subsidy before a child is placed in a home that does.

SAME RACE. This is a controversial requirement. Many practitioners feel that children need the cultural education provided by members of their own race, while other practitioners stress the necessity of finding the right adoptive parents regardless of race. Although the current Child Welfare League of America (1978) policy is that children should not be denied placement if other-race parents are able and willing to adopt, many agencies choose not to risk censorship by black adoption agencies and the publicity of transracial adoptions. Of older child adoptions in Northern and Central California between 1980 and 1984, 80% matched on race. The restrictions on matching parent and child on race are less rigid in public agencies. Race matching is highest for white children, regardless of agency, followed by blacks, and Latinos (State of California Department of Social Services, 1984b). Recent case law is raising new concerns about the legality of placement decisions based primarily on race.

MOTHER'S EMPLOYMENT. The requirement of a full-time mother at home severely narrowed the field of possible parents, and in the case of older children who are at school all day, is completely unnecessary. In fact, in this study of California older child adoptions, 43% of adoptive mothers were working at the time of the placement and 45% planned to be working after placement.

While these requirements might have been genuinely helpful in reducing the field of applicants during the infant adoption boom, they were also promulgated to protect children from unsuitable parents. Instead, they limited the placement of special-needs children. A bigger pool of parents is needed for these waiting children, and is certainly not attainable without flexible requirements. Requirements for adoptive parents have typically been more flexible in public agencies than in private ones. Public agencies supervise adoptions with parents with lower incomes, lower education levels, advanced ages, and more children in the home than do private agencies (State of California Department of Social Services, 1984b).

UNCONVENTIONAL FAMILIES. Agencies are beginning to recognize the potential of unconventional adoptive parents, such as single parents, foster parents, and working-class parents. In the 1983–1984 fiscal year in California, 14% of adoptions were to single parents. Virtually all of these were supervised by public agencies (97%), and most involved adoptive mothers (84%) rather than fathers. An early study of single-parent adoptions (Branham, 1970) found that these applicants have, by self-selection, high levels of emotional maturity, tolerance of frustration, and independence while still linked to a supportive network of relatives.

In our study of older child adoptions in California from 1980 to 1984, 68% of older child placements overall were foster parent adoptions. These increased from 59% in 1980 to 72% in 1984. The median income of adoptive parents in California in 1983–1984 was $27,375. This was lower among public agency adopters ($25,802) than among private agency adopters ($32,029). Fifteen percent of placements were to single parents, especially mothers. Almost one-half of older child adoptive families had working mothers. Clearly, families that adopt older special-needs children are not the stereotypical adoptive parents of not so long ago, causing some concern that a lowering of standards will result in less stable placements and poorer outcomes for children. One response to this concern is a new emphasis on the matching of parents and child.

Matching

With the shift from placing infants to special-needs children, matching of child and family compatability instead of physical similarity is recognized as preferable. Families are thus not judged on some absolute scale of parenting skills or acceptability, but rather are assessed in relation to the ability to meet a particular child's needs (Fitzgerald, Murcer, & Murcer, 1982). In this way, agencies hope to better meet the needs of these older, special children, while opening up adoption to families that could otherwise not afford or meet the requirements for adoption. That every agency and social worker can determine a good match is uncertain. The history of adoption and foster care research is rich with unsuccessful attempts to identify critical components of a good match.

Assessments of many dimensions are made of both parents and child, to find the best fit between parent and child. The parents, when applying, are also asked many questions covering the myriad aspects of family life. This assessment is based on the recognition that different children, especially special-needs children, will require different styles of family life. While some children may need extra parental attention, others may need to be more independent.

Agencies consider many qualities and abilities of parents. This broad brush assessment is partly due to uncertainty about what matters in adoption and partly due to recognition of its complexity. Emotional maturity, which includes the ability to solve problems and adjust expectations, is judged to be important (age and previous parenting experience are often used as indicators). Agencies usually assess the marital relationship, and try to evaluate whether it could continue to flourish without the addition of a child. Parents are asked about their feelings about children, and to assess whether adoption is purely a selfish act or, worse in the eyes of some workers, is only an altruistic one. It is considered important to know whether the decision to adopt is a mutual one and if the motivation to adopt is based on the parents' needs for a family, or whether it might be to replace a dead child or to save a marriage (Child Welfare League of America, 1973). Yet agencies do not have good measures of most of the parental qualities of concern nor evidence to ensure that those qualities are related to better outcomes for children.

A thorough assessment of the child includes information about "the facts of his birth, his health, his early development, his manner of responding to people and situations, any deviations from the normal range of development, and his experiences before the decision was made to place him for adoption" (Child Welfare League of America, 1973, p. 9). It also includes a medical examination, a psychological examination, and pertinent family history. The child's history of abuse is also considered critical (McInturf, 1986). In addition to these analytical indexes of need, the assessment includes the child's current feelings and beliefs about their situation, and future needs.

Once assessments are made, the parents are matched to the child's needs. Optimally, in special-needs adoption, a partnership is created between parent and agency to allow the parents to decide for themselves on this type of adoption. This partnership assumes that the worker fills the role of educator about the child's condition, behavior, and prognosis and also informs the parents about the skills and resources they will need for a special-needs child. Adaptations are made on both sides, as the agency offers children and the parents adjust their standards. Parents are encouraged to "stretch," or adapt their expectations concerning a child's handicaps and needs, in order to shorten their wait for a child (Nelson, 1985). This stretching of standards during the application process if taken too far can result in strained relationships during the trial period, usually a year, between placement and legal finalization. Nevertheless, stretching is an integral part of the matching process, as applicants discover just what children are available for adoption. In the placement decision, the agency predicts that the parents can meet the child's current and future needs, and the child will be able to adjust to this particular family. Given their central role in older child adoption, the effects of matching and stretching on the outcome of the adoption have not been adequately tested, and will be addressed in this study.

Recruitment

Among the 17,000 children free from their parents, and waiting to be placed for adoption in 1984, almost one half were 2 years old or older, and 39% were black (Maximus, 1984). With the need for matching and an increase in the pool of adoptive children, adoption exchanges and networks have begun to fill the need for adoptive parents. Exchanges serve as matching resources, which list children waiting for adoption, and their special needs, and parents seeking to adopt. Nationwide exchange systems, such as the National Adoption Information Exchange System, increase the effectiveness of these regional exchanges (United States Department of Health and Human Services, 1980).

In addition to exchanges, parent recruitment is also effected through community education. There are two types of community recruitment. First, the broad education of the community can reach general groups of potential parents that may never have considered adoption. The One Church, One Child program that involves black churches exemplifies this method. Other agencies sponsor periodic recruitment drives aimed toward encouraging blacks to adopt. These drives may consist of evening meetings advertised in local newspapers. The second mode of recruitment is more individualized, to find the right parents for a particular child. This is attempted through the use of the media, television or newspapers, to present a particular child and a description of his strengths and needs. These media campaigns are modestly successful, but expensive.

Corporate and other group newsletters have begun to address older child adoptions, with the hope of interesting group or company members in adoption of these children (Walton, 1985). Although these newsletters have not had much success, they are only a very recent development, and agencies are fine-tuning their efforts to better reach their audience.

FOSTER PARENT ADOPTIONS AND FOST-ADOPTION.   Recruitment efforts are eased by allowing foster parents to adopt. Foster parent adoptions increased in the 1970s with the growth in the numbers of special-needs children freed for adoption, without an associated increase in adoptive applicants. Prior to that, foster parents were considered inappropriate for adoption. Sometimes the foster parents knew that the placement might become adoptive but, usually the decision to adopt was made after the child lived in the foster home. While some foster parents have felt pressured by the agency to adopt the child (Meezan & Shireman, 1982), others have the intention to adopt from the very beginning. About 70% of relinquishment older child adoptions are now by foster parents.

Fost-adopt placements (or "legal risk adoptions") are becoming more commonplace and involve the placement of a child into a foster home with the plan of adoption if the child does not return home. Many agencies use fost-adoption as an alternative to regular adoption (Child Welfare Task Force, 1985).

There are many controversies surrounding fost-adopt placements. The major objection is that foster parents hoping to adopt will not work toward the child's reunification with the biological family, which is one of the major goals of foster care (Lee & Hull, 1983). The dual goals of reunification with the biological family and the integration of the child into the fost-adopt family impose a strain on foster parents' and children's loyalties. In fact, some professionals believe that beginning an adoption as a foster parent reduces a sense of entitlement to be a parent, resulting in less commitment to parenthood, and a weaker parent–child bond (Ward, 1981). Foster families are also not screened as carefully for compatability with the child (Meezan & Shireman, 1985). The time constraints involved in foster placements allow little matching or placement preparation, both thought to be important to adoption success. Also, there is less confidentiality protection in a foster home adoption where the foster parents and biological parents have met. Fost-adoptions may be disquieting to other foster children present in the foster home. In addition, adoption by foster families may remove them from availability for other foster children, draining the already dwindling pool of foster families.

The advantages of fost-adoptions are the continuity of home life afforded the child, the retention of a familiar community, the ability for on-going assessment of the placement, and the involvement of the child in the decision to adopt. Fost-adoptions can begin when the children are younger and easier to engage in a new family—even if the years-long court battles stretch out ahead. Adoptive parents who were previously foster parents are also reported to be more accepting of on-going supervision. In one study, 90% of foster adoptive parents favored one or more in-person contacts per year with the agency after finalization (Waldinger, 1982).

Given these advantages and disadvantages, there are several situations that lend themselves to fost-adoptions, generally where there is little likelihood of the child's reunification with his biological parents. Those cases where the child has been relinquished by the mother (and the father is unknown, absent, or likely to relinquish in the future) are appropriate for fost-adoptions, as are cases where the child has been abandoned or parental rights have been terminated but are being contested. If the child's birth parents have had their right to parent other children legally terminated, are unlikely to ever be able to parent the child, or have committed a heinous offense against the child, fost-adoption is also an appropriate option (Gill & Amadio, 1983).

Positive reasons given for fost-adoption by the foster parents themselves include the enjoyment of the child by the parents, a strong interest in children (also found in conventional adoptions), and the parent's ability to respond to a particular child. Reasons foster parents have given for not wanting to adopt have included the older age or ill health of the parent, the degree of the child's handicaps, the fact that the child is entering adolescence, an absence of bonding between parent and child, and a fear of losing agency support after adoption (Meezan & Shireman, 1982). Reasons for adopting tend to be child-oriented, while reasons for not adopting tend to belong to the larger interaction of child, parent, and agency.

Fost-adoptions are gaining wider acceptance among professionals, especially concerning older child adoptions, and these placements compare
favorably in terms of stability to conventional adoptive placements. The cost
of potential removal of the family from the foster family network seems to
be overshadowed by the continuity and stability proffered the adopted
child.

Fees and Subsidies

Cost is considered an unacceptable deterrent to giving a child a needed
and well-suited family. Home study, placement, and legalization fees may
be, and often are, waived in special-needs adoptions. Waivers and subsidies
are an indication that no child should be seen as "unadoptable."

California and other states have enacted adoption subsidies in the past 15
years to aid in the adoption of special needs children. States with subsidy
programs provide funds through monthly payments to families that adopt
special-needs children, "based on the needs of the family that can be
attributed to the placement and support of the child (State of California
Health and Welfare Agency, 1977a, p. iii)." In 1980, the federal government
began to reimburse 50% of subsidies to states to promote older child
adoptions. According to the federal government, and most states, this
amount cannot exceed the amount that would be paid to a foster family for
the care of the child. The family can receive payments until the child reaches
majority (Waldinger, 1982), yet adoption subsidies are lower and of shorter
term than foster care payments. Unlike foster care payments, adoption
subsidies do not increase as the child gets older. From January 1969 to
December 1970, the average subsidy payment to adoptive families in
California was $78, compared to the estimated $154 average monthly
payment to a foster family for the same child. The average subsidized family
received payments for 2.7 years, compared to the 15 years that a foster
family would have received payments for the same child (State of California
Health and Welfare Agency, 1977a). At current board rates, the "savings" to
counties are $7680 per adoption per year. What is not known is how many
foster parents do not adopt because they do not want these "savings" to come
out of their pocketbooks.

Subsidies were used in 5% of relinquishment adoptions in California in
1970, in 28% in 1975 (State of California Health and Welfare Agency, 1977a),
and in 54% of adoptions in the early 1980s (Barth, Berry, Yoshikami,
Goodfield, & Carson, 1988). In Waldinger's study (1982), families receiving
subsidies in California had an average income of $13,383 (excluding subsidy).
The majority had other adopted children (76%) and the average age of the
special-needs child was 10. In 66% of the families, the child had not been

told about the subsidy. But 90% of subsidized families said they would encourage other adopters to participate in the program.

Nationwide, adoption assistance funding rose from $442,000 in 1981 to $7 million in 1983 among 40 states (Fales, 1985). Because of federal guidelines, state eligibility requirements for subsidies show little variation in the amount paid to families. A majority of states have, however, expanded their adoption subsidy programs to include certain children not eligible for federal reimbursement. Comprehensive statistics on state level assistance are not available. As our study will show, the standards used to decide the eligibility, duration, and size of subsidies are open to many interpretations.

Postplacement Services

Agencies generally recognize the need for postplacement services in special-needs adoptions. These services take many forms: casework services, parent groups, subsidies, and referrals to community resources and other social networks. Casework services may be the most common and least documented and evaluated form of postplacement service. These invariably include mandatory visits between placement and legalization of the adoption, but the purpose and form of these visits are ambiguous.

Parent self-help groups are becoming more numerous in this country. There were 250 such groups in 1980 (Meezan, 1980), including the Organization for United Response (OURS) (1987) and The Post-Adoption Center for Education and Research (PACER) (1986). OURS, Inc. is a nonprofit organization of over 9000 families and professionals "recognizing a need to share information, support one another and keep the children in contact with one another." OURS provides adoption information, a "help-line," resource materials, a bimonthly magazine, and donations and support to children in need of permanency. PACER is located in Northern California and provides educational resources as well as groups for all members of the adoption triangle: birth and adoptive parents and adopted children. Parents and children find it helpful to meet and talk with people in similar circumstances. Ofter, these groups are organized in the form of a group study prior to placement, and the participants voluntarily maintain regular contact after placement (Trimetiere, 1979). Other groups are more structured and closed-ended, although long-lasting supportive relationships are often formed.

Many postplacement support services involve fostering a support system for adoptive families. Besides parent groups, agencies offer individual and family counseling, retreats, "help lines," reading lists and materials, and video information (Spencer, 1985). The North American Post-Legal Adoption Committee considers postlegal services as a logical extension of preplacement services, that should be offered "at whatever point in their lives these [needs] may arise (Spencer, 1985, p. 5)." They argue that postplacement services should be available, for a (sliding) fee, for the rest of an adoptive family's lives. The call for more available and continuous postplacement services is coming from many quarters, although existing evidence is fuzzy about the type, timing, and effectiveness of such services for older child adoptions. This study hopes to bring some clarity to the picture.

ADOPTION DISRUPTION

The increase in older children placed for adoption does not arrive free of doubt. Practitioners and policymakers are concerned that the effects of the more vigorous and less encumbered pursuit of adoptive placements may have decreased their stability. This concern was the impetus to the study that is the core of this book. The shortage of systematic evidence on the rates and causes of disruption is confounded by the confusion in distinguishing disruption from other placement outcomes. In Chapter 4 we review prior disruption research. In this chapter we consider what disruption is.

Distinguishing and Defining Disruption

A review of adoption nomenclature is necessary prior to any discussion of disruption. The retirement of the term "failed adoptions" was long overdue, since it infers that the family and child were failures despite often admirable efforts to build a new family. Several terms are now in use to describe adoptions that end: disruption and dissolution are the best known. Disruption is often a catch-all phrase used to indicate that any adoptive placement has ended. Most studies of disruption do not distinguish adoptions that ended before or after they are legalized in court (after the 6-month provisional placement period). When the distinction is made, adoptions that end after legalization are called "dissolutions."

Adoptions end in many ways. Common to all forms is more impermanence for the child. Disruption can occur officially or unofficially. Formal disruptions involve returning the child to the adoption agency and are typically all that is recorded in adoption statistics. These types of disruption include prefinalization relinquishments, postlegalization relinquishments (dissolutions), and set-asides.

Most plainly characterized as "disrupted" are those *prelegalization relinquishments* in which the child is placed with an adoptive family but then returned to the agency before the legalization of the adoption which usually occurs after a 1-year waiting period.

After an adoption is legalized, parents may still decide to return the child to the adoption agency. This is commonly called a *dissolution*. Agency policies concerning dissolutions have often been to tolerate this practice, despite the dramatic difference between their response to such families and any other families who wish to be free of the responsibilities of parenting.

Legalized adoptions that disrupt after this and are dissolved by the courts are known as *set-asides*. A set-aside is a type of dissolution. Set-asides have similarities to annulments as they can be granted as a result of inadequate or misinformation or fraud by the agency in making the placement. The right to petition for a set-aside may have a statute of limitations—usually 5 years. At least in intent, these limitations disallow petitions based on parent—adolescent problems that result from normative development rather than the agency's failure to warn the family about such problems a decade earlier. Some judges refuse all set-asides whereas others allow them, assuming that the adoptive situation is hopelessly troubled.

Unofficial disruptions—in which the child's departure from the home is not reported to the adoption agency—may be more common than formal disruptions, but they are not reflected in the statistics. As previously discussed, fost-adopt children are placed with foster parents who identify an interest in adopting a child if the child is soon to be relinquished from his or her birth parents. *Fost-adopt disruptions* occur when foster parents care for a foster child with an understanding that adoption will follow the relinquishment of the child, and then decide not to adopt the child (before or after the child's relinquishment). This is an informal adoption disruption. These are rarely recorded in adoption statistics, but deserve to be tallied to clarify the outcomes of fost-adoption.

Many children in residential care, or under child welfare, mental health, and juvenile justice auspices, are adopted children (Brodzinsky, 1987b). These children have been in adoptive placements that were not successful and that were followed by placement in other settings. States do not typically require residential treatment programs or foster care providers to inform adoption agencies of extended out-of-home services they provide to adopted children. As long as the family maintains legal custody, these *out-of-home care* "disruptions" are not reported in state or county adoption statistics.

When an older adopted child leaves her or his adoptive home voluntarily or under duress before age 18 and becomes *informally emancipated*, this is also a version of adoption disruption. If the child and parent agree that the child is ready for an emancipation and complete the requirements for legal emancipation, then a disruption has not occurred.

OUR DEFINITION.   A study of adoption disruption must grapple with whether an adoptive placement has disrupted if the child is no longer living with the adoptive family but has never been returned to the agency. For example, he or she might be living in residential care or with a relative. In this study, disruptions will include those cases in which the child has been returned to the agency's care either before or after the legalization or when the child is living away from the family without continued family commitment. This includes dissolutions and set-asides but only includes out-of-home care when the family does not continue to view itself as including the adopted child in its future. The designation of disruption indicates that the agency received custody of the child or was informed of the end of the placement when a child informally emancipated.

As a reflection of social change over the past century, adoption continues to evolve. Older children have been allowed to join the world of adoption, but their entrance is coincidental with an apparently increasing adoption disruption rate. Chapter 2 examines the value of adoption to children, families, and society, a scrutiny that is necessary for determining when and whether adoption is worth the risk of disruption and what resources we should expend to place older children in adoptive homes and to prevent disruptions.

2

The Value of Adoption
and Disruption

A permanent, safe, familylike living situation for every child is the goal of current child welfare legislation and practice. The "permanence" in permanency planning is not, however, defined by law. Certain placements are considered more familylike and permanent. Short of living with birth or extended families, adoption is considered to provide the most permanent of homes. Adoption's value to children, adoptive parents, and society has not heretofore been systematically described. We generally assume that older child adoptions save foster care costs and, when they succeed, are a pleasure to the family and child. There is more to it than that. The evidence that adoption provides wide-ranging and great advantages over foster care is compelling and calls for renewed commitment to this program. This chapter clarifies the many benefits of adoption over long-term foster care—the most comparable other "permanent" placement option—and estimates the financial advantages that accrue. This provides but one basis for deciding what level of effort and cost should be put toward maintaining adoptive homes.

Despite priority under the law, adoptions represent relatively small percentages of permanent placements. Long-term foster care and guardianship are far more common. Statutes that give preference to placing children for adoption have such exceptions as: the parents have regularly visited the child and the child would benefit from continuance of the relationship; the child is 12 or older and does not wish to have her or his parental relationship legally severed; and foster parents are unwilling to adopt, but the child would suffer if removed from their custody and placed for adoption (Dodson, 1984). In such cases, and many other cases where the child is deemed unadoptable (especially when no families are thought to be available), guardianship and long-term foster care, respectively, are considered the preferred options. Policy and program guidelines provide practitioners with wide latitude in interpreting the best placement for a child.

THE PERSONAL VALUE FOR
CHILDREN OF ADOPTION

Whereas the de facto desirability of "permanent" placements is defined by law, the true desirability of placements has other determinants. First, the risk that a child will be reabused in any placement is a specter that hangs over all child welfare planners and practitioners. Such abuse may result in permanent handicapping injuries or long-standing behavioral problems (Lamphear, 1985). Second, the stability of permanent placements deserves consideration in the assessment of preferred placements. We know, for instance, that somewhere between 4 and 40% of "permanent" older child adoptions do not last. Since placement moves are often costly to children, families, and communities, the true permanence of placements affects their desirability. A third more neglected aspect of permanence involves the lasting legacy of the placement on the child's development. Childhood ends after one-quarter of a typical life span whereas adulthood encompasses the remaining three-quarters. The influences of a child's development on those last 60 years is critically important. The child's satisfaction with the placement is another indicator of the suitability of placements. This chapter will first consider personal benefits of adoption for children. This analysis will draw on evidence of reabuse, placement stability, developmental outcomes, and the child's satisfaction with adoption as well as the most common alternative: long-term foster care. For one key reason, we do not compare adoption outcomes to the other options of maintaining the abused or neglected child in the home with agency supervision or reunification of the child to the home. Our society has been constructed around the primacy of birth families. Simple comparisons between the costs and benefits of adoption and family maintenance or reunification are precluded by the difference in valuation between the entitlement of living in birth families and other families. Although we would argue that this value often works to the enduring detriment of children and needs reexamination and although we believe that we have shown in Barth and Berry (1987) that family maintenance typically provides inadequate protection to the child, we will not take up those lines of inquiry here. Guardianship is another common alternative to adoption, but so little evidence is available that its benefits cannot confidently be ascertained. The chapter concludes with an estimate of the financial value of adoption for the child, parent, agency, and society.

Reabuse

Child welfare services aim to prevent abuse but, at best, they only reduce it. The amount of reduction is partly related to the child's placement, with reabuse less likely in adoption than in foster care.

ADOPTION. Whereas some authors (e.g., Schneider & Rimmer, 1984) have surmised that adoptive parents are typically hostile to their adoptive children, the evidence is otherwise. Sack and Dale's (1982) adoption disruptions study found that not 1 of 12 children (with an average age of 5½ years) with histories of physical abuse prior to adoption were reabused. Of the 82 disruptions studied by Boneh (1979), 20% resulted from the agency's request for the child's removal but less than 10% involved abuse by the adoptive parents. In Festinger's (1986) study of disruptions, only 1% of adoptions involved agency removals because of "serious reservations about the home" (p. 38). Since adoption disruptions occur in roughly 10% of all older child adoptions, abuse of adoptive children would be about 1%. National studies of child abuse and neglect (Russell & Trainor, 1984) indicate that adoptive parents are alleged perpetrators in 1% of all reports, despite their representation of approximately 3% in the population at large, indicating that adoptive placements are unusually safe. This rate includes infant as well as older child adoptions. Abuse rates are likely to be higher in older child placements, but still below those of the general population.

LONG-TERM FOSTER CARE. McFadden's review of abuse in foster care in 27 states found that complaints were filed against 0.3–6.7% of foster homes with substantiated complaints ranging from 0.2 to 2.7% of homes. The reabuse rates per child would be less than one-half of that since foster homes typically have more than two children. The national studies on child abuse and neglect (Russell & Trainor, 1984) confirm that foster parents are alleged abusers in 0.5% of all child abuse reports while representing less than 1% of all parents. A study of child abuse in Arizona concluded that about 7% of the foster child population is allegedly abused by foster parents (Bolton, Laner, & Gai, 1981). Efforts to estimate abuse rates in residential care yielded a complaint rate of 0.4% among 1000 children and a confirmed complaint rate of 0.9% among more than 69,000 children in care (Rindfleisch & Rabb, 1984). Given that children in group care are more than twice as likely to be identified as difficult to control—as are children in foster care (Fitzharris, 1985)—higher abuse rates are predictable in foster or group care. Overall, children in foster care are probably safer than their counterparts at home but less safe than adopted children.

The Stability of Permanent Placements

A permanent placement is one that is intended, but not guaranteed, to last forever. Even though the law seeks permanence for children, whether in their own homes or with other families, permanence cannot be legislated. Replacement is inevitable in responsible child welfare services. Overall, while all types of placements are subject to disruption, adoption appears to be the most stable.

ADOPTION.   The rate of adoption disruptions has apparently risen since the advent of recent permanency planning reforms. The disruption rate in Kadushin and Seidl's (1971) prepermanency planning study of older child adoptions was less than 3%. Boneh (1979) reported 96 disruptions from 1970 to 1979 in the Massachusetts Department of Public Welfare, with the caveat that this is a low estimate due to the lack of systematic reporting of disruptions. Fein, Davies and Knight (1979) found that 31% of adoptions were disrupted by the end of their 5-year follow-up period; this rate was equivalent to the return-to-care rate for children initially returned home. Cohen (1984) recently reported a disruption rate of 7% per year for older child adoptions in Canada. Boyne and his colleagues (1984) reported a 23% disruption rate in their study of adoptive placements. Older children had still higher rates: 47% of the children aged 12–17 disrupted, compared to 25% of those aged 9–11, 15% of those aged 6–8, and 7% of those aged 0–5.

Block and Libowitz (1983), alternately, found all 32 adoptees who had been discharged from foster care remaining in their initial adoptive homes at the end of the 2-year study period. The Oregon Project's (Lahti, 1982) policy of "aggressive adoption" resulted in 64 adoptions and only 2 disruptions in the following 14 months. California data suggest a rather stable rate of 8.7% across the 1970s (Barth et al., 1986). These figures have apparently increased to over 10% and are consistent with those identified by Partridge, Hornby, and McDonald (1986) and Urban Systems Research and Engineering (1985).

LONG-TERM FOSTER CARE.   Long-term foster care is intended to be permanent. For many children it is not. Fein and associates (1983) reported a 50% replacement rate among their 14 children in permanent foster homes. All replacements involved children aged 9 or over. Block (1981) reported that 28% of foster children who were returned home later returned to care and Stone and Stone (1983) found a replacement rate of 49%. In a study of 87 adolescents in foster care (aged 11–19), the number of placements per child ranged from 3 to 27, with a mean of 9 placements per child (Proch & Taber, 1987). As the age of the child increased, the length of each placement decreased. The general trend was for younger children to experience one or two longer placements in childhood, and then move with increasing frequency and restrictiveness in adolescence. Other reports (e.g., Lawder, Poulin, & Andrews, 1985; State of California, 1985) are far more sanguine about the likelihood that a child will not move more than once during his or her tenure in foster care. Permanence is distinctively more likely when foster parents are well trained and prepared (Jones & Moses, 1984).

Measurable Developmental Outcomes

Although the "best interest of the child" is not the sole determinant, this concept continues to influence placement decisions. Perhaps no placement outcomes are more closely aligned with this standard than the child's health, and educational and social growth. Although longitudinal evidence of adoption outcomes is very scarce, measurable developmental outcomes seem to be more favorable in adoption than in long-term foster care.

ADOPTION. Although most adoptions that result from permanency planning are older child adoptions, the majority of investigations on adoption outcomes are of infant adoptions. Recent writings based on interviews with adult adoptees who are searching for birth parents emphasize the difficulties rather than the benefits of adoption (e.g., Deykin, Campbell, & Patti, 1984). The studies vary in sophistication and tend to rely on adoptee samples who are seeking treatment: an obviously skewed group. The latter are too numerous and generally unrepresentative to completely review here [see Brodzinsky (1987a) for a review] but suggest that adjustment to adoption is usually not simple nor traumatic.

Witmer, Herzog, Weinstein, and Sullivan's (1963) monumental study on independent adoptions made between 1944 and 1947 provides significant evidence about adoption outcomes for infants and only scanty information about special-needs adoption outcomes. In their sample of 484 adoptions, they compared independently adopted children to a control group of birth children, which included only 13 special-needs children. Among those latter placements, only three couples understood the special characteristics of their children, whereas the remainder unknowingly adopted a seriously handicapped child. Several of the children's disabilities were evident to the social worker at placement, but apparently, the adoptive parents did not believe the evidence or believed that the children would overcome their handicaps with sufficient nurturance. The difficulties in explaining why adoptive families so often state that they did not get information about the child remain to this day (Nelson, 1985). Still, among these families, only one mother expressed regret for having adopted a handicapped child. Another mother, after unwittingly accepting a handicapped child for adoption, knowingly brought three other children into her home with varying degrees of physical and emotional difficulties.

Witmer et al.'s (1963) more general findings of the outcomes of adoption 15 years after placement are that, taken as a whole, the adopted children showed no significant difference from a matched nonadopted control group with regard to IQ or school achievement and were only slightly below the control group on adjustment. After excluding the children who had been placed after 1 month of age (21 children were older than 2 years of age at the time of placement), the differences in adjustment disappear. They did find that the least troubled homes had children with the highest overall ratings on adjustment and intellectual achievement. This was especially true for children who were or had been disadvantaged—especially those adopted when they were 2 years or older, those who had been maltreated as infants, and those with serious injuries or defects prior to placement.

Scarr and Weinberg (1976) found that black children adopted into white homes showed considerably higher IQ scores than their birth parents and the mean of the general population, although lower IQs than their adopted siblings. The academic performance of adopted children was also above the national norms. These advantages for adopted children are particularly significant given that the typical occupations of the birth mothers were office workers, nurse's aides, and students—a rather well-positioned comparison group with modal educational attainment of high school graduate. This is approximately the current educational level of foster parents in California and above that of the current population of birth mothers who have relinquished for adoption (State of California Statistical Services, 1984). Scarr and Weinberg (1976) write that adoption is a comprehensive ecological system to promote the welfare of a child.

> The physical environment, the amount and quality of parent–child interaction, the parents' attitudes and practices in child rearing, the neighborhood and community setting of the family, and the larger social contexts of employment, economic security, and cultural values must all be considered in describing the parameters of family effects. Educational interventions alone are unlikely to have the effects reported here for adoption. Schools, as presently constituted, cannot have the far-reaching, intensive impact on the family and home (pp. 738–739).

Rutter (1980) concurs that adoption is the one intervention which clearly makes a major, positive, long-term difference in the life of a child.

A little known French study (Dumaret, 1985) is one of a kind in comparing children born to the same mother who either remained with their mothers, were adopted as infants, or resided in foster or group care. When compared to either control group (or the national norms for the general population) the adopted group surpassed all other comparison groups in school performance and IQ.

Other evidence on infant adoptions suggests that children and parents do have greater difficulty than birth families. Hoopes (1982) found subtle negative effects of infant adoption on self-esteem and identity formation and a larger number—but still within the normal range—of school problems when the children were between 8 and 12 years of age. Brinich and Brinich's (1982) review of a decade of patients ($N = 5135$) served on an inpatient unit found no overrepresentation of adoptees, and Brodzinsky, Schechter, Braff, and Singer (1984a) conclude that the mean adjustment levels of adopted children were lower than those of their nonadopted peers, but still within the normal range. Adjustment problems clearly increase with the age of the child at the time of the adoption. Other studies also identify struggles with self-esteem (Sorosky, Baran, & Pannor, 1975) and constitutional vulnerabilities—like greater hyperactivity (Dalby, Fox, & Haslam, 1982)—that make adoption a less than simple solution to the disintegration of the birth family. Overall, however, infant adoption seems to have many positive and few negative effects for children.

Unfortunately, the evidence on the outcomes of older child adoptions is sparse. Among 30 children placed at 2 years of age or older (Tizard, 1977), 84% showed satisfactory progress and attachment capacity more than 2 years later. In a study involving much older children (placed at 5 years to 12 years), 85% of children made successful adjustments and 73% of parents were much more satisfied than dissatisfied with their adoption (Kadushin, 1970). McRoy and colleagues (1982) found no differences in self-esteem between transracially and inracially adopted children—even when compared to the norm. The sample's mean age at the time of the study was 13.5 years and ages at the time of placement ranged from 1 to 14 years. Lahti (1982) found that children placed in adoptive and fost-adopt placements fared better in family adjustment and emotional and developmental functioning than did children returned home or in long-term foster care. Children in adoptive placements did especially well in school functioning. However, 62% of the adopted children were under 3 years old when placed.

Other evidence that adopted children have higher educational achievement than foster children is indirect but persuasive. Bachrach (1983) found that compared to children living with biological parents, adopted children are more likely to live in two-parent homes, enjoy a higher household income, have fewer siblings, and have an older, more highly educated mother not working outside the home. The latter predicts the likelihood of the child's successful education and employment. In a longitudinal study of transracial adoptees (generally black children in white homes) and their families, Simon and Alstein (1987) found that of 111 transracial adoptees (median age: 14.9), 82% in the study graduated from college, were in college, or planned to continue on to college and 13% planned to go on to some other type of school. The respondents expressed various occupational goals but the most frequently cited fields were law, business, teaching, and computers. The median grade point average for the transracial adoptees in the study was 2.5. In light of the fact that students with a "B" average are 5 times more likely to finish school than students with a "D" average (The Condition of Education, 1986), we expect that most of these youth will graduate. Roughly 20% of Americans ages 18 and over completed a degree beyond high school in 1984 (U.S. Bureau of The Census, 1984). Yet, even if only one-third of those adoptees who aspired to go to college or vocational/

technical school will succeed in completing a degree beyond high school, the rate becomes 28% for the adoptees in the study. In the general population in 1985, the participation rate of high school graduates between the ages of 18 and 24 in postsecondary institution was 21.8%. Thus, adoption seems to promote educational attainment.

LONG-TERM FOSTER CARE.   Studies of children who have grown up in foster care indicate that foster children make difficult but largely normal adjustments to adulthood and appear to succeed more than children who are returned to birth homes and less than adopted children. For the purposes of this chapter, only studies since 1980 will be reviewed; a more complete review of studies on the aftermath of life in foster care is available elsewhere (Barth, 1986a).

Harrari's (1980) study of 34 adolescents who had left foster care within 5 years and not returned to their foster homes found their self-reports on a personality inventory to be indistinguishable from the general population. A large European investigation compared 329 males who were adopted, reared by birth parents, or raised in foster care (Bohman & Sigvardsson, 1980). By age 18, children in foster care had fallen behind adopted children in intellectual ability and evidenced more alcohol abuse and criminality than all the other groups. Kraus' (1981) investigation of almost 500 former foster children found that time in placement and placement continuity were unrelated to later law violations; no comparisons to children raised in their own homes were drawn.

A follow-up study of 61 former foster children from New Orleans who were ages 19 to 29 at the time of the interview found that educational attainment was lower than that of the general population in New Orleans and a group matched according to minority status (Zimmerman, 1982). More than one-half dropped out of school. Students in foster care, on the average, did not complete eleventh grade. Those with the poorest educational preparation had the most problems as adults. Most (75%) members of the sample were self-supporting, although slightly more than one-third lived at or below the poverty line. More than 10% were incarcerated at the time of the study. Nearly one-half reported needing or seeking mental health services. About 5% of the sample were hospitalized for mental illness at some time after foster care. A majority of youth appraised their lives as currently satisfactory or hopeful. Counter to expectations, youth discharged from long-term foster care were more likely to be in the better-functioning group.

Two recent outcome studies provide more sanguine results. Festinger (1983) found no differences between the outcomes of ex-foster children from New York City (and now adult respondents) and the population-at-large on most characteristics including arrests, self-esteem, and life satisfaction.

Former foster children did have significant shortcomings in educational and employment success. Over one-third of the young adults had not completed high school at the time of discharge while 62% of the males in foster care had attained a high school education or less in comparison to 51.6% of those in the population at the time of the study. Only 11% of women in the sample had completed college and remarkably few (2.3%) men had college degrees. When asked about their level of satisfaction with the amount and quality of education they had received while in foster care, more than one half were somewhat or very dissatisfied. Contact with foster parents after foster care or ongoing contact with birth parents during foster care were again associated with better outcomes.

A large study of former foster children in West Virginia (Jones & Moses, 1984) shows that young people discharged from foster care upon achieving majority, after an average of 5 years in the system, have rates of marriage, broken marriages, incarceration, parenthood, and marital satisfaction that are comparable to the general population. Former foster children lagged behind their peers in education by 1 year and often had problems with alcohol (20%). The study also found that 19% of the former foster children's own children were or had been in foster care. Overall, 62% were at least "mostly satisfied" with their lives. Most (75%) of the former foster children were living with family, including a spouse or partner, foster or adoptive parents, birth parents, other relatives like grandparents or siblings, or their own children.

While adoptees may do better educationally than the population at large, foster children fare quite poorly. In a study of independent living services for 291 adolescents between the ages of 16 and 21 (mean age: 18) who were discharged from the care and custody of public child welfare agencies, only 28% of them completed high school at the time of discharge (Westat, 1986). (This sample had also received services that most foster youth do not receive.) Only 37.6% of 18- and 19-year-olds in the study had completed high school at discharge, which matches Festinger's (1983) results and is significantly lower than the 74.6% high school completion rate among those of the general population. Only 4.9% of the youths in the Westat study had some college or completed college. This compares to 10% of the adoptees in the Simon and Alstein (1987) sample who were attending college even though their median age was nearly 3 years less.

Conclusions can be cautiously drawn from studies on foster care outcomes. Continued contact with foster parents and birth parents improves outcomes for foster youth. Educational and employment deficits are apparently most troublesome to adults who were previously foster children. Housing is a significant problem in some urban areas; an estimated 7500 youth who have been discharged from foster care are homeless in New York

City (Demchak, 1985). Criminal behavior and substance abuse are less common, but possibly overrepresented in adults who were foster children. Whereas exposure to foster care does not doom a child to a distressed adulthood—and may provide the child with beneficial developmental experiences not found in their birth homes—foster children are still at risk of short-changed futures.

Children's Satisfaction

Childrens' satisfaction with placements should be weighed in decision making. If other outcomes of permanent placements are equal, childrens' satisfaction becomes particularly salient. Although too little is now known about childrens' preferences, some data are available.

ADOPTION.   In Proch's (1982) study of 56 children adopted by their foster parents, only 8 of the 29 children interviewed could distinguish between foster care and adoption and preferred adoption. Most were old enough to remember living in other foster homes. The essential difference between the two types of placements was stated as foster care being temporary and adoption as permanent. Therefore, to those children who had multiple placements and sought a sense of belonging, adoption was preferable. In Lahti and colleagues' (1978) study, 22% of adopted (formerly foster) children defined foster children as not being treated as well as children in general. In Bush and Gordon's (1982) study of 136 foster children, among 111 judged unlikely to return home, one-half did not wish to be adopted. Most of these were older children removed from their birth family at an older age. These children regarded adoption as destructive to their ties with their birth families. The advent of open adoption might decrease this proportion today. The remaining one-half were more positive about the prospects of adoption citing the security of their tenure in placement and the wish to belong to a real family. Kowal and Schilling (1985) report that 17% of adult adoptees (who had been placed as infants and later contacted an adoption agency or search group) were embarrassed or felt uncomfortable about the fact of adoption, and 25% reported feeling worried or insecure about being adopted. Still, 21% reported feeling differently from nonadoptees but no better or worse, 22% reported feeling no different, and 35% reported feeling "chosen" or "special." Studies that are based on searching adults placed as infants have little relation to older children who know and remember their birth families.

LONG-TERM FOSTER CARE.   Fewer than one-half (43%) of children in the West Virginia study (Jones & Moses, 1984) reported that they were treated differently than other children because they were in foster care. In Fanshel & Shinn's (1978) study, social workers rated foster children—who had been in care at least 1 year and an average of 5 years—as significantly more attached to their foster homes than their birth homes. Although few younger children experienced a conflict in attachments, more older children did. Children living in institutions felt less comfortable, not as happy, less loved, less looked after, less trusted, and less cared about than children in other forms of surrogate care or children reunited with their families (Bush, 1980). Children who had some choice in their foster placement were significantly more satisfied in their placements than were children with no choice (Bush & Gordon, 1982).

THE EVIDENCE IN FAVOR OF ADOPTION

The adoption of older children under permanency planning appears to be a highly favorable form of placement. The positive development outcomes of adoption and children's satisfaction with it seem, on the whole, consistent with current impressions and policies. Additional, improved, and more enduring postplacement services may further these fortuitous results.

Although the benefits of foster care, long the "whipping boy" of child welfare services, are not as great as adoption, we do underscore the conclusions of Lahti *et al.* (1978), "Generally we have not found foster care to be characterized by instable placements affording children limited chance for satisfactory adjustments" (p. 26). In the short-term, foster care is a satisfactory solution. But foster care has an Achilles heel that leaves many young people vulnerable to long-range problems. Foster care ends during adolescence and does not guide youth through the confusing and costly market places of employment, housing, higher education, and family formation. Child welfare policymakers must decide whether permanency planning's primary goal is to create living situations that last across childhood or a lifetime. We agree with Maluccio and Fein's (1983) argument that "(p)ermanency planning is designed to help children live in families that offer continuity of relationships with nurturing parents or caretakers and the opportunity to establish *lifetime relationships*" (emphasis added). As Simpson (1987) writes: "It's not convenient to be an orphan . . . Too much depends on family ties . . . When a young couple marry, their parents set them up. When they begin a career they seek the patronage of relatives. Throughout their lives they know that in an adversity they will have the family behind them" (p. 11). Since future economic success increasingly depends on adequate education (Children's Defense Fund, 1987), the provision of financial support for higher education is important during the postadolescence period.

If permanency planning is a set of services and options to provide "lifetime relationships" rather than services to provide a "continuous family in which to grow up" then the weighting of service options tilts toward greater use of adoption. With greater support, long-term foster care can provide stable, safe, and beneficial places in which to mature. It is far less likely to offer lifetime relationships or corrective educational events. One deleterious result is suggested by the atypical use of foster care among the offspring of former foster children; such use might have been lessened by the involvement of adoptive or birth grandparents.

In sum, the data suggests that adoption is a far more stable and beneficial placement than long-term foster care. We recognize that these are simply aggregated descriptions of outcomes with limited ability to guide social worker judgments on complex cases. The futures for children are also a function of the interaction of their characteristics and needs and the kind of care they receive. Boyne and associates (1984) and Boneh (1979) have shown, for example, that children who have been adopted more than twice are unlikely to find a satisfactory third placement. The appropriateness of long-term foster or group care and guardianship for such children is apparent. Additional profiles that contribute to our ability to make beneficial placements across the range of possible settings will emerge from this study and future experience and research with permanency planning.

THE VALUE OF ADOPTION

Having established that adopted children generally succeed as well as other children and that older child adoptions have superior outcomes to foster care, the question remains: how much are those advantages worth? A complete answer would include a synthesis of evidence on the magnitude and value of differences between adoption and foster care in the financial investment in the child's future, the child's personal and financial benefits, and the return of investment to the agency and society. We focus here on the monetary benefits and costs. For the purposes of explanation, we will assume that a 7-year-old boy, Andy, was adopted by an urban, Northeast, moderately affluent two-parent family. The fost-adopt placement was legalized after 1 year at age 8. What is the value of the benefits for Andy and his family?

Financial Value to the Child

The financial gain to Andy (which is estimated by the agency and family costs) if he were to be adopted again is great when assessed across his lifetime (see Table 2.1). An adoption subsidy of approximately $3264 per year (i.e., $272 per month) is typical in California (State of California Health and Welfare Agency, 1986) and is only a tiny fraction of his total package of benefits. Although all families do not receive subsidies in all years of the adoption, if they did receive this amount over 10 years (when discounted at a 10% rate) the cost to the agency would be $17,397.

The far larger source of resources flows from his adoptive family. The USDA (1986) indicates that the cost of raising a boy from age 10 to age 17 at a moderate-cost level in the Northeast is $42,536. Epenshade (1984) believes these calculations are low and estimates expenditures for a hypothetical child from birth to age 18 that range from $149,150 to $227,700. Since the early years are less costly than the latter, prorating these figures across the last 10 years of a child's youth would leave a range of approximately $87,026 to $132,859 in benefits for the child adopted at age 8. The intermediate point is $109,943. This is nearly double the USDA estimated cost used by the more generous states to set the foster care rate. Thus, the average family spends about twice the foster care rate. Although many foster parents contribute their own resources to the raising of foster children, this contribution would narrow but not eliminate the difference. If Andy subsequently attended a 4-year state university, his parents would be likely to spend an additional $47,330 (Epenshade, 1984) for an intermediate total of roughly $157,273 of financial benefits for the adoption. Admittedly, families that adopt are increasingly not middle class. In our study, however, we found an average family income of $24,000 which suggests that a moderate income level is still typical for adopting families. Also, a minority of adults (about 20%) complete a 4-year college. As such, we will estimate this value at one-fifth the actual cost of college or $9466 for the average child.

In fact, though, these estimates are very modest, in that the financial and personal benefits of family membership last well beyond college. Assistance in finding a first job; provision of housing between jobs or residences; assistance with buying furniture, car, or a home; help with wedding costs; assistance with child care; and personal counsel and support may extend for decades after a youth reaches the age of majority. A few awards have been made to children whose parents died by virtue of personal injury injustices under tort law for "loss of consortium." Recent rulings makes this "loss of a parent's love, care, companionship and guidance" financially recoverable (Ashman & Rubenstein, 1985). This compensation is the most adequate means to estimate the monetary value of the personal experience of having a parent. Because loss of consortium has just recently begun to be granted to children (Ostling, 1986), the awards are still rare and small. Still, in Berns v. Pan American World Airways (1982), three children ages 17, 18, and 20 at the time of their parent's death were awarded $150,000 each for the loss of their parents—a verdict that is considered by trial lawyers to be too small

Table 2.1 Comparison of the Value of Adoption vs. Foster Care

Value of adoption to 8-year-old child[a,b]	
Adoption subsidies	$ 17,397
Parental contribution ages 8 to 18	109,943
Parental contribution to college education for adopted child	9,466
Value of parental consortium after age 18	167,000
Value of adoption	$303,806
Value of foster care to 8-year-old child[a,b]	
Foster care payments	$ 29,688
Value of postemancipation consortium with birth relatives or former foster parents	55,666
Value of foster care	$ 85,354

[a]All values have been discounted to the present at 10% per year.
[b]I have not estimated the value of medical insurance which should be equivalent, since most subsidies and AFDC-FC are complemented by Medicaid.

and "hardly compatible with most persons' concept of fairness" (Kenelly, 1982; p. 465). In the Ueland settlement in Washington State, the awards to two children totaled $385,000. The awards were made on the basis of the loss of relationship through the father's projected life span, not on the loss of financial support for the children's education and the like. An average of the settlements to these five children gives an estimate of the value of a lifetime relationship with a parent or parents of $167,000. Assuming that one-third of foster children develop such a relationship with birth relatives or former foster parents who they recontact, the value of their consortium can be estimated at $55,666 or $111,334 less than it would be if adopted.

This figure does not include the projected value of the education for the adopted child. As previously described, adopted children complete high school at approximately twice the rate of foster children and attend college at approximately five times the rate. A comparison between a hypothetical group of 100 foster children and 100 children adopted after infancy would conservatively result in 35 more adopted children with a high school education and 10 more children with a college education.

Education is generally and accurately regarded as a means for social mobility. In 1986, the unemployment rate for those with 1 to 3 years of high school was 15.4%, while rates were 8.1, 5.3, and 2.5% for those with 4 years of high school, 1 to 3 years of college, and 4 or more years of college, respectively. The greater educational attainment is related to greater annual median income. In 1985, the difference in annual median incomes between high school dropouts and graduates was $4972 for males and $3645 for women. Between high school and college graduates the differences were

$8969 for men and $5908 for women. The rate of annual *increase* in income between 1975–1985 for men who were high school dropouts was 12% higher than that for men who were high school graduates. The same 12% held for high school vs. college graduates. Every 7 years the difference in salary between these groups is doubled. High school graduates with no further education are expected to earn approximately $441,000 more than high school dropouts across their lifetimes (Department of Commerce, Bureau of Census, 1986). College graduates earn approximately three times the monthly wage as high school graduates or $814,000 over a lifetime. The differences are less for women, but as the gap in pay between men and women closes, the discrepancy between more and less educated women will close.

Taken together with the previously described greater proportion of adopted than foster children expected to graduate from high school but not college (51 vs. 33%) and college (25 vs. 5%), the average value of lifetime earnings for the typical adopted child is $242,180.

Moreover, there are several nonmonetary benefits to the child's continued education. Educational attainment is associated with social adjustment, health, improved leadership, and better communication skills. Overall, education not only yields large monetary gain, but also nonmonetary benefits that are essential in promoting well-being. Educational success has increasingly clear implications for positive mental health, and lower criminal behavior in the early adult years (Alpert & Dunham, 1986; CDF, 1987; Spivack & Marcus, 1987; Thornberry, Moore, & Christian, 1985). We did not include these benefits in our calculations.

Typical financial benefits of adoption must be contrasted to the benefits available to children who remain in foster care. Several states base their monthly AFDC-Foster Care payments on the USDA figures (approximately $55,700 across 10 years) and several more are on the way to doing so. We use this generous figure for comparison to adoption. Other foster care programs provide more and suggest this is the difference between the minimum sufficiency of foster care and the possibilities of enriched care. As an example, the Casey Family Program (headquartered in Hartford, CT) is known for its extraordinary commitment to their foster children—most of whom will not return home. They pay higher rates for foster parents, up to $3000 per year for orthodonture, up to $3000 per year for therapy, up to $2400 a month for tutors, and approximately $2400 per year for child development activities like ballet or karate. The children are enrolled in Blue Cross at $912 per year and have a clothing allowance of $70 per month. After age 18 they receive student aid, grants, room and board, and transportation home from college. If they are not in college, they receive $600 per month during the emancipation period. Over a 10-year period from ages 8–19, if Andy were in the Casey Family Program, he would receive approximately $70,000 in benefits that would not be received if he were in an ordinary long-term foster home. This figure would be in addition to the USDA cost of $57,500 that would be paid to a child in more ordinary long-term care. Their sum total of $127,500 is within the range of expenses of the previously computed estimate of $109,943 from Epenshade's (1984) data for a child in an adoptive home and are double the USDA estimated cost of raising a child.

In the years from 8 to 28, society invests more than four times as many resources in a child who is placed in adoption than in virtually the same child who is not. The value of subsidies, daily living to age 18, assistance obtaining a college education ($9466), loss of consortium, and enhanced future lifetime earnings exceeds $500,000. A byproduct of creating a family through adoption is the creation of wealth for a child and society.

Value to the Family

Adoption generally enhances the lives of the adoptive parent(s). Zelizer (1985) has documented the transition in the value of children arising primarily from their economic properties as laborers, to a greater value that principally derives from the parent's sentiment about the child. Even from 1907, little girls were preferred by adoptive parents most probably because they offer greater emotional value in their ability to communicate and reciprocate. When the popularity of adoption began to increase in the early 20th Century, a judge from the Boston Probate Court remarked in 1919, "The woods are full of people eager to adopt children" (quoted in Zelizer, 1985, p. 190). In the 1920s and 1930s sentimental adoption rapidly displaced instrumental fostering arrangements (Zelizer, 1985).

Even the law recognizes the sentimental value of children. In Terrell v. Garcia, a family suing for damages because of an unexpected birth was denied by a court which concluded that, "The satisfaction, joy and companionship which normal parents have in rearing a child make such economic loss worthwhile . . . Who can place a price tag on a child's smile? (cited in Zelizer, 1985, p. 166). Today, adoption of infants is expensive. Although the price of adoption is inelastic (as the free market is constrained by laws against baby selling), it partially reflects the large demand relative to the supply of infants and nonhandicapped children. The approximately 20,000 healthy infants available for adoption each year are sought after by roughly 2,000,000 people (Cole, 1987). That individuals and couples are willing to pay up to $20,000 to adopt an infant, gain a child through surrogacy, or conceive with the use of costly high-tech fertility procedures expresses the desire of would-be adoptive parents to have a young child.

Paying the price to just begin the parenting experience also includes the privilege of spending an additional $100,000 to raise a child. The willingness to expend such money and time is encouraged by several aspects of parenting. While each family's emphasis on the key factors thought to comprise the value of a child are different, the general factors are: the challenge of responding to and rehabilitating children, emotional reciprocity, social status from a child's success, certainty about the future, and bringing the family together in celebration.

Clearly the economic value of a child or of an adoption does explain only a small fraction of the child's or the adoption's overall value. There is more sentiment than supply and demand at work here, although there is certainly some of each. In a 1930 issue of the *Saturday Evening Post*, one observer marveled at the new altruism of adoptive parents: "What do they get out of this bondage? Worry, sickness, a procession of measles, mumps . . . chicken pox . . . scooters and muddy galoshes cluttering the hall . . . financial pressure to give these little strangers the best education in the land. Who would shoulder such burdens voluntarily? . . ." (cited in Zelizer, 1985, p. 170). Yet, the supply of adoptive homes has never been greater. The clergy has long argued for the joys of adoption, "Does the child pay? Yes, surely he pays—a hundred, a thousand-fold. A man's children are his treasure . . . What amount of money would buy them from us? This is . . . almost equally true of those children that come into our homes by adoption" (Lamb, 1905, p. 66).

The Changing Value of Children

Discussion of the value of children must address the limits of that valuation, for if it was unlimited then adoption would be far more common and disruption a one-in-a-thousand occurrence. As long ago as 1875, Homer Folks (1899) explained the significance of ensuring that families realize some kind of gain from placement. He writes, "The great majority of children who are returned after being placed in homes are returned . . . because of their inability to render a certain amount of services which the foster parents rightfully expected. In most cases the boy was not a bad boy, but a bad bargain" (p. 76). Parents continue to require that the placement result in some of "services" although the service has changed from an economic service to service to the cause of family efficiency, togetherness, and satisfaction. In a few placements, the service is more specific—"to be a companion to our only son," was the candid way one couple, who had a disrupted placement, described their reason for wanting to adopt an older child. Another adopting couple expressed the desire for a child "who could eventually go to Princeton" (quoted in Zelizer, 1985, p. 195).

Recent years witness a return to expectations of responsibility in children (Zelizer, 1985). Skolnick (1978) argues that the role of the self-denying adult and the irresponsible child are frustrating for both and that children's rights have been overemphasized to the detriment of their development. There is an overflow of strain from the pressure-packed lives of parents on children to be more adultlike and productive. At least, they should not require any more than the minimum amount of intrusion into the parent's efforts to meet their employment, home maintenance, and marital responsibilities. As such, extra trips in to school to discuss a problem behavior with the teacher is not only a communication about the child's difficulty, but may call for explanations and inconveniences to a dense network of co-workers, customers, and clients. At least within the household, children are again at work. The hope of a growing number of parents is that children will "become invaluably useful participants in a cooperative family unit" (Zelizer, 1985, p. 228). The expectation for productive children may not augur well for older child adoption, unless agencies and families can find means for matching children whose contribution to the family will be delayed or nonexistent with families that can tolerate and enjoy their children's gradual maturation. Preventive actions are needed. The problems of placing older children began to be addressed in the late 19th century. Children at that age were considered too old to serve the family as "pets and means of amusement."

All of these factors may be a part of the impetus for adoption of an older child. Each of these is also threatened by the difficulties that older children often entail. There may be less reciprocity and less social status, as the older adopted child is just as likely to be caught shoplifting as win a National Merit Scholarship. Few parents or social workers fully understand that the environment is a powerful but ultimately imperfect mechanism for changing the life course of a child. Scarr and Weinberg (1976) show that adopted children can make many gains, but that their final IQ is as close to their birth parents as it is to their adoptive parents or their siblings by adoption. In short, in many respects, the value of adopted children may be great but still discrepant from that expected by adoptive parents. For this reason, perhaps, several studies (e.g., Urban Systems Research and Engineering, 1985) suggest that highly educated and upper-income families may be more likely to have adoption disruptions. Their overloaded schedules may not easily tolerate the difficulties, trouble shooting, and disappointments that may arise. These families—even when professional human services providers— may need particularly attentive postplacement services.

To have a family and to become a family are two of the greatest hopes possible in America and all lands where the family stands as the pre-eminent institution entrusted as the purveyor of social and health benefits. Drawing on a range of imperfect evidence we have estimated the advantages that adoption holds over foster care. Adoption is clearly more effective in promoting the well-being of children than foster care. The average resources provided to adoptive children ($303,806) are far greater than those provided to foster children ($85,354). Those resources are primarily offered by the family ($286,409) and not by the government (i.e., subsidies of $17,397). Although the total resources provided to the adopted child are almost four times those provided to the foster child, the amount provided by the agency or government is about one-half. Thus, whereas the purely economic costs of adoption exceed those of foster care, the great majority of those costs are born by the family. The returns of adoption that result from greater educational investment and success surpass those of foster care by at least $242,180. The total value of adoption to the child is $545,986 which exceeds that of foster care by $460,632. The personal benefits of lifetime member-ship in a family are even more salutary. In Chapter 13, the cost of disruption to the agency and the savings from intensive adoption preservation services are detailed. The combined evidence overwhelmingly pronounces that adoption's contribution to children could be far greater if society's support for adoption were boosted.

3

A Social and Cognitive Model of Adjustment to Adoption

Social service providers have long turned to theories to guide them during those lengthy breaks from certainty about what to do and why. Theory building in adoption has been quite limited. Indeed, only Kirk's (1964, 1981) work on the importance of acknowledging the differences of adoptive families qualifies in even the closest way to being a unique adoption theory. Others have made beginning attempts to enlist attachment theory (Fahlberg, 1979; Goodfield & Carson, 1986), loss and grief (Elbow & Knight, 1987), and Eriksonian developmental theory (Brodzinsky, 1987a) to explain adjustment to adoption. In short, theoretical explanations of adjustment to adoption, adoption disruption, and the adoption of older children are largely undeveloped.

Generally, we have no complaints about the lack of unique adoption theories. Instead, we argue for the application of the most powerful existing theories of human development and behavior to older child adoption and disruption. In our view, social learning theory and recent cognitive theories—especially those related to stress and coping—are the most useful for explaining adoption and disruption. After a brief review of previous work, this chapter articulates a social and cognitive model of the adjustment to adoption. In later chapters we demonstrate its power in explaining the outcomes of adoption.

EXISTING ADOPTION THEORIES

Kirk's landmark theory of adjustment to adoption (1964, 1981) stresses the importance of family members' acknowledgment of the difference between birth and adoptive families. Primary consideration is given to the significance of "telling" the child he is adopted and dealing with the feelings that arise from that revelation. "Telling" the child is important in its own right, as well as a precursor of functional relationships between family members based on trust and honest communication. Whereas acknowledgment of differences may reduce the likelihood of disturbing surprises and false hopes for children, this concept fails to account for the complex interplay of blended family relationships and social services that account for older child adoption outcomes.

Brodzinsky (1987a) further develops the role of telling and acknowledgment of differences in his explanation of the adjustment to adoption, which relies heavily on developmental theory. Brodzinsky's attempt is commendable, although his assumptions that psychosocial adjustment to adoption is best explained by drawing on developmental theory does not hold well for older child adoption. Most of the developmental tasks concern the child's unknown past and are specific to infant adoptions. Only a few describe older child adoptions as well.

Like Kirk, Brodzinsky concludes that adopted children are at higher risk of psychological difficulties as a result of an unknown past and the way that the child and family cope with the search for information about that past. Neither fully explain the processes experienced by children adopted when older: children who may remember their birth families and keep in contact with them.

Older adopted children are members of "blended" families, in that they, like the adoptive parents, bring a unique familial history to the adoption. This contributes to the complex task of family integration. Older adopted children cope with psychological and social stressors of adjustment to a new family. Existing models of adjustment to adoption are instructive but provide limited illumination of the relationship between the older adopted child, the family, the agency, and informal social resources. This chapter draws on social learning and stress and coping theories to provide such a framework.

A Social and Cognitive Perspective of the Stressors and Tasks of Adoption

Adopted children and adoptive parents are individually faced with stressors and developmental tasks, and the adoptive family as a whole also experiences the effects of adoption. Although these individual and family tasks are interactive and concurrent, enumerating the individual and family tasks separately is more edifying. First a brief review of important concepts is necessary. *Stress* is defined by Lazarus as "a relationship between the person and environment that is appraised by the person as relevant to his or her well-being and in which the person's resources are taxed or exceeded"

(Folkman & Lazarus, 1985, p. 152). Thus, stress is a function of the individual's (parent, child, or sibling) resources, and his or her appraisal in any given situation. Stress is appraised by the individual, and these stressors are not the same for all children or all adults. Stated simply, in a situation that is important to the individual and where resources are low, stress will be high. The same individual in the same situation, but with more resources, might not appraise the situation as stressful at all. For example, a parent who has organized his or her family for a Down's Syndrome child might view the adoption of a second handicapped child as minimally stressful, compared to a parent without such previous experience.

Adoptive families may face more simultaneous stressors than other families. Adoptive families deal with such universal family developmental tasks as raising children, achieving family unity, and promoting individual growth, as well as difficulties at school and work. They must also manage situations specific to adoptions: for example, relations with the birth parents, formalities of last names, and attitudes of extended family members. These extra tasks contribute to a high "transitional density" (Bain, 1978), or pile-up of stressors, which may overtax resources of adoptive families (Zwimpher, 1983).

Resources can be anything from tangibles like money or time to intangibles like friendship or a hug. Resources fluctuate over time, as they are used up and replenished. In addition, some people simply have fewer resources than others, and need help in acquiring resources from within (like patience and self-management skills) and from their environment (like accurate expectations). If a situation arises when resources are perceived as low (after a long day at work or during an illness or after paying the bills), an otherwise benign situation (a cranky child) may be appraised as stressful.

Available resources influence the appraisal of stress. The support of family, friends, and informal services and agencies can help prevent the appraisal of situations as threatening. Family members can often count on each other to offer information, material goods, emotional support, and other means to solve problems during stressful times. Social institutions such as school and the workplace also support the family by providing models and normative expectations of successful individual and family life. A model of adjustment to older child adoption must, however, recognize the shortage of supportive resources for adoptive (and other "blended") families because of the nature of their unconventional status.

Coping consists of the cognitive and social efforts made to reduce stress. Such efforts are influenced by the resources available to the person as well as the nature of the stressor. For example, a child who has never learned prosocial behavior for solving problems (a resource) will not respond positively to parents (coping) during family negotiations (the stressor).

Alternatively, a fost-adopt child who attends a support group of other adopted children (a resource) will be able to draw on those experiences and better tolerate (coping) the restrictions his family institutes for bad grades (a stressor). One strong determinant of coping efforts is the individual's expectations. Critical expectations relate to one's expected ability to cope effectively, and to the expectations that one will be rewarded when one does cope. Thus, it is not only important that adoptive parents expect that they can parent a difficult child, but that they also have reasonable expectations about how long it takes to develop loving family attachment. If the parent meets the first expectation but fails in the second, they will experience the outcome as stressful.

Coping efforts may be functional or dysfunctional, but to the person using them, they are simply coping efforts. Coping strategies are separate from coping outcomes (Folkman, 1984). If a response reduces stress for the family, they have coped. They have coped well if the response is satisfying to everyone in the family, and they have not coped well if they achieve this reduction of stress as a temporary delay of an eventual disaster. If a family has the expectation that they cannot manage by themselves, they may cope with a difficult child by seeking help from friends or the agency to manage his stressful behavior, or they may cope by returning the child to the agency. Their choice of coping behavior will be determined by many factors and can be influenced by agency efforts.

The more effectively a person resolved past situations, the stronger will be the expectation of success in future similar situations. The stress of an event is not only in its nature, but in our expectation that we cannot handle it. People who stay calm in the face of such seemingly insurmountable events as the adoption of an adolescent are people who engage in fewer self-appraisals of inadequacy and expect to resolve troubles with less stress. Of course, overextended expectations will lead to the experience of failure. Highly successful professionals who rapidly solve many problems each week may find the gradualness of change in older child adoptions distressing.

Our Model

Adoptive families need a range of coping resources to address the primary task for adoptive families: the integration, or blending, of members from two previously separate families into a new family. Often, this primary task involves many other subtasks, such as adjusting to a new home, neighborhood, and school. The successful mastery of these subtasks does not, however, singularly comprise the formula for successful integration. Integration is the main task at hand for most of these family members with the long-term meshing of coping styles and behavior determining the viability of older child adoptions.

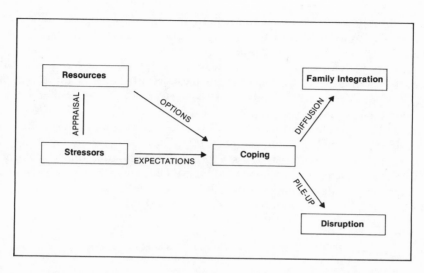

FIGURE 3.1. Individual coping within a transitional task. Adapted from McCubbin and Patterson, 1983.

The resources available to the child in the new home will have a major impact on the child's appraisal of the situation as harmful, threatening or challenging. These appraisals will, in turn, influence the child's coping efforts by increasing or decreasing the options perceived as available. The effectiveness with which the child copes with day-to-day stressful interaction will determine whether stress is diffused and family members are satisfied with each other, or the conflicts are never quite resolved and stressors accumulate leading to eventual global dissatisfaction and, perhaps, disruption (see Fig. 3.1). Of course, as we have emphasized, the child is but one actor in this system. His or her efforts are but one element of family coping and need to mesh with other family member's coping styles to achieve family integration. This will be elaborated when we discuss family tasks.

Kirk's notion of acknowledging differences allows family members to develop their own rules for family life without the constraining expectations about adoption; for example, that the parents and child will never think about birth parents and the parents will never treat the adopted child differently. We build on Kirk (1981) to argue that the family's acceptance and understanding of their unconventionality will allow adoptive families to develop workable relationships that are unencumbered by traditional rules and norms that would not easily apply to them. Our model assumes that there are no "normal" individual behaviors and no "normal" family interactions that, when practiced, will produce a "successful" adoptive family unit.

Instead, it is the functional integration of individual efforts within the context of family tasks and transitions that determines whether everyday difficulties become persisting problems.

This chapter identifies common stressors facing members of older child adoptive families, including the unconventional attributes of the status of adopting or being adopted. Many of these stressors follow from resource deficits typically available to conventional families, since the absence of an expected resource can be a stressor. First, the stressors and developmental tasks facing adoptive children and parents will be considered, followed by an outline of larger familial stressors and tasks. In addition, the formal and informal coping resources that should be available to adoptive children and families will be discussed, with the goal of identifying hypotheses for the study and avenues for improved services (see Table 3.1).

THE OLDER CHILD IN AN ADOPTIVE FAMILY

Adopted children—indeed, all children in unconventional family circum-stances—are burdened with stressors and resource deficits because of the nature of their unique situation. While taxed with these stressors, they also face additional transitional tasks of blending with new family members that other children do not encounter. This combination heightens the vulnera-bility of older children in adoption. The level of stressors will vary, naturally, with children in foster parent adoptions often experiencing more resources and less stress.

Characteristic Stressors for Adopted Children

Older adopted children are not open packages of sculptor's clay willing to be formed into the image of the adopting parents. The effects of the child's prior experience in birth and foster families affects current expectations and cognitive and behavioral responses to stress. In addition to these lasting effects, many resources that are usually available to children are, by definition of belonging to an unconventional family system, diminished for older children. Another resource deficit for these children is the want of social support from lasting family, school, and neighborhood relationships.

MISLEADING EXPECTATIONS.   The older child's history in a maltreating home and in foster care may create or exacerbate resource deficits of frustrating educational experiences and physical and behavioral problems. How the child has coped with past stresses will affect current appraisal and coping. The child learns what reduces or fails to reduce conflict in particular situations. For example, in an alcoholic birth home, a child may learn that

Table 3.1. A Social and Cognitive Model of Adjustment to Adoption

Actor	Stressors	Tasks	Coping resources
Child	Misleading expectations based on: Lack of social skills Low capacity for attachment Behavioral deficits Low sense of permanence Low sense of self-efficacy Lack of social support	Separation and loss Role establishment Developmental tasks	Consistent social worker Siblings Support from biological and/or previous foster parents Preparation visits, life book Support group
Parent	Misleading expectations Instant parenthood Novelty of roles Finances Lack of social support	Role establishment Nurturance of marital relationship	Realistic, accurate information about the child Supportive, strengthening placement process Reasonable waiting period with consistent process milestones Subsidies Consistent social worker Support group Referrals to schools, therapists, groups
Family	Lack of family accord Lack of societal norms Lack of agency support	Role establishment Boundary establishment Integration Attachment	Available yet non-intrusive agency support Skills training Postlegal services Support of extended family Family therapy sensitive to adoption issues

saying nothing or ignoring the problem is the best way to manage. An adoptive home that expects free flowing communication about the child's experience will not reward such avoidance behavior and the child will perceive the experience as quite stressful.

Children who were severely neglected prior to their adoption may never have learned to exchange positive communication with family members (Patterson & Reid, 1970). The lack of positive interactions proves frustrating in the long run, resulting in the parents feeling ineffective with this child and withdrawing efforts toward attachment. As Nelson (1985) found, adoptive parents are least satisfied when the child is unable to engage in a personal way at the level the parents desire. Smith and Sherwen (1983) report that the mother's dissatisfaction with the adopted child's closeness to her was a more significant contributor to disruption than the child's experience of alienation from the mother.

After a likely history of several foster placements, the adoptive child has no compelling reason to believe that the next placement (even if it is called an "adoption") is permanent or will work out. Experience in past placements may have provided few experiences of success in what the older child will perceive as a threatening situation. This lack of confidence may directly affect his appraisal of stressful situations, judging what might be benign to another child as a threat. There are reports on a few children who experienced the "Cinderella Syndrome" and believed that they were severely maltreated in contrast to their nonadopted siblings (Goodwin, Cauthorne, & Rada, 1980). Commitment and motivation bear on beliefs of self-efficacy, and without motivation to continue the placement, coping efforts will not be directed to maintain the placement.

For the child in care, every placement has an element of uncertainty. Uncertainty causes stress and prolonged stress can lead to maladaptive coping. When first taken into care, the foster child is uncertain why he or she is in care and whether he or she will return home. During the months of attempts at reunification with the birth family, the duration and outcome of foster care are uncertain. Trial reunification visits may also leave lasting confusion—one child with 16 trial reunification visits later predictably had a disrupted adoption. The longer this uncertainty lasts, the more stress the child endures, and the more likely it is that behavior problems will develop and the placement will end.

LACK OF SOCIAL SUPPORT.   The newly adopted child also lacks social resources other children have. The move from home to home can mean loss of contact with siblings and extended natural family, and of supportive ties with foster parents and foster siblings. A new school may also mean the loss of support from former teachers and school friends. In addition, workers change frequently, especially in social service systems that assign a new worker to a child as he moves from reunification to foster care to adoption. In short, the child may have few or no continuing social supports.

As for the adopted child, this review of stressors has shown that he or she may have especially few strengths and sources of support. The combination of the accumulation of stressors and few resources with which to cope implicates these children as highly susceptible to the otherwise minor stressors of day-to-day coping, and in need of strong external support as they face the tasks of transition.

Transitional Tasks for Adopted Children

Of all life events associated with a difficult childhood, experiences of family troubles, the addition of a new family member, and entrances into new environments are most significantly related to children's behavior problems (Sandler & Ramsay, 1980). During the adoptive placement, the older adoptive child experiences many major transitions, including major family trouble, entrance into a new adoptive family (perhaps with new siblings and extended family), and entrance into a new school and neighborhood. Each of these transitions carries tasks for the child. As mentioned earlier, these transitions have a compounding stressful effect on the ability of the child to cope with any one transition. During the early stages of the placement, the tasks for the child are numerous: separation from prior caretakers, integration into the new family (composed of numerous subtasks such as his role in relation to the parent and to siblings, and other new roles and rules in this family), and entry into a new social environment.

SEPARATION AND LOSS. An important transitional task for both parent and child in adoption is dealing with the child's separation from the birth or foster parent. This separation can have varying forms, since some adoptive parents allow contact with the child's previous caretakers while other parents and children maintain no contact whatsoever. Whereas the arrangements and outcomes vary, in instances of great conflict between the child and his birth parents prior to separation, noncontact after placement may be a great relief to the birth parents, adoptive parents, and children (Felner, 1984).

One youth described by Howard and Smith (1987) was awaiting adoption, but his birth parents insisted on pursuing custody. The court ordered continued visitation during the birth parents' appeal of the parental rights termination. After an initial and very upsetting visit, the 10-year-old handed letters to his birth parents, telling them that he never wanted to see them, that they had made him unhappy and sick, that he was finally getting better, and that they should get out of his life before he came to hate them even more than he already did. The mother relinquished her rights that afternoon.

Some adopted children may dearly miss the birth parents, glorify their memory so that no parents can surpass them, and wait for those parents to come back. Such children may benefit from disengagement activities— including life book construction (a compilation and explanation of the history of one's life) and review and meetings with birth parents—to allow remembering and letting go of ideas and attachments that preclude joining a new family.

Separation and loss are important events for any child. Separation and loss may become commonplace for the older adopted child who is separated from his parent(s) prior to entry into foster care, and may have left several foster homes thereafter. The multiplicity of separations may not make them any less traumatic for the child, but makes constant readjustment more challenging. Each separation may affect self-expectations as well as his generalized image of parents and families. Even though the adults in the adoptive placement (parents as well as social workers and other professionals) may view the move into adoption as a positive transition, the child may perceive removal from the (prior) foster or biological home as an indication of his own failure or the system's indifference to his or her desire for a stable home.

ROLE ESTABLISHMENT.   In nonsibling, nonfoster-parent adoptions, the adopted child must create a relatively new role from the inception. The parents have the advantage of a past history together, with shared development as a couple and the well-negotiated (if not always shared) values, expectations, and behavior patterns that result. The child is expected to enter into this family, comprised of parents and possibly other children, and make it his or her own. Clearly, the pressure is on the child to integrate. While the parents will certainly try to ease this transition, it is up to the child to conform and to encourage the parents to conform to the his/her style. The latter is facilitated by the child's ability to participate in enjoyable interpersonal exchanges with parents. The more enjoyable the relationship, the more the incentives to reduce conflict and accommodate change.

DEVELOPMENTAL TASKS.   The developmental issues for the child in adoption will differ, depending on age and resolution of previous tasks of development. The adoptive placement and the previous removals from other homes will compound these tasks, resulting in the need for special attention from parents and social workers as to developmental issues.

A successful transition to and through adolescence is considered to be among the most difficult of all tasks for any child, but especially for adopted ones. For all its notoriety, the transition to adolescence is but one of the developmental tasks faced by adopted children. A child's understanding of adoption is very tenuous until about age 10 (Brodzinsky, Schechter, & Brodzinsky, 1986b). Whatever "telling" about the adoption is done in the early years may need retelling and reliving during early adolescence. During adolescence, heightened peer influences may magnify the significance of the differences between adoptive and birth children and contribute to yet greater strain between child and parent. Disabled adopted children experience adolescence as especially troubling as their disadvantages in the dating and mating scene become more pronounced. Adoptive siblings may neglect or reject the support of their birth or adoptive siblings because the adopted sibling highlights the status differences. Most postadoptive services are delivered to adolescents and their families (Fales, 1985).

The Child's Coping Response

Resources are a key element of the appraisal of a situation and coping efforts within that situation. The older adopted child is likely to have a shortage of resources that reduce the child's coping repertoire. Some of these may be constitutional but many are situational. In contrast to the stepchild, a member of another type of blended family, the new adopted child does not remain in the household with either biological parent. Lacking this key resource, the adoptive child might use such social coping sources as siblings (especially if they are placed in the same adoptive home), the social worker, and, when available, support groups. Siblings can be very comforting to each other when placed together (Rosenberg, 1980), although this generates its own stresses for the family. Similarly, the support of a consistent social worker is important. With the increase in foster parent adoptions, moving a child from foster care into adoption typically results in a change of social worker, depriving the child of this source of support. Self-help groups for adopted children are rare, but do exist. Perhaps the best prototypes are the adoption groups and summer camps for Korean-American adopted youth.

Advocates of open adoption emphasize the importance of ongoing contact between the child and previous caregivers (Borgman, 1982; Pannor & Baran, 1984). Those individuals who have taken care of or lived with the child in the past (biological parents and siblings as well as foster families) can give the child a sense of security and familiarity while he is integrating into his new home. The value of open adoption to the child is still being weighed against its possible negative effects on the viability of the placement, however, and many practitioners are cautious about its use (Kraft, Palombo, Woods, Mitchell & Schmidt, 1985).

Coping strategies that the child might use can result in negative or positive changes in their relationship to the adoptive family. The particular coping strategies that children use are, in part, associated with the age and gender of the child (Wertlieb, Weigel, & Feldstein, 1987). Girls use more environment-focused coping (such as asking for help or information), compared to boys, who more often use self-focused coping (such as taking action). Boys are especially likely to say that "nothing helps."

Adoption workers and parents help to promote more functional coping strategies for any particular child through a variety of efforts, including counseling, providing appropriate reading materials, modeling, offering the chance for the child to reconsider expectations and fears, and engaging in anticipatory coping and rehearsal. Through this rehearsal, the child is helped to anticipate many of the possible problems that may arise, and can rehearse how not only to respond in these situations but how to successfully negotiate through them. The child adds the resource of preparedness to his coping repertoire. This is the rationale for the use of age-appropriate books and stories for adopted children, like *Who is David?* (Nerlove, 1985) and *Why Was I Adopted?* (Livingston, 1978). These help children to identify with other adopted children who have questions but are basically happy, and provide models of children with prosocial coping skills specific to situations in adoptions. Such anticipation and rehearsal helps to remove the novelty of situations, thus decreasing the stress and increasing adaptive behavior.

THE PARENT IN AN ADOPTIVE FAMILY

Children are often initially seen as the vulnerable party in adoptive families but are soon viewed as responsible to change their behavior to suit that new environment. Parents also face stressful transitional tasks that arise from their new family constellation. This vulnerability can be a precursor to adaptive or maladaptive coping on the part of the parent. This outcome depends on many variables, including the level of stressors that parents can manage.

Characteristic Stressors for Adoptive Parents

Adoptive parents share many stressors common to adoptive children, especially concerning misleading expectations and the lack of social support. Other stressors unique to parents include instant parenthood, the novelty of new roles, and financial costs.

MISLEADING EXPECTATIONS. Adoptive parents may not treat themselves as the "real" parents—and may be told so by adopted children. They may feel different or lacking in parental qualities (Cole, 1984). Children may encourage adoptive parents' diminished expectations by informing them that they are not going to do what they are told because "You're not my mother." Experienced adoptive parents will treat this comment as if it were from a birth child lamenting the same parental ordinance by proclaiming "I wish I were never born;" that is, as a complaint about the mother's effort to socialize her child, not as a challenge to her right to parent. In the adopted child's adolescence, this inadequate feeling may be pronounced, as the parents deal with problems that all parents experience, like the child's emerging sexuality (Schneider & Rimmer, 1984), as well as the issues more unique to adoptions such as a different appearance and whether to reestablish or maintain ties with the biological family.

Adoptive parents' expectations of success may also be tread upon in the application and waiting process. While this is never the intent of the preplacement process, the partial goal of the application and associated interviews may be interpreted as a questioning of parents' competence. This process necessarily entails asking parents to identify children they are most and least interested in and able to parent. The uncertainty about when a child will be found and what the child will be like also contribute to stress.

One very tangible resource that adoptive parents often lack is adequate information about the child's special needs, childhood history, medical and educational records, and history in foster care. Adoptive parents often complain about the dearth of accurate information provided about the adopted child (Meezan, 1980; Nelson, 1985; Trimetiere, 1979). Adoptive parents may read a child's scanty case history but not understand their implications. They may, instead, focus on the poor child who has undergone such deprivation and disappointment.

Parents with no prior experience in older child adoption may have unrealistically high positive expectations of themselves and their child (Nelson, 1985; Ward, 1981; Kadushin & Seidl, 1971; Lawder, 1970). These are encouraged by the beatification of adoptive parents by friends, fellow worshippers, and neighbors—"You are a saint to do this", "The kids are so lucky", "There isn't a better set of parents anywhere." Parents with high expectations for immediate and full integration of the child into the family are at risk.

Not only do parents have high expectations of the child, but these parents also impose high expectations for themselves to meet the child's many needs (Smith & Sherwen, 1983; Hepworth, 1980). Their measure of their own self-worth is contingent upon the child's response to them, which is a rather unreliable yardstick. Parents who are inadequately prepared for the child's lack of responsiveness to them will certainly be frustrated (and even those who are prepared will find the transition trying). Their initial expectations that the adoption will work out may be quite positive (other adoptive parents develop close, loving relationships with children), but they seem to be ineffective at achieving such an outcome with their child. After a while, they may believe themselves to be ineffective parents.

The risk of error and its consequences adds to the probability of an appraisal of threat. For example, most parents expect that positive routine displays of affection on their part will elicit positive returns from their children. Since older child adoptions involve many children with limited ability to receive and give affection, parents are cautioned not to expect too much affection initially. In fact, some children will react quite negatively to affection. A display of parental affection followed by the child's angry rejection adds dollars to the bank of pessimism.

INSTANT PARENTHOOD.   Like stepparents, adoptive parents share the burden of instant parenthood and the "myth of instant love" (Jacobson, 1979). Adoptive parents may feel pressure to treat the child as their own, with "instant love" exhibited at every home visit to prove the viability of the placement. This may seem simple enough until the adopted child rejects them or, worse, physically or sexually assaults a birth or previously adopted child. This challenges the adopted parents' identity as being an equal parent to all of the children in the household. More commonly, parents worry that the continued drain on the family's resources are reducing the overall quality of family life. Adoptive parents may be hesitant to express such concerns to themselves, to each other, or during agency visits for fear that the mention of problems will invalidate their claim to be loving, committed parents.

Birth parents typically have the child's history to draw on in interpreting new behavior or problems. Adoptive parents have only a case record and other information from the adoption worker, which tends to be more factual, regarding the medical and placement history. More everyday information about the child's behavior is often glossed over. For example, the "instant" adoptive mother does not know if her child's lying is just a temporary lapse in honesty or an indication of a deeply ingrained habit.

Many adoptions involve new sibling relationships. Those that do not, where siblings are adopted into homes with no other children, seem to fare rather smoothly (Kadushin & Seidl, 1971). When other siblings are involved, children have new siblings to love and hate. The overnight conglomeration of many people into one household imposes myriad stresses and strains, as well as struggles for power and property. The parents are suddenly in charge of delegating privileges and property, which tax their diplomatic resources. This is especially difficult when the adopted child's behavior is less responsible than the birth child's, or when the older birth child has more privileges because of age, which can be easily misconstrued as favoritism.

NOVELTY OF ROLES.   Regarding role ambiguity in stepfamilies, one researcher notes, "the present situation approaches chaos, with each individual set of families having to work out its own destiny without any realistic guidelines" (Bohannon, 1970, p. 137). The same can be said of some older child adoptive families—especially those with open adoption plans. Such families share the problem of a lack of guidelines concerning roles for parents and children. They lack models to follow when accepting the role of parenting "someone else's children." Whereas there are no definitive guidelines for parenting of any sort, adoptive families have fewer TV shows, books, friends, and personal experiences to draw upon.

For new adoptive parents without other children, novelty will be the rule. Parenting is not completely novel to any parent, because each has at least an abstract knowledge of parenting through their own parents and other parents they know. The novelty of parenting an older child generates much guesswork, however, and one's guess will be based on old expectations modified by new information.

FINANCIAL COSTS. Finances are stressors in adoption. Zwimpher (1983) found that the families with the fewest financial resources had a higher rate of disruption. The special medical and psychological needs of the child may strain the financial resources of the family, one of the most difficult strains with which any family must cope (Olson *et al.*, 1983). Subsidies for special-needs adoptions are granted in the majority of cases, and are federally funded in recognition of these stressors and their effect on the ability to make and keep adoptive placements. Yet, following the discussion of the costs of raising children in Chapter 2, subsidies (which cannot be higher than the foster care rate) hardly approximate the actual costs of adoption.

LACK OF SOCIAL SUPPORT. Social support strengthens adoption (Partridge, Hornby, & McDonald, 1986). Although agencies screen adoptive parents to ensure that they have adequate sound support, subtle factors may undermine the value of this support. Adoption is not sanctified in our society (Cole, 1984), and formal programs that provide social supports are lacking (North American Council on Post-Legal Adoption Services, 1984; Feigelman & Silverman, 1979). Even when available, these groups may not be used. Somewhat ironically, single parents in Nelson's (1985) study were less likely to participate in adoption support groups because of more pressing familial demands.

One social support that may be lacking in older child adoptions is a norm for the relationship between the adopted child and his or her biological parents, in addition to the relationship with his or her adoptive parents (Borgman, 1982). Also, some relatives disapprove of or are just not thrilled by the adoption of an older, difficult child (Katz, 1977). Alienation from the extended family may result in a lack of social support where and when it is most needed (Feigelman & Silverman, 1979). Even families with social support prior to the placement may lose that support as they tend to the demands of the parenting role.

Transitional Tasks for Adoptive Parents

Since adoptive parents usually do not face the additional stressors of moving to a new home or school, their tasks of adoption focus more on their role in the family. These roles include both parenting and marital roles, and are affected by the adequacy of resources and coping repertoires.

ESTABLISHMENT OF THE PARENTING ROLE.   Becoming parents is a role transition like none other, affecting intra- as well as extrafamily relationships. This transition is considered to be extremely stressful, even under "normal" conditions (Holmes & Rahe, 1967). Becoming a parent to an older child magnifies this stress, accelerating the development of the parental roles to the speed of light. Not only are parents new to their role, but they are parenting a child who is not new to that role. Older adopted children are once empty slates now covered with strong beliefs about typical family life and norms of family interaction. Parents seasoned by their own or foster children may have more success in this role, given the acquisition of more resources for the situation and a likely appraisal of the placement as challenging and manageable. Those who have experienced a previous disruption may be more tentative about the strength of their efforts. Parents with no prior adoptive or parenting experience will probably rely heavily on vicarious learning from books, social workers, other parents, and self-help groups.

Smoothly functioning couples seem to agree about parenting. This is partly an illusion resulting from incremental rule development in their homes and due to their children's infrequent testing of the rules. The introduction of a new member into the household who does not share those rules may result in reconsideration of more rules than the family ever knew they had.

MANAGING NOVEL CHILD BEHAVIOR.   Older children bring novel behavior into every adoptive home. Some of these may be talents that they possess and that are appealing to the adoptive family. Some older adopted boys in our study were terrific caregivers for little children, for example. More often, the novel behaviors are deviant and discordant with the family's expectations. Whereas these expectations may need to be adjusted in recognition that these behaviors will not change quickly, the family will also have to cope with the behavior. Children who have become eroticized as a result of severe sexual abuse are a case in point. These children may assault other children in the home or be expelled from school because they stimulate themselves publicly. More common are adoptive children with explosive tempers that cause conflict in the family and community. Indeed, incidents that precipitate disruptions often involve attacks on parents or siblings (Holmes, 1979). Families certainly need to know about these problems before the placement, but they also need skill to manage the difficulty. Most families of older adopted children expect to have a therapeutic effect on their older children but few expect to have to become skilled in changing behavior or to act as case managers. Most adoptive families will not need to become that sophisticated, but when they do, the stressors created by novel child behaviors can disrupt an adoption.

NURTURANCE OF MARITAL RELATIONSHIPS. Adoptive parents, like all parents, face the task of nurturing the marital relationship. Even though the marriage has preceded the adoption and is presumed to have some stability, adoption can place severe strain on marriages (Rosenthal, 1982). One parent can devote so much time and energy to the child that the spouse resents the neglect. The adoption worker is sometimes guilty of working closely with one parent (often the mother) to the exclusion of the other. This can alienate the other parent from the adoptive as well as the marital relationship. When the child's behavior is egregious to one parent but not the other, this parent's behavior may be interpreted as being too rigid or too unconcerned about the rest of the family ("You are as hypercritical of Jackie as you are of me"). Issues of loyalty and commitment to a child may spread to become issues of loyalty and love between spouses ("If you can't stick by Lee in thick and thin, how do I know you will stick by me if the going gets tough?").

Adoptive parents must come to grips with the fact of their infertility. While adoptive parents today are seldom screened for infertility, a sizable proportion of adoptive parents of older children cannot have children of their own. The placement of the adoptive child, while sought by the parents, is also a reminder of this inability of the marital couple. Since infertility is increasingly viewed as a mismatch between the couple's reproductive characteristics and not a trait of an individual, infertility raises such questions as, "What if I had married someone else (or did in the future)? Could I have a birth child who is more like me? Wouldn't that be more rewarding than this?" These and related doubts draw on parents' and couples' personal commitment and resources.

The Parents' Coping Response

The lack of societal norms and guidelines for adoptive parents can become a resource instead of a stressor. If adoptive families are helped to downplay the myth of the normal family (which is becoming extinct among all families), and helped to form their own roles and rules, their acknowledgment of differences can liberate them from expecting to be like "the Joneses."

Parents can be helped to cope through agency preparation prior to placement and availability during the time of and post-placement. Referrals to other coping resources such as special education for the child and support groups will also help to promote adaptive coping. Provision of other, more concrete resources, such as subsidies and respite care, can boost the parents' store of resources to lessen the impact of stressful situations.

Parents in older child adoptive families may need help to realize the special circumstances of this situation, and modify their expectations, which are typically based on experiences that do not accommodate this special case of parenting. Parents must treat these children as individuals, not as stereotypes of abused or neglected children, and must respond to the specific behavior of the child at the time. As such, successful adoptive parents emphasize the necessity of living "one day at a time," and appreciate signs of love and progress "one inkling at a time." The belief that "we would all have settled in after about a year or so" can be amended to recognize that adoption is a lifelong process and, at least, families can expect that it will take as long for a child to unlearn negative coping styles as it took to learn them.

Our model suggests that parents who have received an adequate preplacement orientation and, ideally, have participated in parent support groups, will know that they may need to alter their expectations of the outcomes of their parental interactions. Their adopted children may not respond like other children to affection or discipline. Parents can expect a delayed return of what they give their children. Armed with this expectation they may be less likely to prematurely withdraw their offerings to the child.

The Adoptive Family

Beyond the stressors and tasks for individuals in adoption are those facing the family as a system. While children and parents may cope successfully with their transitional tasks on an individual level, larger environmental and internal stressors also affect the family.

Stressors for the Family

LACK OF FAMILY ACCORD. The most successful families have an implicit agreement about family norms and communication (Olson *et al.*, 1983). This understanding is absent at the beginning of adoptive placements. New adoptive families, especially those who adopt sibling groups, do not have time to warm up to the task by parenting a single nonverbal infant. Communication skills take time to develop. The old and emerging norms of dyads and triads of the newly formed family have customs and rules that will be tested by other members of the family. Through the conflict of everyday life, new customs and rules will eventually be ironed out. In the meantime, these conflicts contribute to family stress.

LACK OF SOCIETAL NORMS. Without societal norms for the unique relationships in adoptive families, day-to-day interaction will require constant adjustment and adaptation. People in all kinds of families are always looking to others in their school, work, or church for approval of their life style. When, instead, they find themselves constantly explaining and/or excusing their family style, the lack of understanding can be isolating. In fost-adopt families, for example, children have different last names than their parents. If the parents describe the placement to others as an adoption, this may be confusing and awkward. The unusually varied appearances of family members also need explanation.

LACK OF AGENCY SUPPORT.   The social institution that sponsors the stressful life event is the adoption agency, a primary consideration in examining the stress and adjustment to adoption. Bain (1978) recognizes the important (often negative) role of social institutions in defining a family transition. The definition of transitions in these such institutions are typically "located on one side of the transitional boundary, with primary tasks defined in terms inappropriate for coping with the transition as a psychosocial event. This has the result that the experience for the individual and family is one of fragmentation" (pp. 682–683). Adoption agencies are typically located on the preadoption side of this transition since the main agency tasks are the assessment, approval, and preparation of the adoptive family and child. After the placement, a minimal number of required agency visits occur and, barring complications, the adoption is legalized. Adoptive parents and child sometimes feel free of agency interference, but may as often feel deserted and in need of support from the social agency that best understands the situation. Thus, the agency, which is the social institution of most import to the transition, will better promote adaptation when organized to deal with the transition as an ongoing process.

Family Tasks

While adoptive families must find their own way, the overall framework of family tasks is, in a general sense, the same for all families. Among the tasks Elbow (1986) lists as involved in moving from caregiving to parenting are role establishment and boundary establishment. In addition to these tasks, adoptive families address the broader task of integration and attachment between all family members.

ROLE ESTABLISHMENT.   The entry of the child into the adoptive family affects many roles and relationships. Family systems theorists like Jackson (1967) emphasize that roles are essentially individual rather than interactional concepts. However, it is within the family context that family members' individual roles are developed. While there may be culturally set roles ("parent," "child"), the establishment of unique roles within each family is important to the overall family functioning.

BOUNDARY ESTABLISHMENT.   Like members of remarried families, adoptive families have more complex family structures with which to cope

(Cherlin, 1978), including other parents and children external to the household. Adoptive families retain an awareness of the biological parents, former foster parents, the agency, and other siblings. Family members must cope with the separation from these people and develop new forms of relationships with some of them. The issue of open adoption revolves around these concerns. It is important for the child to have the continuous support of people who were important to him in the past, but if the boundaries of the adoptive family are too open, integration of the child may never occur (Elbow, 1986). Adoptive parents may find contacts between the child and biological parents to be stressful, but these contacts are often beneficial to the child and the placement.

In addition to intrafamily role transitions, special-needs children involve the parents in additional extrafamilial roles within the medical, educational, and mental health systems. Agencies are a part of adoptive family life for a while (sometimes a long while), whether families like it or not, but this model suggests that agencies provide services without usurping the family's right to independence.

INTEGRATION AND ATTACHMENT. Adoptive families have the dual family task of attachment and separation (Elbow, 1986). While conventional families move from complete attachment toward separation and individuation of the children, the adoptive family of older children is striving for attachment to the child at the same time that they must support the development of independence and self-sufficiency. These dual goals conflict in everyday life, making seemingly benign choices stressful.

Adoptive families are unconventional and encounter different problems and role transitions than other families. Accepting the status of an unconventional family may, of itself, be an added stressor for families, seeming to isolate them even more. Understanding the liberating aspect of being unconventional, can, however, lead to creative attempts at integration and attachment. For example, promoting contact with a birth mother may help the older child to resolve feelings of loss or rejection and learn to resolve those issues within the family rather than in isolation. Efforts to strengthen overall family commitment will need to focus these creative energies on the integrational aspects of individual behavior. Disruption can be considered the result of nonintegration of the child, since most parents in disruptions agree that the child "just never fit in."

The Family's Coping Response

Figley (1983) identifies eleven characteristics which differentiate successful and unsuccessful family coping styles. The most crucial characteristics to this discussion of adoptive families are: viewing the situation as a family problem rather than merely a problem of one or two of its members; adopting a solution-oriented approach to the problem rather than simply blaming; evincing role flexibility; and using appropriate resources inside and outside the family. These characteristics of functional family coping show the outcome of a successful adoption rather than the starting point. Many of these functional coping characteristics are easier to develop in conventional family structures. The adoptive family is coping with the absence of many of these characteristics in addition to the day-to-day stressors of family life. In striving to develop these coping styles, other supports may be needed.

Coping efforts within the family must mesh if there is to be a satisfactory interaction. Not only must coping efforts prove successful to each individual member, but the process of coping must eventually be satisfying for all in order for all members to adapt to one another. For example, if one parent never develops a positive relationship with a child, periods of unusual stressors may lead to a less than acceptable relationship and the suggestion of a disruption. The long-term quality of family interaction depends upon the short-term effectiveness of individual coping, and this depends not only on one's own satisfaction, but the effects one's coping has on the environment, which includes the response of other family members. For example, a child may cope with a curfew by sneaking in the window after hours. This strategy may be satisfactory to her, but not to her mother, who will respond by nailing the window shut, leading to a further response from the child. This chain of coping efforts, or "pile-up," may eventually be unsatisfactory for all, resulting in a call for change. Whether this "change" is a demand for a family conference, severe sanctions by the parents, or outright disruption depends on a myriad of factors, including the resources on which each person can depend.

The Utility of the Model

A useful model of adjustment to older child adoption should improve our ability to make decisions about the design and delivery of services. It should also generate hypotheses. Yet, given the complexities of child, parent, and family resources, stressors, tasks, and coping responses, parsimonious predictions seem improbable. However, the model is still useful in generating questions that this study will address. Although we lack sufficient longitudinal design to use a helpful statistical program like LISREL and test the relative strength of all the contributing factors in our model, the data we will present are able to test parts of our study. The hypotheses we consider include the following.

1. Children adopted by their foster parents have an added resource and are thus less likely to disrupt.

2. Children with more historical problems of abuse and neglect will display more behavior problems and will be more likely to disrupt.
3. Children who have developed close relationships to prior caretakers will benefit by retaining contact with them. Thus, open adoptions, for children attached to prior caretakers, will be more stable than closed ones.
4. Children who have been in foster care longer will have endured more prolonged uncertainty and stress, and will be more likely to disrupt.
5. Families with continuous sources of support (no changes in social workers) will adjust to the placement, with less likelihood of disruption.
6. Children with unresolved separations from prior caretakers will be more likely to disrupt.
7. Adoptive parents with prior experience as foster or adoptive parents will use those resources to create a more stable placement.
8. Parents with inadequate information and/or preparation prior to placement will have misleading expectations and will be more likely to disrupt.
9. Sibling placements into homes with no other children will go more smoothly than sibling placements into homes with other children.
10. Subsidies will be associated with smoothness of placements, with a lesser association to disruption.
11. Adoptions will proceed more smoothly when families have the social support of friends, relatives, and informal networks (church, school, etc.).
12. Families in which the marital relationship is strained by the adoptive placements will be more likely to disrupt.
13. Parent support groups will provide resources that help families to maintain adoptions.
14. Adoptions in which the agency is available throughout preparation, the trial period, and in postlegalization difficulties will be more likely to remain intact.
15. Placements in which the child is reported to increase reciprocity toward his parents will be more likely to proceed smoothly and remain intact.

We begin the model-testing process in Chapter 5 with the data from the large intake sample of older child adoptions. We test the contribution of stressors and resources pertaining to the adopted child, the family, the match between birth and adoptive parents, and subsidies. In Chapters 6–9 we look at parents of the model in great detail. After our interviews with parents and social workers in disrupted and stable adoptions, we are better able to assess the influence of services—a key element in our overall model—on outcomes (Chapter 10).

Permanence and family life are considered optimum for the healthy development of children. The large numbers of older child adoptions attest to the societal consensus on this issue. For the most part, in fact, these unconventional families remain intact, and thus contribute to the healthy development of their members. Almost all of these families are, however, likely to experience stress as a function of the many transitions and tasks involved in this endeavor. The value of successful adoptions and the modest but significant proportions of disruptions that occur bear witness to the problems of nonintegration and stress in these families.

Disruption may be wise or unwise. What is not desirable, however, is when the avoidable failure to provide adequate resources results in a parent or child's decision to cope by way of disruption. Even with the best of resources, some adoptive children and families will best separate. That condition is sad but far less distressing than adoptions that break up because the family and child had grossly unrealistic expectations and little and diminishing support. That is tragic and preventable.

II

The Study

4

Disruption Research:
Past and Present

The child welfare grapevine has recently been buzzing with estimates that as many as 50% of all older child adoptions disrupt. Other informal estimates have been a bit more reassuring, but still indicate that a large proportion of older child adoptions fail. "We recently heard from adoption agencies in the New York City area that they are estimating their disruption rate to be approximately 35 percent" (Children's Home Society of California, 1984, p. 74). Systematic evidence on the rates of disruption and disruption's correlates are slowly accumulating. This chapter reviews key studies of disruption rates and family, child, and service contributors to disruption. A few studies have attempted to estimate disruption rates, whereas others have compared disrupted to stable placements. Our study does both and so we address both issues in turn.

Kadushin and Seidl (1971) provided the first significant review and study of adoption disruption. Overall, the disruption rate across 7 years of placements in a public agency was 2.8%. The majority (66%) of the 2734 children in their sample were adopted before age 2; they had a disruption rate of less than 1%. Among children adopted between 2 and 6 years, this percentage rose to 7%, and among the 10% of children adopted after age 6, the percentage that disrupted was 10%. Almost a one-third of older child placements were of children who had been adopted before, and these placements tended to be more likely to disrupt. Combining their findings with those of six other pre-1970 reports of children returned to public and private agencies in the United States, the U.K., and Canada, the authors compute an overall disruption rate of 1.7% of all children placed. Fewer than 1% of families experience a disruption since many disruptions involve more than one child.

Cohen (1984) recently reported a significantly higher disruption rate of 7% per year for older child adoptions in Canada. Tremitiere (1984) reviewed almost 2500 adoptions from 1979 to 1983 and found that 6- to 12-year-old children had a disruption rate of 9.7% and 12- to 18-year-old children had a rate of 13.5%. Boyne, Denby, Kettenring, and Wheeler (1984) identified a 23.2% disruption rate among 219 hard-to-place children. The rates increase from 7 to 15% to 25 to 47% for children adopted at ages 0–5, 6–8, 9–11, and 12–17, respectively. A review of nearly 500 adoptive placements in Britain shows a 9% disruption rate (Fitzgerald, 1983). Fein, Davies, and Knight (1979) found that 4 of 13 adoptions were disrupted (31%) by the end of their 5-year follow-up period. Block and Libowitz (1983), alternately, found all 32 adoptees who had been discharged from foster care remaining in their initial adoptive homes at the end of the (2-year) study period. The Oregon Project's (Lahti, 1982) policy of "aggressive adoption" resulted in 64 adoptions and only 2 disruptions in the 15 months following the end of the project.

Evidence of increasing rates of second adoptions also suggest higher dissolution and disruption rates. Of the 1937 children placed in adoptive homes from 1980 to 1981 in California, 151 (7.8%) were children who experienced adoption dissolutions—that is, they had previously been placed for adoptions that were never legalized (Barth, Berry, Carson, Goodfield, & Feinberg, 1986). Comparative rates of new placements of children who had previously been placed for adoption were 3.0% ($n = 202$) and 6.7% ($n = 176$) in 1970 and 1975, respectively. Adoption of children whose earlier adoptions were legalized but then disrupted also increased from .4% ($n = 28$) to 1.3% ($n = 33$) of relinquishment adoptions from 1970 to 1975 and then leveled off at 1.2% in 1980. These incidence rates are conservative insofar as they do not reflect (1) dissolutions or disruptions not followed by another adoption; (2) second or third or more disruptions for a child; (3) children who no longer live in their adoptive homes but whose adoption has not been reported as dissoluted or disrupted. Further, Kadushin and Siedl (1971), Donley (1983), Kagan and Reid (1984), and Groze (1985) suggest that from one-half to two-thirds of older child adoptions that follow previous dissolutions or disruptions for the child will fail.

A state-by-state review of disruption rates was completed by Urban Systems Research and Engineering (USRE) in 1985. The study considered four states and one New York county. They found that between 6 and 20% of placements disrupted—a rate which varied by state. Overall, children over 12 were 11% of the placements and 36% of the disruptions.

Partridge, Hornby, and McDonald's (1986) study on adoption disruption involved six study agencies (a blend of private and public). A sample of 684 nondisrupted cases were randomly selected to compare with the agencies' list of disrupted placements ($n = 64$) which began and disrupted during a 2½-year time period. They calculated a disruption rate of 8.6%. Case records of 212 children (representing 235 placements because some children had two placements during the time frame) in that sample of 748 placements were reviewed. In addition, 12 parents involved with disrupted placements and 12 families involved with nondisrupted placements were interviewed. The average age at placement was 7.8 years.

CONTRIBUTORS TO ADOPTION DISRUPTION AND STABILITY

Some of the aforementioned studies and numerous smaller studies have also compared characteristics of disrupted and stable placements. The lessons of these studies shaped our inquiry and are reviewed below.

Family and Child Characteristics

Various dimensions of adoptive family life are cited as potentially useful indicators of adjustment and outcome. Disruptive adoptions reportedly occur in families with less flexible family roles and rules (Boneh, 1979; Sack & Dale, 1982; Cohen, 1981), in families with insufficient training or information about the child (Nelson, 1985; Pardeck, 1983), in families where the parents feel excessive internal demands to meet the child's needs (Smith & Sherwen, 1983), in families where the parents and child are each too "different" to foster a good relationship (Unger, Dwarshuis & Johnson, 1977), and in families with too many stressors and too few resources (Zwimpfer, 1983). In general, adoptions seem more successful in families whose parents expect and accept behavioral and emotional problems in response to the stresses the child has experienced (Smith & Sherwen, 1983; Cohen, 1981). This may be learned from prior experience as adoptive parents (Partridge, Hornby, & McDonald, 1986). Parental flexibility and patience help promote attachment to the child and to incorporate the child into the family (Gill, 1978; Fanshel, 1962). College education was associated with a slightly higher disruption rate in the USRE study (1985). In Arizona research, young affluent, educated parents had higher disruption rates. The USRE (1985) report concludes: "Further research should be conducted to determine if younger parents of higher socio-economic status have unrealistically high expectations, particularly if they are adopting older children who have had a history of emotional or behavioral problems" (p. 43). Groze (1985) also found that the higher the income the more the chance of disruption.

Religion may also be significant. Regular church attendance is also associated with favorable outcomes (Nelson, 1985; Howard & Smith, 1987). Boyne, Denby, Kettenring, and Wheeler (1984) found that Catholic parents did significantly better than Protestant parents with younger children and worse with teenagers with psychological problems.

USRE (1985) found that parents over the age of 40 accounted for 30% of the total placements, but only 16% of the disruptions; minority parents accounted for 25% of the placements but only 8% of the disrupted placements; parents with incomes under $20,000 had a slighly lower disruption rate (they were 20% of the placements but only 13% of the disruptions) and single parents were equally represented between disrupted and stable populations. Groze (1985) also concluded that older adoptive mothers are less likely to experience disruptions. These studies failed to distinguish between foster parent and new adoptive placements.

Research consistently indicates that adoption disruptions increase with the child's age at the time of adoption (Kadushin & Seidl, 1971; Bass, 1975; Feigelman & Silverman, 1983; Groze, 1985; Zwimpfer, 1983). Children's characteristics associated with older age and adoption instability include their behavioral and emotional problems (Kadushin & Siedl, 1971), the experience of multiple preadoptive placements (Boneh, 1979; Nelson, 1985), and previous adoptive placements (Donley, 1983). Children with emotional problems were 19% of all adoptions and 29% of disruptions in the USRE (1985) study. Boyne and Associates (1984) found a child's age, experience of a previous disruption, and psychological handicap to have a cumulative effect on the likelihood of a subsequent disruption. About three-fifths of children with eating disorders and sexually promiscuous behavior disrupted in Partridge, Hornby, and McDonald's (1986) sample. A history of serious physical abuse was associated with disruption by Kagan and Reid (1986). Research has uniformly shown that race is not associated with disruptions (e.g., Howard & Smith, 1987), although USRE (1985) did find that minority placements disrupted at an 18 rate vs. 36% for all children (but they did not control for relative placements which are more stable and more common for minority children).

ATTACHMENT. Some families and children make speedy and steadfast attachments to each other despite backgrounds or problems that predict otherwise (Fahlberg, 1979). It would appear that these families seem most able to withstand the strains inherent in the older child adoption process. Alternately, families and children where bonding does not occur may be at the greatest risk of disruption. Children removed from their homes because of neglect, abuse, or abandonment may have underdeveloped abilities to make attachments (Kirgan, 1983; Kirgan, Goodfield, & Campana, 1982). Attachment impairment may result from and contribute to subsequent placement disruption. Difficulties in the development of parent–child attachments may influence adoption disruption. In support, Nelson (1985) found the strongest predictor of parental dissatisfaction with adoptions was the child's psychological or social isolation from the parent and peers. Service delivery also influences the development of attachments. The rush to place a child is one detriment to forming a lasting parent–child bond (Coyle & Lyle, 1983; Powers, 1983). Howard and Smith (1987) report that strong attachment to the birth mother and difficulty attaching to the adoptive mother was associated with disruption. The importance of the father is far less.

TRANSRACIAL ADOPTION. The evidence from 10 years of studies on black children adopted by white families suggests that parent and child satisfaction and adjustment do not significantly differ from inracial adoptions (reviewed in Feigelman & Silverman, 1983). Still, transracial adoption may present an additional strain on family resources and may contribute to disruption in previously burdened families. The rarity of transracial adoptions makes this hypothesis difficult to test.

Preadoption Experiences

Children's and parents' experiences in the child welfare system influence adoption outcomes.

PARENTAL RIGHTS TERMINATION. Adoption is cited as the major contributor to reduced long-term foster care in pilot permanency planning projects (Fein *et al.*, 1983; Lahti *et al.*, 1978; TenBroeck, 1981). These increases in adoption often follow renewed agency efforts to terminate parental rights. Many such adoptions are of older children who have served lengthy tenures in out-of-home care; Californian children in the 4- to 13-year-old group adopted during the period 1980–1981 were in foster care for a median time of 29 months. Adoptions following contested parental rights terminations are increasing. For example, court actions to terminate parental rights had been taken for 29% ($n = 563$) of children adopted in 1980 in California (State of California Department of Social Services, 1978, 1984a). This represents a significant increase over similar court actions and percentages of all adoptions in 1970 (4%: $n = 279$).

These placements may be particularly vulnerable to disruption. Borgman's (1981) report of outcomes for children freed for adoption showed that 9 of 11 adoptive placements following contested parental rights terminations were later disrupted. A few ($n = 7$) disrupted adoptions identified in Nelson's (1985) study suggest that they disproportionately followed involuntary terminations or the deaths of biological parents.

FOSTER PARENT ADOPTIONS. Foster parent adoptions are relatively new to child welfare (Meezan & Shireman, 1982). Foster parent or "fost-adopt" placements assume at least two forms: (1) adoptions by foster parents who first cared for children without the intent of adoption, and (2) adoption by foster parents who begin care of a child with the intent of adopting but before the termination of parental rights (a.k.a "risk-adoptions," see Lee & Hull, 1983).

Data on outcomes of foster parent adoptive placements are sparse. Nelson (1985) found that adoptive parents of children who were not legally freed at the time of placement were less satisfied, but her data do not show greater disruptions among fost-adopt families. Raynor (1980) interviewed 14 fost-adopt parents who had not initially planned to adopt who were less satisfied than other fost-adopt parents. Proch (1980) also concluded that agency pressure either to adopt or lose foster children was a source of significant dissatisfaction among adoptive families. Lahti and associates (1978) found no difference in the permanency of fost-adoptions, reunifications, and new family adoptions. In Illinois (USRE, 1985) regular adoptive homes had a 14.5% disruption rate for new adoptive homes, a 6.6% rate for foster parent adoptions, a 17% disruption rate for fost-adopt placements, and a 3.3% rate for relative adoptions. In Illinois in 1984–1985, 34% of placements were new adoptions and represented 84% of disruptions. Howard and Smith (1987) found that disrupted placements were more likely to be with new adoptive parents (76% of disrupted placements vs 58% of not disrupted placements were with new adoptive parents). This study will provide useful additions to the data on fost-adopt homes vis-à-vis adoption disruption by taking the child's age at the time of placement, race, and level of problems into account.

Formal Adoption Services

Family recruitment, preparation for adopting parents, preplacement visitation, postplacement services, and the availability of postlegalization services are but a few of the many aspects of services that vary across cases, social workers, and agencies. The contribution of formal services to adoption outcomes may result from direct effects on the child or parent or indirect effects through referral to other community agencies or self-help groups (Chestang & Hyemann, 1976; Jones, 1979; Katz, 1977). Agency support, caseload size, and other system factors are likely, but unstudied, influences on adoption outcomes.

PARENT PREPARATION. Nearly one-third of the disrupted adoptive families in Cohen's (1982) study reported unrealistic expectations of the child, and more than one-third reported an inability to cope with the child. Dashed parental expectations were also cited by the least satisfied families in Nelson's (1985) study. She found that parents that had been misinformed about limitations in the child's functioning or past experiences or had been otherwise poorly prepared had less satisfaction with the placement. Lahti (1982) found that the child's well-being is powerfully influenced by adoptive parents' knowledge of the child's past and by preparation for the child's arrival in the home. USRE (1985) asked families and social workers about the reason for the disruption and families consistently reported that they had not been fully informed about the child's problems and that they had sought to adopt younger children without disabilities but had agreed to adopt older children with disabilities—that is, stretching. Social workers, on the other hand, listed the problems as the child's behavior, lack of bonding between parent and child, and the child's inability to meet the parents' expectations.

PREADOPTION GROUPS. Adoptive parent group training sessions before placement help prepare parents for typical problems they will encounter with their child and help foster friendships with other adoptive parents who can support and understand them after the placement. Specifically, preplacement groups serve to assess parents' motivation and potential for adoption (Jarrett & Copher, 1980). These groups also provide general information on the adoption process, advice on problems to expect with children, and specific information on specific children (Jarrett & Copher, 1980; Tremitiere, 1979). Perhaps most importantly, these groups may also provide the framework for informal support networks after placement (Tremitiere, 1979; Gill, 1978). Use of groups led by fellow adoptive parents lessens the burden of the social worker and enhances the involvement of potential adoptive parents.

ADOPTION SUBSIDIES. Despite changes in adoption policies and practices that follow from the Adoption Assistance and Child Welfare Reform Act of 1980, the use of adoption subsidies seems to vary markedly across workers, agencies, and counties. Adoption subsidies have increased roughly twentyfold since 1980 (Penelope Maza, pers. commun., October 31, 1984). Waldinger (1982) notes that 14% of families in California suffer delays in obtaining payments and Nelson (1985) reports that several parents cited that social workers functioned to cut red tape to ensure adoption subsidies, for which they were grateful and which reduced the difficulty of their placement. We do not know if higher subsidies are given for the more difficult children, nor is there much information about the relationship between subsidy and disruption after controlling for the risk of the placement.

SIBLING PLACEMENT. Placing children in sibling groups is considered preferable; in California, more than 20% of all older child placements include siblings. However, placement in a sibling group (Boneh, 1979; Kadushin & Seidl, 1971; Nelson, 1985) appears to predict adoptive disruption. Further analysis by Boneh (1979) indicates that all 9 sibling placements into homes with birth children disrupted. USRE (1985) found that children placed with siblings represented 20% of the placements, but 43% of the disruptions. These findings are consistent with those indicating that families with multiple additional stressors are, not surprisingly, more likely to have adoption disruptions (Zwimpfer, 1983). Boyne and colleagues (1984) found that the size of the sibling group was significantly associated with disruptions that occurred in 37% of the 96 sibling placements. They conclude, however, that sibling placements are no more likely to disrupt than other placements, but sibling placements that do disrupt typically require the replacement of the full sibling group which increases the number of disruptions for children who were placed in sibling groups. Because disruptions often do involve the entire sibling group, the disruption rate for children is not, nonetheless, inflated; only the number of adoptive parents who suffer a disruption is inflated by this method of calculation. Howard and Smith (1987) found little difference between sibling and nonsibling placements but found that children who still have sibs with their birth family are at greater risk of disruption. Kagan and Reid's (1986) high-risk sample stands alone among adoption studies in finding that sibling placements tended to be associated with stability. The size and ages of the sibling groups certainly influence the outcomes.

POSTPLACEMENT SERVICES. Formal postplacement services are important and often neglected contributors to placement success. The importance of these services is noted by Sack and Dale (1982) who provided family therapy to 12 older child adoptive families. The families began treatment an average of 21 months after the child's placement in the home. The more successful outcomes were for younger children who were referred earlier. Knowledge of current pathways to formal services may increase the rate of timely and helpful referrals. Nelson (1985) found that the inability to obtain needed services, usually counseling for the child or special education, was linked to decreased parents' satisfaction with the adoption. These difficulties were significant contributors to parents' dissatisfaction. Children who were receiving educational counseling were less likely to disrupt (Partridge, Hornby, & McDonald, 1986). Adolescent birth children of adoptive parents also report the need for more contact with social workers since they often care for the adopted child (Cohen, 1984). The Massachusetts Adoption Resource Exchange (Funaro, 1984) convenes 4-hour "Disruption Meetings" when disruptions are imminent, to (1) identify factors that contribute to the break-up of the placement; (2) help the family and professional staff recover from the experience; (3) make short- and long-term plans for the child. These meetings have been designed to improve later placements but their success in accomplishing that purpose or in preventing disruptions has not, at this writing, been evaluated. Howard and Smith (1987) found that disrupted and not disrupted placements had no difference in the rate they used family counseling, nor did they differ in the amount of postplacement agency services they obtained.

Informal Networks and Services

Most available research on adoption disruption gives limited attention to the influence of social support and informal services on the adoption outcome. Available studies focus, above all, on demographic characteristics and motivations of the adoptive families. This focus is in keeping with the highly psychological perspective on the causes for behavior. Although these contributors to adoption outcomes should not be dismissed, current theory and research suggest the added importance of the social environment on family behavior (Bronfenbrenner, 1979). The connection of the family to social support networks has direct and indirect influence on the functioning of children and parents (Sandler, 1979). The growth of the self-help movement and the recognition that families in need often do not call on formal services (Veroff, Kulka, & Douvan, 1981) further attest to the importance of informal services to families.

Several authors point to the importance of extended family and social support to the success of an adoption (Feigelman & Silverman, 1979; Coyle & Lyle, 1983). This seems particularly true for single-parent adoptions (Feigelman & Silverman, 1979), yet single adoptive parents use parent groups at a lower rate than other adoptive parents (Nelson, 1985). Families who can turn to extended family and friends for support during times of stress have fewer adjustment problems (Cochran & Brassard, 1979). Fellow adoptive parents, often introduced in preplacement groups provided by adoption agencies, are especially helpful in providing nonjudgmental understanding and empathy during difficult times. Parents report appreciation of the contacts made during preadoption group experiences for use in later times of trouble (Tremitiere, 1979; Jarrett & Copher, 1980). Contact with biological parents or kin is also in increasing favor as a means of providing social support during the stressful transition for children (Baran, Pannor, & Sarosky, 1976; Borgman, 1981). The number of people willing and able to offer assistance to the adoptive family was associated with placement stability for emotionally disturbed youth by Kagan and Reid (1984). The effects of open adoption have not, however, been adequately evaluated.

Conclusions from Past Research

Although the evidence is not conclusive, and needs supplementation by research with probability samples, adoption disruption has apparently increased over the last two decades. The extent of the increase is unclear. The importance of this problem in child welfare is more certain. Significantly reducing adoption disruption—especially in an era of more challenging adoptive placements—will require additional information and program and practice developments. The current quest is not to decide whether older child and special-needs adoptions are disruption-prone, but rather, recognizing their central place in permanency planning, to determine what adoption practices reduce this tendency.

The available literature, provides, at best, a starting point for adoption decision making. Among the most important clues it offers is that the matching of difficult children with already burdened families is unwise without providing significant additional resources in the form of subsidies and services. Concerted efforts by adoption workers to expedite subsidies and to identify special education and counseling resources and thereby promote parent satisfaction may well contribute to adoption stability. The potential psychological benefits of sibling group placements must be balanced against their possible contribution to less stable adoptive placements. Since as many as 1-of-5 older child adoptions may involve siblings and since disruptions of these placements often involve all children, greater understanding of their stability is urgently needed. Research on comparisons between older children with siblings in care but placed in different homes— preferably with opportunities for contact—would help answer this question. Evidence on whether risk-adoption is a contributor to disruption is especially equivocal and also deserves more intensive scrutiny. Transracial adoptions appear to be no less stable than inracial adoptions. Postplacement groups, training, and informal services are often touted as important to the quality of the adoptive experience. Their relationship to adoption disruption is less definite. This study explores these concerns.

Just as we know that "love is not enough" to make a successful placement, we know that singular relationships between child, family, and service characteristics are not enough to explain adoption outcomes. Yet, we want them to be. We want to be able to say with some confidence "children like this are at high risk for disruption or homes like that are at high risk for a disruption." Some such singular relationships do have statistical significance and have been reported in other studies. We reviewed them in this chapter without the intent to fuel false hopes that adoption decisions can be made with this "red-flag" method. That is, no checklists of factors standing alone or together should ever rule out an adoptive placement. We conceptualize the prediction of adoption outcomes as resulting from a combination of unitary family and child risk factors that indicate a greater likelihood of disruption and of services that may reduce or increase that likelihood. The better we understand the risks, the better we can devise a service plan. Our study design and analysis and subsequent discussions reflect this view.

THE STUDY DESIGN

The study has two integrated parts: the intake study and the interview study. Simply described, a pool of adoptive placements of older children were identified from placement records, basic demographic data (e.g., the age of the child), and outcomes (disrupted or stable) were determined, relationships between basic data and outcomes were computed, and some of the families were interviewed to gather information about additional indicators of disruption. The design of the intake and interview studies are described in this chapter. Results of the intake study and interviews are presented in subsequent chapters.

Sampling and Data Collection

The sample was drawn from the population of adoptive placements in 13 Northern and Central California counties from January 1, 1980 to June 30, 1984 as identified from the adoption placement forms that are filed at the time of placement. (The total population of these counties from the 1980 census was 7,903,000: U.S. Department of Commerce, 1982). Eliminated from this sample were all adoptions of children younger than 3 years of age at the time of placement and all children placed from out of the state leaving a final sampling frame of 1156. Lists of case ID numbers were sent to adoption units of 13 public county-operated child welfare agencies at the end of FY 1985. Cases were verified by adoption unit supervisors and social workers as (a) not disrupted ($n = 831$); (b) disrupted before legalization of the adoption—which occurs after 1 year in California ($n = 79$); (c) set aside after the legalization ($n = 16$); (d) could not determine outcome ($n = 154$), and (e) could not identify case number ($n = 76$). Thus, the final study sample on which outcomes could be determined was 927 children.

The form on which the placement data was collected is completed at the time of placement by the adoption social worker. Although the state did provide guidelines for completing the form, and most items are quite straightforward, we did not test for the reliability of adoption workers' responses. The data items were used from that form.

The Interview Study

Families were recruited for interviews in two rounds. Initially, the 13 contiguous San Francisco Bay Area counties that participated in the previously described prediction study were engaged in contacting families for the interview study. Each was asked to send letters to the families in the sample from the 1980 to 1984 period requesting that the families contact the project to indicate their interest in participating. During this recruitment period, letters were sent to families who reportedly had disrupted placements and to a like number of randomly selected families with stable placements in those counties regardless of the apparent risk of disruption. We also asked agencies to send follow-up letters within 2 weeks to families

Table 4.1 Interview Samples and Disruptions

	Disrupt	Stable
Social worker *or* parent interviews ($n = 120$)	57	63
Social worker *and* parent interviews ($n = 69$)	18	51
Parent interviews only ($n = 22$)	13	9
Social worker interviews only ($n = 29$)	26	3

that did not send the return postcard indicating that they had either accepted or refused our request. Upon receipt of postcards indicating interest in the project, staff called families and arranged interviews within a few weeks. This first round of recruitment resulted in 81 interviews. Stable families had a higher response rate than disrupted families. The response rate for stable families was 29% and for disrupted families 22% (excluding potential respondents who now had unknown addresses). The smaller counties had the widest range in responses (from 0 to 50%) and the larger more metropolitan families had rates that were closer to the mean rates.

During the second round of recruitment, disrupted and high-risk families were oversampled to strengthen our ability to draw conclusions from family interviews about the difference between difficult placements that did and did not disrupt. For the purposes of this sampling, high risk was identified as involving placements of children over 10 years of age or of any child who had previous disruption(s). Six additional large Southern California counties (total 1985 population = 7,121,900), were contacted and five agreed to send letters to the families that they identified as disrupted or at high risk of disruption. This second round of recruitment led to 39 more cases: 21 more interviews with disruption families, 17 more interviews with stable families, and 23 interviews with social workers.

In our efforts to reach as many families with disruptions as possible, two private agencies who specialized in placing older children were also enlisted. They helped us to identify 15 families who were contacted: of those, 7 agreed to be interviewed (6 disruptions and 1 nondisruption). The percentage of social workers interviewed for these cases was 43%—significantly lower given the greater turnover in these smaller agencies.

These efforts yielded an overall sample and three subsamples in the interview part of this study: (1) the overall sample of the cases in which we interviewed the social worker *or* parent(s) ($n = 120$); (2) all cases in which we interviewed *both* the parent(s) and the social worker ($n = 69$); (3) the cases in which we interviewed just the parent(s) ($n = 22$); and (4) the cases in which we interviewed only the social worker ($n = 29$). The proportion of cases which disrupted or were stable are shown in Table 4.1. Unless specified, we use the first sample described above.

FAMILY INTERVIEWS. When families were contacted they were informed that either or both parents were welcome to participate in the interview and that we would interview them at home, at work, or at an agreed upon community site during the day or evening. A total of 91 families were interviewed. The bulk of interviews were conducted in the evenings and at client homes, although some were done in neutral sites (like a hotel lobby), interviewer's offices, or at the job site. About 1-of-10 interviews was conducted on the telephone with families that had moved out of state. One interview was completed by one out-of-area family who wrote directly on the interview form to fill in the blanks.

SOCIAL WORKER INTERVIEWS. Agencies were contacted and asked to arrange interviews with the social workers who worked with the adoptive family in our interview sample or with adoptive families who we could not reach but who had disruptions (the identities of these cases were never revealed). If the family worker was not available, then an interview with the child's social worker or supervisor was requested. In total, we had 98 social worker interviews: 37 interviews with the family's worker, 32 with the child's worker, 9 with the case supervisor, and 20 with others. Social workers were asked to bring the case records to the interviews and most were able to do so.

Description of the Sample

In the sample of 120 cases, there were 57 disruptions (47%) and 63 nondisruptions or intact families (53%) (see Table 4.2). The majority of children (59%) were male, and the mean age at placement was 8.2 ($SD = 3.2$). The large majority of children were White (72%), followed by Black (11%), Latino (10%), Asian (2%), Native American (2%), and Other (11%). The majority of placements (56%) were new adoptions, followed by foster parent adoptions (32%), and fost-adoptions (12%). Most placements involved a single child (77%); another 27 (23%) involved siblings placed together. Most children had some problem, usually emotional problems (43%), behavioral problems (26%), a medical condition (14%), physical disability (8%), or were mentally retarded (6%). Over one-fifth had a previous adoptive placement (21%). Of this total sample of 120 children, only 13% were in a transracial placement, and only 13% were in a single parent adoption. Many (66%) were placed with adoptive parents whose education levels were not the same as those of the child's biological parents. The average age of the adoptive mother at the time of the placement was 37 ($SD = 8.1$), and the average age of the adoptive father was 39 ($SD = 7.6$). The modal number of other children in the home was 1. The average annual family income was $30,099 ($SD = $18,074), and most families (61%) received an adoption subsidy.

Table 4.2. Disruptions by Placement Type

Type of placement	Total ($n = 120$)	Stable ($n = 63$)	Disrupt ($n = 57$)
Foster care	38	24	14
	(32%)	(38%)	(25%)
Fost-adopt	15	12	3
	(12%)	(19%)	(5%)
New Adoption	67	27	40
	(56%)	(43%)	(70%)
Total (%)	100%	100%	100%

PLACEMENT DIFFERENCES.   Fost-adoptions are different from foster parent adoptions and new adoptions in their nature as well as their outcomes. The parents entering into a fost-adopt arrangement are more likely than foster parent adopters or new adopters to know other foster or other adoptive parents (67% fost-adopters vs. 59% of new and 56% of foster parent adopters: $p < .001$). In other respects, the fost-adopt relationship was much like that of foster parent adoptions. The number of other adopted children in the home was smaller for foster parent and fost-adoptions than for new adoptions ($t = 1.99$, $p < .05$). Foster parents and fost-adopt parents were slightly more likely, however, to report someone new (besides the adoptive child) moving into the household around the time of the placement (14 vs 2%, $p < .07$). This new person could have been another foster child, but the specific nature of the new person is unknown. Previous adoptive experience tended to be less likely among foster parent and fost-adoptions than among new adoptive parents (22 and 20 vs 41%).

Among boys, more were placed in new adoptive homes (65%) than in foster parent homes (19%) or fost-adopt homes (16%). Girls were more likely to be placed in foster parent (43%) or new adoptive placements (40%), but less likely to be placed in fost-adopt placements (17%; $\chi^2 = 6.55$ $p < .04$). Sibling placements were equally likely among fost-adoptions, foster parent adoptions, and new adoptions. Children waited for new adoptive placements the longest ($M = 917$ days); more than in fost-adopt or foster parent adoptions ($M = 523$ days, $t = 2.91$, $p < .005$).

CURRENT STATUS.   Collapsing these data among the interview sample, 52% are in their current placement; 8% are unknown or other; 17% are in foster, group, or institutional care; 13% are in new adoptions; and 7% are with birth family members (see Table 4.3). Of the children, 72% were, at the time of the interviews, with birth or adoptive families.

Table 4.3. Current Residences of Children in Interview Sample (n = 120)

Current Residence	n	%
Don't know	7	5.8
In same adoptive home	63	52.5
On his/her own	3	2.5
With birth parent	5	4.2
With birth relatives	3	2.5
In foster home	10	8.3
In group home	4	3.3
In institution	7	5.8
In new adoption	15	12.5
Other	3	2.5
Total	120	100

Study Variables

Frequencies from individual items provide useful descriptive data. These were complemented by scales computed from several conceptually related variables for additional theory-testing.

ATTACHMENT. Because no instruments are available to assess the attachment of children older than 3, an Attachment Rating Scale was created to capture parent's assessment of their children's attachments. Parents completed a 13-item scale that was comprised of six behavioral specific items reflecting the dimension of reciprocity, three items reflecting separation, and four items reflecting exploration. Each item ranged from 0 (never true) to 2 (often true). Parents were initially asked to indicate their observations of their child during the child's first 3 months in the home (time 1) and, then, the child's most recent or final 3 months in the home (time 2). The three scales were tested for internal consistency; only the reciprocity scale had an alpha which was above the commonly accepted minimum of .50. The reciprocity alpha was .52 at time 1 and .50 at time 2. The separation alphas were .26 and .29, and the exploration alphas were .40 and .36, respectively, indicating that parents did not respond to items in those scales in a similar way. Summary scale scores were, therefore, computed only for the reciprocity items at time 1 and then at time 2. The reciprocity scale at time 1 had a mean of 1.04 (SD = .46) and at time 2 had a mean of 1.17 (SD = .44).

STRETCH. A composite scale was computed by taking the base similarity score (very different = 4 and very similar = 1) and adding a point for specific differences that the family identified as worrisome between their child and the child they planned to adopt that are known correlates of a high–risk placement—specifically, the child was older or the child was behaviorally disturbed. The mean stretch score was 1.9 (SD = 2.0) and ranged from 0 to 6.

CHILD PROBLEMS.   This is a composite score from intake forms about the child's problems. Each item received a no (0) or yes (1): emotional problems, mentally retarded, behavioral problems, physical disability, medical condition, and other. Therefore, the number of child problems ranged from 0 to 6 with a mean of .95.

SAME EDUCATION.   This was computed from questions on the intake forms about the adoptive and biological mother's educations. If the adoptive mother's education was within one level (higher or lower) of the biological mother's education, it was considered a match. The levels were: under 8th grade, 8th grade, some high school, high school graduate, some college, college graduate. Same education was scored higher than the lack of a match. The majority of placements did not match on education (66%).

DIFFERENCE.   This was computed from several questions to the family concerning differences of the child from their expectations that worried them. The range is from 0 to 8, with the higher number indicating more of a difference. The mean score is .57 (SD = .86).

INFORMED.   This variable was computed from the family questionnaire concerning various information that the family received about the child prior to placement. The higher the number, the more informed the family. The score ranges from 0 to 1 with a mean of .35 (SD = .16).

DIFFERENCE BETWEEN INFORMATION GIVEN AND INFORMATION RECEIVED.   A summary score was computed, reflecting the number of the following historical facts and characteristics that the family and the child exhibited which the adoption worker said he did not exhibit: physical abuse, sexual abuse, developmental disabilities, learning disabilities, and emotional/behavioral problems. The highest possible score was thus 5. The actual values ranged from 0 to 4, with a mean of .72 (SD = .21).

LACK OF INFORMATION.   This is a sum of the number of conditions that the child exhibited after placement about which the adoption worker had not informed the family before placement. The possible conditions included: physical abuse, sexual abuse, neglect, multiple placements, medical problems, developmental disabilities, learning disabilities and emotional/behavioral problems. This variable had a mean of 1.26 (SD = 1.44) and a range from 0 to 6, although the possible maximum was 8.

PREPARATION ACTIVITIES.   This score was computed by summing possible preplacement activities that parents engaged in to prepare for the child's coming to live with them. These include meeting the child's former caregivers and meeting other adoptive parents. The variable had a mean of 4.30 (SD = 2.51) and a range from 0 to 11.

DIFFICULTY. A placement difficulty score was computed to estimate the overall difficulty of the placement, as indicated by parents' and workers' responses to general outcome measures. This is a composite mean score from six items on the family and worker questionnaires. Each item was rated on a four-point scale, with higher numbers indicating a better outcome, resulting in a score of placement difficulty ranging from a possible 1 (very difficult) to 4 (not very difficult). The specific questions follow.

FAMILY

If you had it to do again, would you adopt this child?

Overall, would you say that the impact of this adoption on the family has been . . . ?

Overall, compared with what you expected, how well has this adoption worked out?

WORKER

If you had it to do again, would you have placed this child for adoption?

Would you say that the impact of this adoption on the child has been . . . ?

Compared with what you expected, how well has this adoption worked out?

The alpha coefficient for the scales was .74, indicating acceptable internal consistency. The correlation between difficulty and disruption is strong $r = .63$, but pleasantly imperfect. Difficulty ranged from 1 to 4 and had a mean score of 3.05 ($SD = .79$) with a higher score indicating less difficulty.

DEGREE OF OPENNESS OF THE ADOPTION. Families were asked whether there were contacts between the child and people from his past, including birth parents, birth siblings, foster parents, foster siblings, other relatives, and others. A contact with each of the groups was multiplied by the score on a three-point scale of frequency (1 = less than monthly, 2 = once a month, and 3 = more than monthly), resulting in a possible range of values from 0 to 18. This variable actually ranged from 0 to 10, and had a mean of 2.08 ($SD = 1.99$).

Risk, Prediction, and Surprise Outcomes

A discriminant analysis was run on the intake sample and rerun on the interview sample, twice: first, in the original form, and second, with minor changes reflecting the improved information from interviews. Given the generally similar results of the two analyses (with the exception of age), but the somewhat better information from the second model, the probabilities and predictions of the second analysis were used to compute additional variables—RISK, PREDICT, and SURPRISE. (In the 32 cases omitted from the second analysis, the values from the first analysis were used.)

RISK.   This variable is taken from the discriminant analysis and reflects the probability of disruption, based on the five discriminating variables. As such, it ranges from .00 to 1.00. The mean level of risk for stable families was .39 vs. .60 for disruption placements, $t(111) = 5.58$, $p < .001$.

PREDICT.   This variable is a result of the discriminant analysis, and is the predicted group, disrupt or nondisrupt, to which a case is assigned, based on its inclusion in the five discriminating risk groups. Therefore, its value is either -1 (nondisrupt) or 1 (disrupt). There were 52 predicted disruptions and 62 predicted nondisruptions.

SURPRISE.   This variable is a comparison of the predicted (PREDICT) and actual outcome for each case. The relationship between the child's predicted outcome and actual outcome was recoded so that placements that were expected to disrupt but did not were coded as 1, placements that were predicted to be stable and were stable were coded as 2, placements that were predicted to disrupt and did were coded as 3, and placements that were expected to be stable and disrupted were coded as 4; hence a higher score is worse. Among the larger sample of 898 classifiable cases, 149 (17%) were 1s, 657 (73%) were 2s, 64 (7%) were 3s, and 28 (3%) were 4s. For the interview sample, 18 (18%) did not disrupt despite the prediction, 46 (47%) were stable as predicted, 18 (18%) did disrupt as expected, and 16 (16%) disrupted despite the prediction of stability.

Differences in risk might partially explain the outcomes of disruption and membership in one of the surprise categories. That is, the cases that did disrupt may have had the highest risk among the placements predicted to disrupt. Similarly, families that had surprisingly bad outcomes may have had the highest risk among the families that were predicted to be stable. This appears to be only partially the case. There is no significant difference in risk between cases that were predicted to disrupt and did vs. those that were predicted to disrupt and did not. There was a tendency for the placements that were predicted to be stable but disrupted to have greater risk ($M = .37$) than those that were stable and predicted to be so ($M = 30$; $t = 1.81$, $p < .08$).

The Analysis Plan

The data analysis that will be described involved scores of variables and tests of significance. To reduce the likelihood of chance findings by resetting alpha levels according to the number of statistical tests completed, we would change the conventional alpha level to .01 or less. In such a case, we would have few statistically significant findings. Instead, we take quite the opposite position and argue that the complexity of the phenomenon that we are measuring yields a tiny likelihood that any single characteristic of a child, family, or social worker would be strongly associated with disruption. As such, using conventional signficance levels as indicators of what the reader should and should not consider is worthwhile is not wise. Instead, we prefer to help readers maintain an awareness of the likely contributors to adoption outcomes by discussing bivariate relationships that are trends, not just statistically significant. We discuss relationships as "suggesting an association" or "tending to be associated" when the "p-value" is .15 or less. We reserve the terms "statistically significant" and "significantly" for relationships that are at the $p<.05$ level or less even though this alpha level allows for approximately a 1 in 20 chance that these findings would occur by chance.

Although a range of data analysis approaches are needed to answer different questions, a general strategy was employed. Relationships between single variables and the outcomes of disruption and overall placement difficulty were first tested. Possible differences in these relationships for new adoptions, foster parent adoptions, and fost-adopts were then examined (if there were none, they are not mentioned in the text). When appropriate, univariate relationships were controlled for by risk to see whether the relationship to disruption or difficulty is determined more by the characteristics of a high-risk placement than by pre- or postplacement service characteristics. When possibly interesting relationships existed between risk, service variable, and outcome, the variable SURPRISE was added to the analysis. This variable helped to ascertain if the way services were provided was related to better or worse outcomes than predicted.

5

Predicting Disruptions

Information that is readily available to social workers before they make decisions about placing an older child is badly needed. Although the characteristics of the eventual relationships between children and adoptive parent(s) will not be fully discernable from such intake data, any assistance that such data can provide to child welfare professionals will reduce the financial and personal costs of adoption disruption. The analysis in this chapter uses the intake sample described in the prior chapter to predict adoption disruptions.

Preliminary inferential statistics checked the representativeness of the placement data by comparing the combined STABLE (n = 832) and DISRUPTED (n = 94) groups against the MISSING (n = 229) group on the aforementioned variables. The final sample differed from the missing cases by having significantly ($p < .05$): fewer previous adoptions for the child (7 vs. 12%); less matching on religion (26 to 34%); proportionately fewer families receiving subsidies (54 vs. 61%); fewer parental rights terminations (70 vs. 83%); and a shorter mean time that the child waited (621 vs. 731 days). Among these differences, the most noteworthy is the higher number of prior adoptions among the missing sample; 27 of the 229 missing cases would have had prior disruptions. Since prior adoptive placement has been shown to be highly associated with disruption, the study sample is likely to underrepresent the percentage of disruptions that occur.

Children in the final sample were most often: male (53%), placed alone (66%) rather than with siblings; beginning their first adoption (93%), in a same race placement (81%), in a placement in which the adoptive parents were not the same religion as the birth parents (74%), or in a placement in which the educational levels were not the same (79%); adopted by foster parents (68%) rather than new adoptive parents (32%); and freed as a result of a nonvoluntary parental right termination (45%). The mean age at placement was 7.2 years with a range from 3.00 to 17.87 years. The median family income reported was $24,370, with 54% of families receiving adoption

89

Table 5.1. Percentage of Placements Made During 1980–1984 that Later Disrupted

Fiscal year[a]	No. of placements	Percentage of all placements that disrupted	Percentage of foster parent placements that disrupted	Percentage of new adoptive placements that disrupted
1980	96	18.8	17.5	20.5
1981	195	14.9	9.2	24.0
1982	186	9.1	7.9	12.8
1983	245	6.1	3.0	12.8
1984	204	7.4	3.4	17.2

[a]1980 data is only available for second half of fiscal year.

subsidies and 9% having their adoption subsidies deferred. Most children were White (63%), followed by Black (17%), Latino (14%), Asian or Pacific Islanders (3%), Native American (2%), and other (1%). Only 15% were single parent adoptions. The average time in foster care prior to adoption was 35 months. Adoptive mothers had a bimodal educational level of high school graduate ($n = 291$) and some college ($n = 294$).

The ages of the adoptive parents at the date of placement ranged from 22 to 78. The mean age of the mother was 38 and of the father was 40. About 75% of the families had at least one other child in the home. Almost one-half had biological children (44%), while 20% had other adopted children, 26% had other pending adopted children, and 14% had foster children. Most of the sibling placements (85%) involved placing siblings in a home with no other children. Of the nonsibling placements, 67% involved placing one child into a home with other children.

For the majority of adoptive parents, this was the first marriage for both parents (64%). Most adoptive parents were White (69%). The majority of adoptive families received an adoption subsidy (54%), with a mean monthly award of $125. Subsidy amounts ranged from $1.00 to $920.00 a month, and the majority of awards were expected to extend 3 years or less. Only 11% of the subsidies were expected to extend until the child's majority.

The percentage of placements that disrupted was 10% ($n = 94$). The percentage of cases placed in each year that were later identified as disrupted are shown in Table 5.1. Placements made in earlier years have more frequently disrupted ($\chi^2 = 18.9$; $p < .001$). This simply may result from the passage of time during which a disruption could occur. Yet no significant differences exist between the percentage of placements from each year that disrupted after legalization and the proportion of adoptions that disrupted before finalization. This would not be true if disruptions continued to accumulate at a substantial rate during each year following placement and suggests, therefore, that elapsed time is not the sole contributor. Still, since the average time to disruption in our interview subsample is 18 months, we can expect additional disruptions from placements in the last year of the study. These would increase the rate to 11%. Change in such services as foster parent adoptions—which increased from 59% of placements to 72% of placements ($p < .01$) during those years—may explain more of the downward change in rate. When the relationship between disruption per year is computed separately for foster parent and new adoptive parents, the trend toward a lower adoption rate is best for the foster parent placements (see Table 5.1).

Across counties, the difference in disruption rates was great, ranging from 13 per 100 adoptions to 3 per 100 adoptions: $\chi^2 = 30.5$, $p < .002$. This partly reflects the varying use of foster parent placements. Among foster parent adoptions, county differences in disruptions were less, but still significant.

Foster parent placements may have lower disruption rates because the child and family learn if the placement will work during the foster care stage. This would result in replacement of children during foster care which is not counted as adoption disruption. More foster parent adoptive placements are subsidized ($p < .01$). The difference in stability of fost-adopt placements holds, however, only for nonminority children who had a stability rate for foster parent adoptive placements of 94 vs. 81% for new adoptions. Minority children had 90% stability rates for both fost-adopt and new adoptions. Foster parent adoptions are less stable for boys than girls but more stable than new adoptions for children of either gender. The low rate of disruptions for foster parent adoptions occurs despite the generally older age of children adopted by foster parents ($p < .01$). Foster parent adoptions were no more stable for children who had previously been placed for adoption ($n = 62$) or for children older than 12 ($n = 99$).

The intake data form does not distinguish legal-risk adoptions. To estimate differences between foster parent and legal-risk adoptions, adoptions by foster parents that occurred after the child had lived with the family for shorter periods of time were separately computed. Among the 81% ($n = 524$) of children in foster parent adoptions who had been in the home for 1 year or more at the time of the adoption, the disruption rate was 6.3% ($n = 33$). For those children adopted by foster parents after less than 1 year in the home, the disruption rate was 11.6% ($n = 14$; $\chi^2 = 3.30$, $p < .10$)—this approximates the overall disruption rate. The greater stability of foster parent adoptions, then, appears to hold primarily for those with longer preadoptive relationships between foster parent and child.

Bivariate statistics were computed to summarize differences between single characteristics of disrupted and stable placements (see Table 5.2).

Table 5.2. Characteristics of Disrupted (n = 94) and Stable (n = 832) Groups

Characteristic	Disrupt	Nondisrupt	χ^2 or t
Child			
Age of child	9.29	6.93	−6.67***
Gender of child[a]	Male (63%)	Male (52%)	3.56*
Child's ethnicity[a]	White (62%)	White (63%)	8.61
Parental rights termination[a]	No (60%)	No (55%)	.56
Months in foster care	34	35	0.64
No. of children's problems	.89	.59	−3.31***
Previous adoptive placement	No (75%)	No (95%)	56.11***
Child's wait (days)	642	621	−0.27
Placement			
Foster-parent adoption[a]	no	yes	24.77***
Sibling placement[a]	No (70%)	No (66%)	.64
Single parent placement[a]	No (86%)	No (85%)	.02
Financial resources per child	$14,160	$13,290	−0.62
Annual family income	$30,132	$26,728	−1.91
Mother's education[a]	College grad.	High school grad.	18.34**
Mother working[a]	Split	Not	1.98
Parent's wait (days)	377	365	−0.29
No. of other children in home	2.00	1.90	−0.51
Age of adoptive mother	36	38	1.72
Age of adoptive father	39	40	1.28
Match between birth and adoptive parents			
Same education[a]	No (82%)	No (79%)	.344
Same race[a]	Same (82%)	Same (81%)	.03
Same religion[a]	No (76%)	No (73%)	.13
Same county placement[a]	Same (86%)	Same (91%)	1.64
Subsidy			
Received subsidy[a]	Yes (59%)	Yes (53%)	1.40
Monthly subsidy	$119	$125	0.37

[a]Modal values given *p < .05; **p < .01; ***p < .001.

Previous placements, age, number of child problems, foster placement adoptions, and education of adoptive mothers were significantly different by group.

The relationship between previous placements and subsequent disruptions was considered further. Previous placements increased significantly with age and the number of child problems. There were no differences by gender or race. Only 3.2% of foster parent adoptions vs. 14% ($p < .001$) of nonfoster parent adoptions involved children with previous adoptions. Children with previous adoptions were less often placed in sibling groups (13 vs. 36%) than children in their first adoptive placements. Somewhat, but not significantly, more children with prior adoptions were placed in single-parent adoptions and given subsidies. The relationship between previous disruption and disruption of the placement does not hold for children over 12, or for placements with siblings together. It holds for boys and girls and single- and two-parent adoptions and regardless of subsidies.

That age is a strong associate of disruption was expected. Older children have consistently been more likely to require replacement in foster care and adoption. The relationship between age and disruption is further shown by examining disruption rates per 3-year age group. Between ages 3 and 5, 4.7% of cases disrupted, between ages 6 and 8 the rate was 10.4%, between 9 and 11 the rate was 17.1%, between ages 12 and 14 the rate of disruption was 22.4%, and between ages 15 and 18 more than one in four (26.1%) adoptions disrupted.

Age also interacted with other associates of disruption. Before the age of 12, previous adoption has a strong association ($p < .001$) with disruption; children under 12 who have had a previous adoptive placement are far more likely to disrupt than are their peers without such a history: 41–7%. After the age of 12, however, the association weakens. The presence of multiple child problems does not significantly contribute to disruption among 3- to 5-year-old children, or children 9 to 11, or children 15 or older but is significantly associated with disruption for 6- to 8-year-old ($p < .01$) and, to a lesser extent, 12- to 14-year-old children ($p < .10$). Among children ages 3 to 5, those 6 to 8, and those 9 to 11, fost-adopt children are significantly less likely to disrupt. The significant differences are attenuated for children 12 years old or older. The number of child's problems differentiated disruptions from nondisruptions ($\chi^2 = 26$, $df = 5$, $p < .001$). Certain types of special problems were also significantly associated with disruption. Disruptions were significantly more likely among children with emotional problems (16 vs. 8%: $p < .001$), behavioral problems (21 vs 9%: $p < .001$), and mental retardation (23 vs 10%: $p < .03$), but not more likely among children with a physical disability (14 vs. 10%), or a medical condition (13 vs. 10%).

Previous findings that sibling placements are more likely to disrupt were not confirmed. But, most sibling placements were for younger children ($p <$ .05) and fewer had previous adoption disruptions ($p < .001$). Sibling placements for children older than 15 tended to disrupt more than single-child placements. The data do, however, support Boneh's (1979) and Kadushin and Seidl's (1971) finding that sibling placements into homes with other children are significantly more likely to disrupt for one or both children (28 of 268: 10.4%) than sibling placements into homes with no other children. In our study, *none* of the 47 children placed in sibling groups into childless homes disrupted. A strong and counterintuitive finding—albeit on a small subsample—was that no sibling groups in our study ($n = 8$) with a previous adoptive placement disrupted. Caseworkers apparently made good judgments about which sibling groups could succeed together; the data cannot inform us, however, about outcomes for siblings who were separated after an earlier disruption.

Single-parent adoptions ($n = 137$) were no more prone to disruption than two-parent adoptions but had several unique characteristics. Single parents were significantly ($p < .001$) more likely to adopt older children—only 24.5% of the children adopted by single parents were younger than 9 years of age—and more likely than were couples to adopt boys (61 vs. 52%: $p <$ .05). Single parents less commonly adopted siblings or were involved in fost-adopt than were couples. There were no differences on the previous adoptive status of the child. Single- and two-parent adoptions had the same likelihood of having a disruption regardless of the age, gender, and race of the child, sibling placements, subsidy or no subsidy, and previous adoptive placements.

Higher disruption rates are associated with mother's education. The disruption rate among those having some college or a college degree ($n = 501$) was almost double that of mothers with a high school diploma or less ($n = 394$) (13 vs. 7%, $\chi^2 = 8.31$, $p < .01$). Children adopted by highly educated foster parents are no more likely to suffer disruptions than children adopted by less educated foster parents. Foster parent adoptions were, however, far less likely among more highly rather than less educated parents (63 vs. 76%; $\chi^2 = 18$, $p < .001$). Among new parent adoptions, parents with college degrees have a disruption rate of 26%, followed by parents with some college (19%) and high school graduates (11%). Nonfoster parents with less than a high school diploma ($n = 22$) had no disruptions! College-educated parents are somewhat less likely than less educated parents to have children with special needs or problems placed with them. They also experienced a sharply higher disruption rate with children aged 3 to 9 (11 vs. 4%: $p <$ .001), but not for children 10 and older. These findings fail to confirm those of Boyne *et al.* (1984). The higher disruption rate for college-educated parents is lessened in placements of children with prior adoptive placements and among adoptions by non-white parents.

Table 5.3. Contribution of Child, Placement, Match, and
         Subsidy to Disruption

Characteristic	Standardized canonical discriminant function	Wilks Lambda	Correct classification of cases (%)	Squared canonical correlation
Child		.89	80	.11
Age	−.63			
Gender	.18			
Parent rights termination	.07			
Time in foster care	.18			
Child problems	−.21			
Previous adoption	.64			
Placement		.97	65	.03
Foster parent program	.87			
Single parent adoption	.25			
Sibling placement	−.18			
Family financial resources	−.30			
Mother is working	−.47			
Parent's wait for child	.11			
Other children in home	.21			
Match between birth and adoptive parents		.99	50	.00
Same education	−.42			
Same race	−.24			
Same religion	.22			
Same county	.83			
Subsidy		.99	57	.00
Receives subsidy	1.40			
Amount of subsidy	1.20			

DISCRIMINANT ANALYSIS

Discriminant analysis was next used to determine the contributions of
adoption characteristics to adoption outcome. The variables used in the
analyses were chosen because of modest or strong bivariate relationships to
the adoption outcome. The variables were entered in four groups: (1) child
characteristics; (2) placement characteristics: (3) match between child and
placement; and (4) subsidies. The ability to explain each of these models, the
variance in outcomes—as indicated by the squared canonical correlation
coefficient which describes the proportion of variance between the two
outcomes that each set of variables explains—and the ability to correctly
classify cases is shown in Table 5.3.

Variables whose importance to predicting adoption disruption were indicated by strong standardized canonical discriminant functions for individual

Table 5.4. Reduced Prediction Model

Characteristic	Standardized canonical discriminant functions	Squared canonical correlation	Wilks Lambda	Correct classification of cases	
				Disrupt (%)	Total (%)
Previous adoption	−.66	.06	.94	26	88
Age	.58	.09	.91	50	77
Non-foster parent adopt	.45	.12	.88	66	78
Child problems	.29	.12	.88	69	80
Education of adoptive mother	.29	.13	.87	70	80

models or by previous research were entered into a reduced model (see Table 5.4). The five variables for the reduced model accounted for 15% of the difference between the groups; Wilks Lambda $= .87$, $\chi^2 = 124$, $df = 5$, $p < .001$. This model correctly classified 80% of the cases (see Table 5.4). The model is superior at indicating which placements were likely to be stable rather than at indicating which placements were likely to disrupt. This is deceptive, however, since a prediction that all 926 cases would be stable would be accurate in 89.8% of the cases. This prediction would, however, be accurate in 0% of the disruption cases. The current model—which may yield a somewhat inflated estimate of its ability to predict disruption because the model was tested on the same data from which it was developed—could accurately predict about 2 of 3 disruptions (see Table 5.5). Adjusting for expected correct classification due to chance, the Kappa is .32. This indicates that using the model to predict adoption outcomes would result in a 32% overall improvement above simply assuming that 9 of 10 placements will be stable.

Table 5.6 shows disruption rates for children given the five characteristics identified by this model. (Age and special problems were recoded as

Table 5.5. Classification of Stable and Disrupted Adoptions with Reduced Model[a]

		Predicted membership	
Actual membership		Stable	Disrupted
Stable	806 (89.8%)	657 (82%)	149 (18%)
Disrupted	92 (10.2%)	28 (30%)	64 (70%)

dichotomous variables; the latter by distinguishing between children with no special problems or one or more special problems.) The percentages reported at each level indicate the proportions of the subgroup who disrupted and not the proportions of the total sample who disrupted. This table shows changes in the number and percentage of disruptions as additional information is added. For example, 8% of the 718 children from 3 to 9 years old ($n = 56$) and 21% of 175 children older than 9 ($n = 36$) will suffer disruptions. This rate is higher (35%) for older children who are not adopted by foster parents ($n = 37$) but lower (17%) for those adopted by foster parents ($n = 138$). The latter rate approximates the 14% rate for younger children not adopted by foster parents.

Among the older group, the disruption rate is 46% among the children who also had a previous adoptive placement and 55% among the 11 who also have special problems. The last column—the match between birth and adoptive parents—results in some marked differences, especially for children not identified as having special problems. The small cell sizes that result from adding this criteria suggest cautious interpretation.

The prediction substudy indicates that adoption disruptions apparently occur with less frequency than many have feared. Also good news is the failure to show that these rates are increasing. They may be decreasing. Several explanations are apparent. First, adoption workers may be more adroitly selecting families and children for adoption. The use of older-child, fost-adopt, and single-parent adoptions has increased markedly in recent years and agency placement practices may simply have needed time to catch up. Agency practice for delivering pre- and postadoptive services—which are not part of the prediction model but which may influence outcomes—may also have improved.

Second, the advent of legal-risk or fost-adopt adoptions may result in preadoptive placement moves that do not appear in these statistics but that reduce later disruptions when successful matches are made. Such children may try several families until they find one that will work and never have the trial placements register in the official statistics as disruptions. (These replacements may nevertheless register in the hearts and minds of families and children.) This study clearly demonstrates the significant role of foster parent adoptions for older children. Still, the self-satisfaction about child welfare practice that appears justified from the study's findings of a declining disruption rate must be enjoyed tentatively until more information about the preadoptive replacement rate and its effects on children are more fully understood.

Third, not enough time has transpired to determine how stable these adoptions are; some of the stable group may yet disrupt. Cohen's (1984) findings that the mean time to disruption is 6 months after placement

Table 5.6. Disruption Rates by Reduced Model Characteristics

Age	%	Cell (n)	Foster parent placement	%	Cell (n)	Prior adoptive placement	%	Cell (n)	Special problems	%	Cell (n)	Education of adoptive mother	%	Cell (n)
3–9	8	(718)	No	14	(240)	Yes	40	(25)	Yes	40	(15)	H.S. or less	0	(5)
												College	60	(10)
									No	40	(10)	H.S. or less	0	(2)
												College	50	(8)
						No	11	(215)	Yes	9	(88)	H.S. or less	0	(34)
												College	15	(54)
									No	12	(127)	H.S. or less	3	(36)
												College	15	(91)
			Yes	4	(478)	Yes	38	(8)	Yes	40	(5)	H.S. or less	50	(2)
												College	33	(3)
									No	33	(3)	H.S. or less	0	(0)
												College	33	(3)
						No	4	(470)	Yes	6	(203)	H.S. or less	6	(108)
												College	7	(95)
									No	2	(267)	H.S. or less	1	(119)
												College	3	(148)

98

10–17	21	(175)	No	35	(37)	Yes	50	(12)	Yes	60	(10)	H.S. or less	50	(4)
												College	67	(6)
									No	0	(2)	H.S. or less	0	(0)
												College	0	(2)
						No	28	(25)	Yes	31	(16)	H.S. or less	29	(7)
												College	33	(9)
									No	22	(9)	H.S. or less	0	(3)
												College	33	(6)
			Yes	17	(138)	Yes	33	(12)	Yes	33	(9)	H.S. or less	40	(5)
												College	25	(4)
									No	33	(3)	H.S. or less	0	(1)
												College	50	(2)
						No	15	(126)	Yes	23	(48)	H.S. or less	23	(22)
												College	23	(26)
									No	10	(78)	H.S. or less	14	(44)
												College	6	(34)

suggest that these later disruptions will not occur in large numbers. Our findings indicate, however, that many disruptions occurred after 1 year. Thus, for placements made in the last year, the likelihood of further dissolutions remains. If the average disruption rate for prior years is substituted, then the disruption rate would increase from 10.2 to 11%.

The findings on foster parent adoptions may be deceptively sanguine since the disproportionate stability of these placements does not hold for children with a shorter stay as a foster child prior to adoption, for children with a previous adoptive placement, or for older and minority children. Additional research on the frequency and impact of preadoptive moves among children in legal-risk adoptions and better outcomes for placements that are specified as legal-risk is needed to provide clarity about this increasingly frequent practice. That the risk of adoption disruption increases as age, prior placements, and children's problems increase is a predictable finding. These findings should not discourage clinicians from placing older, special-needs children for adoption but can instead help to guide their placement. The knowledge that previous adoptions are a less strong predictor of disruption for white children, for siblings, and for children older than 12 can assist in placement. Knowing that the effects of child problems on disruption are least significant during the earlier and later childhood years is also useful to social workers. (Such information can also be provided to parents who are considering adoptive placements of children with prior adoptions and who want to know what their chances are of succeeding with such placements.) These findings also highlight the importance of placing children in adoptive homes with minimum delay. Further, agencies will do well to allocate additional services to placements of older children with prior disruptions who are at the greatest risk of suffering another disruption.

That single-parent or sibling placements do not disrupt more than other placements is interesting and hopeful. Because sibling and single-parent placements are not made randomly, we cannot conclude that they are just as stable as other placements. Separating siblings was associated with less difficult placements, but keeping two siblings together did not increase the disruption rate. Families are apparently able to cope with sibling groups. Given the current use of sibling placements in the sample counties, however, they are as stable as other placements. Adoption agencies might now proceed to test the durability of single-parent placements under additional conditions which are underrepresented among single-parent adoptions— especially in fost-adopt placements and placements with younger children.

The finding that more highly educated, white, adoptive parents may have less success with younger children who they did not care for as foster parents is provocative and worthy of further study but cannot—given the contradictions with previous research—provide a reliable rule for practice. These findings are partly accounted for because of the higher risk children that these parents adopt. The findings do argue against overlooking less educated adoptive appliecants for more educated applicants and for not assuming that professionals—yes, even human service providers—are beyond the need for adoption subsidies and complete pre- and postplacement services.

The decidedly imperfect ability of the discriminant analysis to distinguish between placements that would and would not disrupt indicates that the relationships between placement characteristics and outcome are quite complex. When all the placement factors in our model are taken into consideration, and the adoption worker has the choice of options to choose placements that are not associated with disruption risk, the risk of disruption can be lessened. As much as is practical, workers should be mindful of these findings as they negotiate with the harsh adoption marketplace and its often intractable shortages of homes. A good part of the remaining unexplained variance in adoption outcomes may arise from preplacement, postplacement, and postlegal agency services, personal and interpersonal (rather than demographic) qualities of the child and family, and available community resources. These are considered further in the interview substudy.

6

Preplacement Assessment and Decision Making

Child welfare workers have long understood the importance of judicious preplacement assessments of child and family and the fit between them (Bass, 1975; Bell, 1959). For new and fost-adopt placements, a collaborative assessment process in which the agency provides information to the family about several possible children, expresses interest in learning more about some children, and finally meets a child or sibling group has become the standard. This process differs somewhat for foster families who adopt their children, although in Meezan and Shireman's (1985) study of such families, at least one-half of the foster families thought they would like to adopt the child at the time of placement. Given the increasing use of fost-adopt and foster parent adoptions, there is a growing concern about assessing the possible benefits of foster homes for children as adoptive homes. The study considered several issues related to the match between parental expectations and the children who came to live with them. We looked at parent and social worker ideas as well as at the assessment and decision-making process that was followed. We also consider preplacement services in this chapter.

At this time, no one knows (but most of us assume that we have a fair idea of) what factors need to be considered when deciding which families and which children should be placed together. Our inquiry about the preplacement assessment and decision period drew on a broad pool of assumptions from practitioners and previous researchers.

DECIDING TO ADOPT

A nearly universal interest of adoption workers concerns the family's reason for adopting. We suspect that no agency adoption has ever been consummated without the family being expected to explain to the adoption worker why they want to adopt a child. We were also curious about this,

Table 6.1. Reasons for Wanting to Adopt

| | Percentage Indicating YES | | | |
Reason	Total YES (%) (n = 91)	Foster parent adoptions (n = 27)	Fost-adopt (n = 15)	New adoptions (n = 49)
Religious or humanitarian convictions	44	15	53	57*
Unable to have a child of your own	37	29	24	47
Emotional attachment to a specific child	18	56	0	2*
Your children wanted you to adopt	15	21	21	57
Attraction to a specific child	11	30	0	4*
Ability to choose the sex of the child	11	7	27	8
Agency urged you to adopt a specific child	9	11	7	8
Wanted younger children because your own children were adults/ near adults	2	0	0	0
Agency planned to remove (foster child), so you decided to adopt	1	1	0	0

*$p < .001$ for difference between placement types.

despite our assumption that people's ability to explain why they act is usually overestimated. Families report that they decided to adopt for many reasons (see Table 6.1). The reasons most often indicated were that they had religious or humanitarian convictions, were unable to have a child of their own, or were attracted or attached to a specific child (often a foster child). Despite concerns expressed in the child welfare literature, adoption because the agency planned to otherwise remove a foster child was most infrequent.

When further queried about their decision to adopt an *older* child (Table 6.2), families most often reported that an older child fit in better with their family, that few infants but many older children were available for adoption and that they had an emotional attachment to a specific older child. Least often cited as a reason was parent's interest in children with special needs regardless of age.

Table 6.2. Reasons for Adopting an Older Child

Reason	Total YES (%) ($n = 91$)	Foster parent adoptions ($n = 27$)	Fost-Adopt ($n = 15$)	New adoptions ($n = 49$)
		Percentage indicating YES		
Older child fit in better with family	56	22	60	63*
Few infants, but many older children available for adoption	33	4	45	47*
Emotional attachment to a specific older child	24	96	0	5*
Had special talent for working with older and/or difficult children	15	0	13	2
Attraction to specific older child	13	30	13	4*
Success with previous adoption(s)	8	0	0	7
Older child part of sibling group that included younger child	4	0	1	3
Interested in children with special needs, but age not a major consideration—child with special needs happened to be older	3	0	0	3

*$p < .01$ for difference between placement types.

Fost-adopters were much like new adoptive parents regarding reasons for adopting. New adopters and fost-adopters were much more likely than foster parent adopters to adopt for religious or humanitarian convictions. On the other hand, foster parent adopters were much more likely than fost-adopters or new adopters to adopt because of an attraction or emotional attachment to the child.

Reasons for adopting an older child differed by type of placement. New adopters and fost-adopters, compared to foster parent adopters, were especially likely to adopt because infants were unavailable. New adoptive parents were also especially likely to adopt an older child because of previous adoptive success. New and fost-adopt parents were also much more likely than foster parent adopters to adopt an older child because he would fit in with the family.

Again, foster parent adopters were especially likely to cite attraction or emotional attachment to the child as a reason for adopting an older child.

Extended family, relatives, and friends were more in favor of the adoptions than they were opposed, with a mean response of 3.1 ($SD = .97$) with four indicating very much in favor. The reported opposition or support of families and friends was not strongly related to disruption, difficulty, or risk for new adoptions but was for foster parent and fost-adopt adoptions.

Among fost-adopt parents (also known as "legal-risk" parents: Lee & Hull, 1983), all said that they entered into a fost-adopt agreement because they understood that the child was soon to be freed for adoption. None said that they became fost-adopt parents because of the poor functioning of the child, to test whether adoption was a realistic goal, or any other reason. The reasons for becoming a fost-adopt parent were not related to the stability of the placement.

We did not consider parental reasons to apply for fost-adopt status or for the status of a new adoptive parent. Our knowledge of child welfare services in California suggests that decisions about the type of adoption that a family will engage in is, in large part, determined by the policies and practices of the agencies. For example, in some counties white families who wish to adopt pre-teenagers are routinely assigned to the fost-adopt program because of the recognition that very few white children who are legally free will be available for adoption. We know that some families do not want to tolerate the risk entailed in such a program, but do not know whether they decide not to adopt or whether they sign on for the often long wait for a free child. Meezan and Shireman (1985) describe rather relevant differences between foster families that do and do not adopt. A study of families that do and do not agree to participate in fost-adopt programs would be a useful companion piece, but ours is not such a study.

THE WAITING PERIOD

We also considered the amount of time that families had to wait for a child, anticipating that such waiting might have direct and indirect influences on their decisions and the outcome of the placement. Foster families who adopted first talked to the agency about adopting after the child had been living with them for an average of 8.4 months with a range from 0 (for the foster-adopt families) to 60 months. The mean time to the decision to adopt was only 1 month after the initial discussion with the agency.

Children placed into fost-adopt were in care, on the average, a total of 25 months with an average of 19 months since their last entry into foster care. The longer children had been in care the higher their risk ($r = .65$, $p < .05$)

and the more difficult their placements, ($r = .83$, $p < .001$). The relationship between longer waits and actual disruption was not as strong. The relationship between prior foster care and fost-adopt placements and current placement difficulty was modest but primarily determined by associated risk factors. New adoptive parents waited for an average of 18 months between their request and the actual placement. Their adopted children had been in care 37 months and had four placements on average. Contrary to expectations, for new adoptions the greater number of months from the parents' request to the actual placement tended to be associated with less difficulty and fewer disruptions ($p < .05$), despite more risk ($p < .10$). The waiting period was apparently used productively by the agency or parents or both. A possible cost that we did not measure is the loss of adoptive homes caused by delays.

For all children the average number of entries into out-of-home care prior to the referral for adoption was 1.5. They spent an average of 31 months in foster care before their cases were sent to the adoption unit and spent those months in an average of 2.89 placements. The mode was, however, just 1 placement. Of the total of 336 placements that our study children were in prior to their referral for adoption, only 14 (4%) of those prior placements were fost-adopt placements. On the average, 2 years had passed between the referral for adoption planning and the child's placement into a fost-adopt or new adoptive home. For children placed in new adoptive homes, a modest positive relationship ($p < .09$) existed between the difficulty of the adoption and the length of time that children were in foster care prior to adoption after controlling for risk. This indicates that longer stays in foster care worsen the adjustment to the adoptive home regardless of the placement risk.

On the whole, social workers judged that the adoption referral was at the appropriate time in 78% of cases. Social workers indicated that it could have been made earlier in 18% of cases and by an average of 29 months. These responses were typically accompanied by comments that the delay predated permanency planning statutes and would not currently happen. In 4% of the cases, the referral was thought to have been better if delayed by 6 months. These were for cases that had prior adoptive or fost-adopt disruptions or sudden placement changes.

INFORMATION

The importance of providing quality information to the family about the child—an importance which might overshadow the specific characteristics of the match—has been shown by other investigators. In Katherine Nelson's (1985) study, families given the information needed to decide whether or not they can care for a child who is not exactly or even nearly like they expected were more likely to have satisfactory adoptions than were families deprived of that information. Nearly one-third of the disrupted adoptive families in Cohen's (1984) study report that they had unrealistic expectations of the child, and more than one-third reported an inability to cope with the child. Our model of adjustment to adoption predicts that those families with less accurate preplacement information about the child will have less realistic expectations about behavior, resulting in long-term frustration for both parent and child. In principle, we agree with Bass (1975) that "If the life and future of a child are to be entrusted to his new parents, they can be trusted with all the information pertinent to his individuality" (p. 509). The significance of the relationship between information and adoption outcome clearly deserves greater understanding.

Our parent interviewees commented often and, at times, vehemently that they were not provided with adequate information about the child they adopted prior to the placement. Families do not only appear to be reporting that they were not given enough information as a result of sour grapes following an adoption disruption; many intact families have a similar grievance. In the most dramatic of these cases, one family did not know of their child's history of arson and another family reported no knowledge of their child's prior residential placements spanning 6 years. In some cases, the social workers appeared not to have known the information, and in others they appeared to be aware of the information but did not choose to provide the family with it. The provision of information to families was queried in several ways. Families were asked to indicate whether or not the children they adopted had any of the following experiences or conditions: physical abuse, sexual abuse, neglect, developmental disabilities, multiple placements, learning handicaps, or behavior problems. If they responded YES, they were then asked whether they had been told this information prior to the placement or whether they had learned this after the placement. Table 6.3 shows family responses to these items. More than one-half of children were physically abused—families did not know about it in almost one-third of those cases. About one-third of children had been sexually abused—families knew about the sexual abuse in less than one-half of the cases (more than one-half of the cases where sexual abuse was found out later subsequently disrupted). Neglect and a history of multiple placements were the most common of the experiences and were generally known to families. Physical and developmental disabilities were less common problems and were more often known to families. Still, a small but surprising percentage of families did not know about these conditions at the time of placement. More than one-half of the children were reported to have learning disabilities and, among those, more than one-third were not known to adoptive

Table 6.3. Parental Knowledge Before the Placement[a]

Available information	Known history (%)	Found out later (%)	No history (%)
History of sexual abuse	15	17	68
History of physical abuse	42	18	40
History of living in many different places	58	8	34
History of neglect	69	13	18
Physical/medical disability	24	9	67
Developmental disability	32	8	60
Learning disability/educational difficulties	37	22	41
Emotional/behavioral problems	52	32	16

[a]Percentages do not sum to 100 because of multiple responses.

families before the placement. Perhaps most striking was families' reported ignorance about the emotional and behavioral problems of their adopted children. The great majority of the children were identified as having behavioral or emotional problems. Far more of the children who disrupted (100 vs. 75%) had such problems according to their adoptive families. Of families that reported such problems and indicated that they were told of them ahead of time, the disruption rate was 35% whereas those who discovered the problems after placement had a disruption rate of 45%.

On the average, families reported learning about 1.3 of these conditions after the placement. Most (59%) of the families reported one such information gap—16% reported that they did not know of three or more of these situations. Among families that reported no information gaps, the disruption rate was only 19%. Among families reporting one or more gaps, the disruption rate was 46%. Better information was associated with more positive surprises regarding outcomes. Families predicted to be stable were less likely to have disrupted if they had no information gaps (13 vs. 21%) whereas placements predicted to disrupt were more likely to be stable (22 vs. 16%) when provided complete information.

Responses that workers made about the presence of a problem were contrasted to reports of information gaps by parents to better understand if the worker's failure to provide information was because the worker did not know of the problem. In 23% of the cases in which families reported finding out about at least one child's condition after the placement, the worker did not indicate to us that such a condition was known to them. In 6% of the cases, the worker reported that the problem was very severe or severe but the family did not report knowledge of this information at the time of placement.

When parents were queried about whether the additional information that they were not provided would have affected their decision to accept the child, 34 of the 55 parents (64%) who reported an information shortage indicated that it definitely would have affected their decision to accept their child. Among those reporting such a reaction, the disruption rate was 35%. Contrary to our expectations, this is somewhat lower than is the disruption rate (50%) for those who indicated that the information would have had less of an impact. They may have been so eager to adopt that the information would not dissuade them. The dilemma that workers face is clearly shown by the evidence that many families that were able to maintain a difficult adoption might not have entered into that adoption if they had known more about their adoptive child. Whereas this is not justification for deceiving families about the characteristics of their new family member, this does argue for encouraging families that might underestimate their ability to cope with difficult children's behavior. The encouragement should focus on an informed assessment of the family's and child's strengths and shortcomings.

The importance of realistic information is also evinced by families' responses to a question about the overall quality of information they received about their child. One-quarter reported knowing virtually nothing, 9% thought that the information was too negative, 42% judged it as realistic, and 24% found it too positive. Among the latter group, the disruption rate was 59%. Among the other groups, it ranged from 21 to 27%. Families that our model predicted to have disrupted placements were far more likely to report that what they were told was too positive and less likely to report that it was realistic ($p < .01$). This relationship was stronger than the relationship between the accuracy of the information and the outcomes of the placement ($p < .05$). This suggests that reporting inaccurate information is not just a post hoc strategy to reduce self-blame about the end of the placement. Information about the highest risk children seems to be less carefully gathered and communicated to families than is needed. Also overrepresented were families who reported realistic information and were predicted to disrupt but were stable. There was a strong relationship between responses about the accuracy of the information and the difficulty of the placement as judged by the prediction model ($\chi^2 = 12.3$, $df = 3$, $p < .01$). The cases that were predicted to disrupt were far more often likely to report that the information they received was too positive (42 vs. 11%) and far less likely to report it as realistic (24 vs. 54%). Social workers should be especially careful to provide full information when the prediction model suggests a high-risk placement. Currently, there are no differences in reports of preparation according to the predicted difficulty of the adoption. The correlation between risk and preparation was −.04. That the relationship is stronger for the prediction of

Table 6.4. Percentage of Families Receiving Information Prior
  to Placement[a]

Available information	Parent YES/ worker YES (%)	Parent NO/ worker NO (%)	Parent NO/ worker YES (%)	Parent YES[b]/ worker NO (%)	χ^2	p
Psychological report	23	48	19	10	9.11	.00
Birth history	29	32	33	6	5.62	.02
Neurological report	7	74	12	7	5.23	.02
Foster care history	62	12	17	9	5.16	.02
School report	32	30	29	9	5.01	.03
Physical therapy report	3	87	7	3	3.49	.06
Family background	52	13	26	9	2.47	.12
Dental history	3	49	32	16	1.71	.19
Medical history	45	13	29	13	0.27	.60
Typical behavior	36	16	33	15	0.01	0.94
Early childhood history	25	17	49	9	0.00	1.00
Other background	0	91	7	2	0.00	1.00

[a]Rows sum to 100%.
[b]Includes cases with both social worker and parent interviews ($n = 69$).

disruption than it is for the actual disruptions indicates that the interviewees can distinguish between the process and outcome of the adoption.

Despite the 30 disruptions, only 16 families reported that they would definitely not adopt this child again, and only 6 indicated that they would probably not adopt this child again. The vast majority (64) of families indicated that, if they had it to do over, they most likely or definitely would adopt this child again.

Directly related to this, families indicated in overwhelming numbers (67%) that they would have been better prepared to care for the child if they had "better, more accurate information." Unfortunately, the question does not specify whether that information should be about adoption or about the child or both. This is a far higher percentage than those who indicated that they wished they had knowledge about resources for the child (16%), for themselves (17%), parenting skills training (23%), or, even, more preplacement visits (19%).

Sources of Information

Parents were also asked to identify the kinds of information provided (see Table 6.4). Fewer than one-half of the families received psychological reports, dental histories, educational reports, neurological reports, birth histories, reports on early childhood development, or physical therapy reports.

Although the absence of any single kind of information about a child is not significantly associated with disruption, many of the relationships suggest a positive association between more information and more stable placements. Social workers much more often reported that families had received information about the child than did families (see Table 6.4). The majority of parents and workers agreed that information had been provided regarding only two items: foster care history and the child's family background. They also often agreed that neurological and physical therapy reports were not provided. Parents seldom said that information had been provided when workers did not. On the contrary, parents often said that they were not provided information when workers said it had been provided, especially concerning early childhood history, birth history, typical behavior, dental history, medical history, and school report. Yet, when social workers were queried about ways that preparation might be improved, a scant 15% indicated providing the families with more accurate child information. A slightly higher percentage (17%) indicated that providing more information about adoption in general would have improved preparation.

What explains these discrepancies? We suspect that the definition of what constitutes "report" may have differed for families and workers. Workers may have argued that they provided a "report" when they told the family about the child's education (e.g., that he/she was or was not in special education). This is partly borne out by worker's indication that they provided educational reports in 63% of the cases since this very high figure is unlikely given the infrequency of written educational materials getting forwarded when foster children change placements (see Barth, 1985).

Family and worker figures on the provision of educational reports include written and oral reports received. Adoptive families much more rarely had the experience of receiving a report (whether oral or written) than did adoption workers have the experience of providing one. The ambiguity about what is a report would certainly be clarified if more materials were transmitted in writing with cover checklists regarding the type of information enclosed. Even if workers used a checklist that the adoptive family could initial after they had received an oral report on key adoption matters, the discrepancy would be reduced and, we suspect, the thoroughness of the information would be enhanced. The checklist could also include a column for indicating that no information is available. We present a sample cover checklist in Chapter 12.

STRETCHING

Nelson's (1985) investigation identified an association between disruption and the discrepancy between a family's idea of the child they initially planned to adopt and the child they did adopt. She called this discrepancy "stretching" and indicated that the more the family was stretched as a result of misinformation or lack of information the greater the detriment to the placement. Stretching that was informed was less detrimental. In our study, two items helped to estimate the effects of stretching on disruption and difficulty of placements. Families indicated how different or similar the child was to the kind of child they originally had in mind. More than one-third (35%) indicated that the child was very similar, 15% indicated that the child was similar, 32% indicated that the child was different, and 18% indicated that the child was very different. When queried about any differences that worried the family at the time of placement, 11% of the 40 families that reported a difference indicated that it was concern about the child's older age that worried them, 19% worried about the child's behavior problems, and virtually none worried about race, siblings, gender, or developmental disabilities.

Stretching does not only occur among high-risk placements. There were no significant differences between the amount of similarity reported by families with higher risk and lower risk placements. The reported similarity between the child and the family's original notion tends to be related to disruption ($\chi^2 = 8.68$, $df = 4$, $p < .07$). This relationship stands for disruptions that were predicted to be stable as well as for those that were predicted to disrupt. Stretching may be as significant, then, for families who are seeking lower risk adoptions as for families involved in higher risk placements.

Stretching was highly correlated with the difficulty of the placement ($r = .34$, $p < .01$). This relationship is somewhat worsened if you remove the effects of information provided during the preplacement period ($p < .005$). That is, the provision of information partly reduces the effect that reported stretching has on the difficulty of the placement. For new adoptive placements, the relationship is the strongest. This confirms Nelson's (1985) findings that the effects of stretching are most dramatic when considered in the context of the amount of information provided.

PREPARATORY ACTIVITIES

If actions speak at least as loud as words, then preparation activities like visiting with children and meeting other adoptive families should also influence the outcome of the adoptive placement. We queried social workers and parents about the kinds of preplacement activities they engaged in and looked at associations with outcomes. Workers and families were much more closely matched when asked to indicate which adoption activities the agency

Table 6.5. What Did Agency Do to Prepare You For Child's Placement?[a]

Preparation	Parent YES/ worker YES (%)	Parent NO/ worker NO (%)	Parent NO/ worker YES (%)	Parent YES[b]/ worker NO (%)	χ^2	p
Meetings with child	49	22	12	17	8.28	.00
Discussed child's past	59	10	19	12	1.92	.17
Met former caretakers	35	24	19	22	1.59	.21
Reviewed life book	9	61	16	14	1.06	.30
Given reading material	3	81	6	10	0.83	.36
Read case record	0	70	7	23	0.53	.47
Preadoption counseling	1	80	18	1	0.05	.82
Met other adopters	3	68	20	9	0.00	1.00
Movies, videos, slides	0	91	3	6	0.00	1.00
Other activities	0	87	9	4	0.00	1.00

[a]Rows sum to 100%.
[b]Includes cases with both social worker and parent interviews ($n = 69$).

did for or with the family in preparation for the adoption (see Table 6.5). Parents and workers usually agreed that the following were provided prior to placement: a discussion of the child's past and meetings with the child. More often, however, parents and workers agreed that the following activities did *not* occur: movies, videos, or slides, provision of reading material, preadoption counseling, reading the child's case record, meeting other adoptive parents, and reviewing the child's life book. Differences were slight (providing some reassurance that families and workers could agree about specific practice activities), although worker recollections about whether they helped the family contact other adoptive families or find preadoption counseling was much greater than was indicated by the family's reports.

A few aspects of preparation were associated with disruption. When a case record was provided (23% of the cases), the likelihood of a stable placement was 82 compared to 67% for those in which no case record was provided (phi = .17, $p < .05$). The correlation between the summary preparation score and placement risk was .45 ($p < .001$). This indicates that the higher the risk of the placement, the greater the number of activities. The bivariate relationship between preparation and difficulty is not, however, significant. Thus, preparation has a general effect in reducing difficulty that is disguised by the level of placement risk (since more preparation is often given for riskier placements). Whereas the difficulty of the placement is clearly related to risk ($r = .24$, $p < .05$), this relationship is reduced somewhat for families with high levels of active preparation; after controlling for preparation the relationship between risk and difficulty is not significant. Among low-risk placements, preparation tended to be lower for those that disrupted (F, 1.95, $p < .10$). More active preparation may have reduced these disruptions.

Assessment Meetings

While almost one-half of adoptive parent applicants (43%) reported that they were introduced to other adoptive parents in preparation for adoption, only 12% said that they met with these other parents to learn more about adoption, only 10% turned to adoptive parents' groups, and 2% turned to parent self-help groups, for help in dealing with difficulties during the placement. Meeting other adoptive parents as preparation was especially likely for foster parents who adopted (16%; $\chi^2 = 7.50$, $p < .05$). Meeting with other adoptive parents was not associated with disruption rates. Parents in difficult adoptions were very likely to meet with other adoptive parents singly ($r = .19$, $p < .05$) or in groups ($r = .30$, $p < .05$). When the strong relationship between risky and difficult placements is controlled for by meetings with other adoptive parents, the magnitude of the relationship declines, suggesting the importance of these contacts.

Children's Preparation

According to adoption workers, about one-tenth (9%) of the children met other adopted children in preparation for adoption, and another 9% would have benefited from this type of contact during preparation. However, meeting other adopted children was not related to a lower likelihood of disruption. Meeting other children was more likely in fost-adoptions (21%) and new adoptions (14%) than in foster parent adoptions (0%; $\chi^2 = 5.31$, $p < .07$).

Assessment Visits

About one-third of the families (32%) and social workers (35%) said that parents did not meet the child prior to placement. Meeting the child prior to placement was especially likely for fost-adoptions (93%), followed by new adoptions (78%), and foster parent adoptions (37%; $\chi^2 = 18.41$, $p < .001$). Contrary to our expectations, parents who did meet with the child had a higher disruption rate (40%) than did those who did not meet with the child (17%; $\chi^2 = 3.78$, $p < .05$), regardless of placement type. Among parents who said they could have been better prepared for the adoption, almost one-fifth (19%) said that they could have been better prepared by more visits with the child prior to placement. This sentiment was not significantly more common, however, among families with disrupted adoptions.

Although adoption workers did not arrange face-to-face meetings between children and families prior to placement as often as might be expected, they were somewhat more likely to arrange those for placements in which disruptions were predicted. Only 25% of those placements did not involve meeting the child first, whereas 42% of less risky placements did not include such meetings. Meeting the child had no singular relationship to disruption among the high- or low-risk placements. The older child and family appear to be as well informed about each other from hearing as they are from observing.

In preparation for the adoption, over one-half of the adoptive families (57%) report meeting with the child's former caretakers prior to placement. This was much more common among fost-adoptions (80%) and new adoptions (61%) than among foster parent adoptions (37%; $\chi^2 = 7.99$, $p < .05$). Workers also report that more than one-half (55%) of the families met with the child's former caretakers, especially among fost-adoptions (79%) and new adoptions (59%), compared to foster parent adoptions (35%; $\chi^2 = 7.57$, $p < .05$).

Assessment of the Child

Adoption workers reported that most of the children (69%) had some special qualities, although this level is lower than that reported by adoptive parents (88%). Among the 57 children for whom the parents remarked upon some good point(s), adoption workers said 25% of these children had no special qualities. Among the 8 children for whom parents could identify no good points, adoption workers said that 3 (38%) had special qualities. Clearly, family and worker appreciation for children could be bolstered with more attention and discussion of children's strengths.

The majority of children were assessed as being either somewhat (32%) or very much in favor of (61%) the adoption. All of the children in stable adoptions were assessed as being somewhat or very much in favor of the adoption, compared to 87% of the disruptions ($\chi^2 = 7.07$, $p < .10$). Almost one-half of the adoption workers (43%) had concerns about the potential effect of the adoption on the child. Most of these concerns focused on attachment issues: whether the child would bond to the parents (30% of cases), that the child was still attached to the foster parents (14%), and that the child was still attached to his biological parents (14%). When workers had concerns about the effect of the adoption on the child, the disruption rate was 38%, compared to a 48% disruption rate for those adoptions where the worker had no concern about the effect on the child.

Assessment of the Family

Adoption workers were asked to rate families on a four-point scale in each of several areas concerning the ability to respond to the child and use help.

Table 6.6. Worker Concerns About Family (Mean Scores)[a]

Concern	Total (n = 93)	Disrupt (n = 42)	Stable (n = 51)	t
Recognizing emotional needs	2.95	2.36	3.43	5.71*
Managing difficult behaviors	2.79	2.17	3.29	5.69*
Ability to use services	2.97	2.46	3.37	4.54*
Understanding separation and attachment	2.87	2.41	3.25	4.48*
Willingness to seek out help	3.13	2.71	3.47	3.89*
Support among family members	2.90	2.43	3.24	3.77*
Available informal help	2.82	2.44	3.16	3.43*
Support of racial identity (n = 49)	3.43	3.25	3.60	1.57

[a]Scale: 1 = poor to 4 = very good.
*$p < .01$ for differences between disruptions and nondisruptions.

The mean scores are shown in Table 6.6. The vast majority of adoptive families (90%) were assessed by adoption workers to bring some strengths to the adoption. There were few differences in the presence of strengths between disrupted and intact placements. Many families were said to have expertise or experience with children (37% of cases), be highly motivated (16%), be sensitive or loving (14%), be flexible (13%), and have a religious background (12%) that would be a source of strength in the adoption. These were not, by themselves, related to the outcome of disruption. Only families considered to be strong because of wealth had a high disruption rate (86% disrupted).

Just over one-half of the adoption workers (53%) had some concern about the family selected to adopt. There were no significant differences in the presence of concern between disrupted and intact placements. Regarding specific anxieties many worried if the family knew their own limitations (21% of cases), or if they were too rigid (17%) or had too high expectations (15%). Many workers were also apprehensive about the financial status of the family (10%). Disruption rates were high among families where adoption workers had misgivings if the family knew their own limitations (60%), had high expectations (71%), or were too rigid (63%). New adoptive parents were more likely than other parents to be reported as having high expectations or being too rigid.

Social workers report that only four families needed to be encouraged to adopt. Those that did needed encouragement because of the child's aggressive behavior, the financial burden of the child's medical problems, the family was stretched to accept siblings, and the adoptive mother was unsure of bonding. The family with a financial burden (a foster adoption) did not disrupt, while the other three placements (new adoptions) did.

MATCHING

When adoption workers were asked why the particular family was chosen to adopt the child in question, responses were varied. The most common responses were: the family was available at the time (19% of cases), the child responded to these parents (13%), this family had had the child for a large portion of his life (11%), and this was a strong couple (10%).

About one-tenth ($n = 11$) of the placements about which social workers were queried were reported as transracial placements. Transracial placements were considered for 4 (5%) of the children in same race placements. For the children in transracial placements, the following reasons were cited: a same race placement was not available, a same race placement that also met the child's other needs was not available, the child was attached to these parents, and finding a same race placement would delay placement too long. Disruption was no more likely for transracial adoptions or among transracial new adoptions (21%) rather than transracial foster parent adoptions (15%). There were no transracial fost-adopt placements. When a transracial placement was made because the child was already attached to the family, there were no disruptions. This reason was given frequently among foster parent adoptions.

Discussion of the Possibility of Disruption

Workers reported discussing the possibility of disruption with 59% of the families. Two of three workers who mentioned disruption indicated that the discussion was not at all important or slightly important; 21% indicated that the discussion was very important. The bulk of discussions related to adoption disruption were for children who had been adopted before or for families that had adopted before. Oddly, there was no relationship between the presence or absence of a discussion of disruption or the amount of importance the worker placed on discussing disruption and the prior experience of the family or child with a disruption.

AGENCY IMPROVEMENT

When parents had the opportunity to volunteer ideas about how the agency could improve, information and preparation were most often identified. Of 147 responses given by 83 families, only seven responses received more than 10% of all responses. They included: more preparation (33 responses), more and consistent workers (17 responses), and more information on the child (16 responses).

The greatest complaint of interviewees who had high-risk placements that succeeded was for more information about the placement. One family commented, "they thoroughly investigated us, but we hardly had a chance to investigate the children." Some families indicated that they received records on the child only after the agency had placed the child with them. Others indicated that their meetings with workers focused on screening and matching and not on what to expect once the placement occurred.

CHILD PREPARATION

Social workers commented on the preparation of the children placed for adoption. Most children were judged to be very much, (61%) or somewhat (32%) in favor of the adoption; only a few children were rated as somewhat against (3%) or very much against (4%) the adoption. In view of the comments by some adoptive parents that the disruption was a direct result of the child's ambivalence or antipathy toward the idea of adoption, this relationship was tested and found lacking. Workers also indicated how well prepared the child was, with 46% judged as very well prepared, 36% as well prepared, and 9% judged as moderately or poorly prepared, respectively. The relationship between the child's preparation and disruption was tested and a mild association found ($\chi^2 = 5.10$, $p < .15$).

When the relationship between disruption risk and placement difficulty is controlled for by preparation activities, the overall correlation decreases from a bivariate $r = .39$ to a partial correlation of .37; this is a nonsignificant reduction in difficulty due to the amount of preparation. Preparation had the most significance for foster-adopt parents, reducing the relationship between risk and difficulty from $r = .37$ to $r = .23$. Preparation activity was modestly associated with disruption as more of the stable families had higher preparation scores. Also demonstrating the association between information and stability, 66% of the predicted and stable families had a difference in information score of zero whereas only 40% of the predicted stable but disrupted families had a zero score; 40% of the disrupted families had scores of 3 or 4 whereas only 5% of the stable ones did, indicating that a difference between workers' and parents' reports of information provided is related to disruption and should be closely watched.

Among placements predicted to disrupt, the strongest relationship was when little information was provided ($p < .05$) which shows that more families predicted to disrupt that did disrupt had no or one source of information whereas placements that were stable despite the prediction of disruption were more likely to have two or more sources of information. This collection of findings shows that information is important to stability, whether or not that information is positive or negative. Families want accurate information and when workers and families agree that accurate information has been provided, adoptive placements generally work out. The provision of relevant and accurate information by workers helps to prepare families for the placement, and fosters a positive helping relationship between agency and family that can also be utilized by the family after placement.

Our findings strongly support those of previous investigators that the amount and type of information and preplacement preparation provided to families is crucial to the welfare of the placements. Social workers and families have vastly different ideas about what information was provided to the family. Admittedly, some of these cases required a recall of almost 5 years. Still, there is little reason to expect that selective recall would make the results so different for each respective group. The absence of certain kinds of information was followed by difficult placements. When not informed ahead of time, sexual abuse and behavioral problems were surprises to which families had difficulty adjusting. Disrupting families often reported that they received information that was far too positive. This was especially true for the highest risk placements. Families that adopted children who were considerably different than the kind of children they had planned on when they began the adoption process has more difficult placements. The increased difficulty is evident for both high-risk and low-risk placements. This relationship is mitigated by providing more information about the child. Agencies should maintain systematic records that indicate what information was provided and should use these records to assess their own performance.

Activities to prepare families for the adoption were important to the stability of placements. This was most true among low-risk placements. Placement preparation that included meeting with other adoptive families seemed to lessen the difficulty of the highest risk placements. Preparation infrequently included discussion of the possibility of disruption and these discussions were no more common when children had prior disruptions or were at high risk for disruptions.

Families and social workers are optimistic at the time of placement. This makes discussing disruption as unappealing as signing prenuptial financial agreements at the time of marriage. Yet, such discussions provide an invaluable forum for considering many key issues. Families can preview indicators that the adoption is developing problems from learning about disruptions in other families. Adoptive families will also come to understand in a most vivid way that the adjustment to adoption is lengthy and uneven. Conferences between the family and worker will help to focus on resources available for weathering the challenges of a high-risk placement. Families and social workers can also use the discussion of disruption to identify critical incidents that might call the future of adoption into question—an assault by the adopted child, sexual molestation of a birth child, or an allegation of abuse against the adoptive parent by the adopted child. Anticipatory-coping strategies can then be devised. Discussions of disruption help all parties to take a hard look at what they can expect and what they can tolerate and to initiate plans for preserving the placement.

7

Birth and Adoptive Parents

Our model of adjustment to adoption places great importance on the characteristic stressors and resources of adoptive parents. The strengths and vulnerabilities that adoptive parents bring to the adoption will affect their ability to adopt to family life. We examined parent characteristics and their relation to the difficulty and outcome of the placement, recognizing that characteristics are not only a snapshot indication of parental qualities, but are indicators of the larger sphere of parenting style and family environment.

BIRTH PARENT CHARACTERISTICS

While we did not examine associations between birth parent characteristics and adoption outcomes, we did review birth parent information for an overview of children's backgrounds. State records on birth parent information is limited, particularly concerning any medical or economic conditions. The most reliable data on birth parents concerns their ages and the source of the referral to the adoptions branch. Even then, the data about the birth father is sketchy. Of course, information about birth parents was obtained only at intake, not during the interviews.

Among the cases in the interview sample, the ages of the birth mothers at the birth of the child ranged from 15 to 39, with a mean age of 22 ($SD = 4.8$). The birth father's ages ranged from 17 to 66, with a mean of 28 ($SD = 8.4$). As expected, the typical source of referral of the birth mother to the adoption agency was a public welfare agency, with 57% referred by these agencies. Over 10% of the birth mothers had been adopted themselves, although lack of certainty by adoption workers on mother's adoptive status leads to cautious interpretation of this finding.

ADOPTIVE FAMILY CHARACTERISTICS

In addition to the services provided before and after the adoptive placements, the characteristics of the adoptive family bear on the outcome of the placement. The study examined family characteristics, including demographic data, social support, and previous experience as a foster or adoptive parent.

The ages of the adoptive parents in the interview sample ranged from 22 to 74 at the time of the placement, with a mean age of the adoptive mother at 37 (SD = 8) and the mean age of the adoptive father at 39 (SD = 8), demonstrating the growing flexibility in age requirements in older child adoptions. Often, parents who were older thought it would be "inappropriate" to adopt younger children. There was a significant correlation between the child's age and parent's ages (r = .18 and .19, $p < .05$) illustrating (a) the prevalence of the preference for "age-appropriate" children; (b) the reluctance of the agency to place small children with older parents; or (c) both.

The majority of women were homemakers (54%), while the men were either professional/managerial (41%) or craftsmen (14%). Age and occupation level had no relation to disruption. The median family income was $27,600, which also had no relation to disruption. Most women who reported their employment plans (n = 78) did not intend to work after the placement of the child (53%), while about a quarter (27%) planned to work full-time and the other 20% planned to work part-time. The mother's work plans were not associated with disruption.

The majority of adoptive mothers were white (82%) followed by smaller percentages of black (10%) and latino (5%) adopters. Ethnicity of the mother was not associated with disruption. Most mothers had either attended (18%) or graduated (34%) from college. Mother's education level was related to disruption, but only in foster parent adoptions, where a higher education level was associated with disruption (χ^2 = 10.94 $p < .01$).

About one-half (40%) of adoptive families were Protestant, and another quarter (24%) were Catholic. Contrary to other studies' findings (e.g., Boyne et al., 1984), disruption rates did not differ by religion of the parents. Most families reported going to church once a week or more (57%), with another 32% reporting church attendance of less than once a month or never. Church attendance did not differ by placement type. However, among foster parent adoptions, more frequent church attendance was significantly related to adoption stability (χ^2 = 12.8, $p < .005$). This relation was not present for fost-adoptions or new adoptions.

Household composition was modestly relationed to disruption. There were 12 single-parent placements (13%) in the interview sample, and they were no more likely to disrupt than were two-parent placements. The number of people in the household beside the adoptive child at the time of placement ranged from one to eight, with a mode of two people. In the majority of families, there were two adults (60%), and either no other children (25%) or one other child (22%). The number of other children in the home ranged from 0 to 6. Overall, the number of people, adults or children, in the home was not associated with disruption. However, the number of other adopted children in the home was associated with disruption ($t = 2.83$; $p < .01$). The relationship is mitigated (but still holds) after controlling for placement risk, as families with multiple previous adoptions adopted more difficult children. Adoptions that had a negative effect on the closeness between the parent and the other children were less stable regardless of the number of other adopted children in the home.

Parents were asked about stressful life events occurring around the time of the placement. Few families reported a stressful event, although 22% reported someone changing jobs or job status. This is often the case, when one parent quits a job or changes to part time in order to stay with the child, or when a parent increases job responsibilities for better financial resources for the placement. No stressful life events were significantly associated with disruption. The majority of families experiencing a stressful life event ($n = 38$) said that the stressor had no effect on the placement (68%) or that it was helpful in developing the relationship (11%) or expediting the placement (3%). Only a few families said that the stressor delayed the placement (8%) or made the child uncertain about the placement (8%).

Informal support of adoptive families has had limited attention in previous studies of disruption. Several authors have pointed to the importance of extended family and social support to the success of an adoption (e.g., Tremetiere, 1979), but this has not been rigorously tested in outcome studies. In this study, adoptive families varied in their number of relatives residing nearby, ranging from 0 (22%) to 50 (1%) relatives within visiting distance, with a mean of 6 ($SD = 9$). On average, disrupting families had significantly fewer relatives within visiting distance (4 vs. 7; $p < .05$). Among families with nearby relatives, the frequency of contact with those relatives was fairly frequent, with 79% reporting contact of once a week or more. Contact was least frequent among foster parent adoptions, compared to fost-adoptions and new adoptions ($\chi^2 = 12.62$, $p < .05$). Frequency of contact was also related to stability of the adoption, but only among foster parent adoptions ($\chi^2 = 6.71$, $p < .10$) and not among fost-adopts or new adoptions. The relationship between frequency of contact and disruption held after controlling for risk.

Families were asked about the overall family opinion toward the decision to adopt. This could include household members as well as extended family. Opinion was generally favorable, with 46% of respondents reporting that families were very much in favor, and another 32% somewhat in favor. Only 13% were somewhat opposed, and 9% were very much opposed. Four families declined to answer because family opinions were too varied for one general response. Family opinion did not differ significantly by placement

type, but within foster parent adoptions and fost-adoptions, family opposition to the adoption was significantly associated with disruption (foster
parents: $\chi^2 = 7.1$, $p < .10$; fost-adopts: $\chi^2 = 9.4$, $p < .05$), a relationship not
present among new adoptive parents. This difference may be due to the
familiarity of the child to the family of foster parent adopters. If the extended
family of a foster parent objects to the adoption of the foster child, it may be
due to their dislike of the specific child's behavior or other characteristics,
while extended family of new adoptive parents may be more likely to
disapprove of adoption in general. These extended family members may
lend their support after the placement.

Frequency of contact with friends was high, with 77% of families
reporting contact with friends once a week or more often. Unlike contact
with relatives, frequency of contact with friends had no relation to the
stability of the adoption or to the type of placement. When it comes to
adoption, the support of family members appears to be more important than
the support of friends. This is consistent with the idea that extended family's
approval of the adoption facilitates attachment between family members.
The number of friends on whom families could call for help ranged from 0
to 50 with a mean of nine ($SD = 11$). This number was unrelated to adoption
stability or type of placement, even after controlling for risk.

The majority of families reported belonging to a professional or social club
or group of some variety. Among those belonging to a group, the degree of
involvement was usually high (73%) or moderate (15%). Belonging to such a
group and the degree of involvement were unrelated to adoption stability or
to the type of placement.

We predicted that previous experience as a foster or adoptive parent
would help parents to anticipate problems, and would be associated with
stability. In fact, most parents who adopt special-needs children are well
acquainted with the child welfare system. The majority of adoptive families
(53%) had been foster parents to other children, especially foster parents
(67%) and fost-adopt parents (60%). However, even new adoptive parents
frequently reported previous experience as foster parents (43%). Among
those with foster parent experiences ($n = 48$), most (77%) had fostered an
older child, many (46%) had fostered a disabled child, and some (27%) had
fostered siblings. Previous experience as a foster parent was not a significant
associate of adoption disruption, but tended toward significance ($p < .10$)
when controlling for risk.

Almost one-third of adoptive families (32%) reported a previous adoption.
Previous adoptive experience was slightly more frequent among new
adoptive parents (41 vs. 22% of foster parents and 20% of fost-adopt parents),
although not to a significant degree. Among those with adoptive experience
($n = 29$), many (52%) had previously adopted an older child and/or a disabled

child, and some (17%) had previously adopted siblings. Previous adoptive experience by itself was not related to adoption stability of the current placement, even when controlling for risk. Only two families had experienced a prior adoption disruption; one of these families had a disruption in the current placement.

The majority of families ($n = 42$) with prior experience with either foster care or adoption said that the experience was either very helpful (38%) or helpful (21%). However, one-third (33%) said the experience was not helpful. Just as many disrupters as nondisrupters found prior experience helpful. Most families who found the experience helpful said that it helped to learn how the placement would be (42%), or that they learned to overcome problems (17%). Those that said that the experience was not helpful said that the previous experience involved a child of a different age (27%).

The support of families who are knowledgeable about older child adoption can be quite encouraging. Families were asked if they knew other adoptive or foster parents at the time of the placement. Over one-half (59%) reported knowing someone, with 36% knowing adoptive parents, 11% knowing foster parents, and 12% knowing both. Knowing other foster or adoptive parents was significantly more likely among fost-adopt parents (67%) than among new (59%) or foster parent (56%) adopters ($\chi^2 = 24.2$, $p < .001$), and was mildly associated with adoption stability ($\chi^2 = 7.5$, $p < .10$), especially when controlling for risk ($r = .37$, $p < .01$).

SUMMARY

Only a few aspects of the choice of placement discriminated between stable and disrupted placements. Adoptive parents in families with disrupting placements had higher education levels—this was primarily true for foster parent adoptions. Disrupted placements more often had other adopted children in the home. Parents in disrupting placements had fewer contacts with relatives. Foster parents in disrupting placements went to church infrequently or not at all. Also, among foster parent disruptions, other family members were more often opposed to the adoption.

The following placement characteristics did not differ between disruptions and nondisruptions: the ethnicity, age, religion, and marital status of the parents; mother's work plans after the placement; the number of other children in the home (except for adopted children); previous experience as a foster or adoptive parent; simultaneous stressful life events at placement; frequency of contact with friends; or the reason for adopting. Placements into homes with nonadopted biological siblings were not more prone to disrupt.

The associates of disruption indicate the importance of social support to adoptive families. Disruptions often occurred when the parent did not have the support of his or her spouse, children, other family members, relatives, or church members. In view of the finding that social workers almost never had contact with anyone in the families' support networks, adoption workers may do well to reduce the emphasis on personal information of applicants, and instead focus on assessing, building, and enlisting familial and social support for the placement. Adoption workers rarely had contact with members of the family's social support system during assessment or in order to strengthen the placement. At least two of our cases did disrupt because families did not have adequate contingency plans in the event of a serious illness or death. The assessment of families must include greater efforts to document the commitment on behalf of persons identified as interested in the child's welfare.

8

The Children:
History, Behavior, and Attachment

In older child adoption, the child is thoroughly assessed as to their history and its effects, current needs, and potential for development in an adoptive family. All of these concerns are assessed in light of choosing an appropriate home for the child. Thus, the characteristics of the child are felt to influence his contribution to an adoption, but the process and extent of their influence is not clear. Our examination of child characteristics identified which qualities are most important to the outcome of the adoption. These characteristics could be more concretely and accurately assessed at pre-placement decision making as well as being addressed in postplacement services to families. Besides static characteristics of the child, we examined the development of reciprocal attachment behavior over time and its effect on adoption stability.

Child Characteristics

The ages of the children in the interview sample ranged from 3 to 16, with a mean age of 8.2 years at placement (SD = 3.2); about two-fifths of the children (41%) were aged 9 or older. As found in many other studies, a higher age was associated with disruption. Disrupting children had a mean age of 9 at placement compared to a mean age of 7 for nondisruptions (t = 2.63, p < .01).

The majority of children were male (59%) and white (74%). Boys had a 54% disruption rate while girls had a 38% disruption rate. Among boys, there was no difference in disruption rate by type of placement. Among girls, however, over one-half of those in new adoptions disrupted (56%), compared to 14% of fost-adoptions and 12% of foster parent adoptions (χ^2 = 8.77, p < .01). White children had a 41% disruption rate, black children had a 62% disruption rate, and Latino children had a 58% disruption rate.

These differences were not significant but approached significance when grouped as white (41%) and nonwhite (65%).

The length of total foster care for these children prior to relinquishment ranged from less than 1 month to 11 years, with a mean of 27 months ($SD = 27$). There was no difference between disruptions and nondisruptions on length of time in foster care. The mean number of days that passed between adoption agency acceptance of the case and placement of the child was 756 days ($SD = 719$), or about 2 years. There was no difference between boys and girls in the length of wait for a placement or in the length of time they were in foster care. However, boys were significantly younger at placement (mean age of 7.7 vs. 8.9 for girls), suggesting the continuation of the age-old practice of older boys being considered unadoptable and not being placed for adoption (Zelizer, 1985). Girls were significantly more likely than boys to be adopted by their foster parents ($\chi^2 = 6.5$, $p < .05$). The majority of this sample of children (64%) were perceived by the adoption worker at intake to have some special problem, either behavioral, emotional, physical, medical or intellectual. Of these problems perceived by the worker at intake, only behavioral problems were mildly associated with disruption. Over one-half of those with behavioral problems disrupted (61%) compared to 43% of those without ($\chi^2 = 2.49$, $p < .15$).

The majority of children were referred for adoption because of biological parents' incapacity to care for the child (53%) and/or willingness of the parent to care for the child (47%). According to families, the majority of children in the interviewed sample had a history of neglect (82%), multiple placements (66%), and/or physical abuse (60%), and had emotional or behavioral problems (83%) and/or learning disabilities (59%). Developmental disabilities (40%), physical/medical disabilities (33%), and a history of sexual abuse (32%) were less common. Similar to worker's perceptions, families' reports of the child having emotional or behavioral problems were significantly associated with disruption and placement difficulty especially among new adoptions; the disruption rate for children with emotional or behavioral problems in new adoptions was 55% while in foster-adoptions the rate was 21%.

Almost all parents said that the adopted child had some good qualities. Children were most often reported as being well-mannered, curious or smart, or cute or attractive. Children were seldom reported by parents to have a sense of humor (6%). The presence or absence of any of these qualities was not associated with disruption of the placement, but the absence of being viewed as cute at the time of placement ($p < .10$) was associated with difficulty in the placement.

In the interviewed sample, 24% of the placements were sibling adoptions, with 20% involving two siblings, and another 4% involving three siblings.

Consistent with the larger sample, sibling placements were no more likely to disrupt than were single-child placements (33 vs. 35%), nor were they more difficult, regardless of foster adoption or new adopt status. The majority of children in the interviewed sample (78%) had other siblings not placed with the same family. Having nonadopted siblings did not significantly increase or decrease the likelihood of disruption or difficulty in the adoption, and did not have any relationship with placement type.

PLACEMENT HISTORY

According to social workers, the mean amount of time that the child spent in care prior to referral was 30.7 months ($SD = 23.3$), or 2 1/2 years. There was no significant difference between disrupted and nondisrupted adoptions in time in care (33 vs. 29 months).

The number of foster care placements a child experienced prior to referral averaged 2.9 ($SD = 2.4$) with 30% of children having one prereferral placement, and 24% having two such placements. There was no difference between disruptions and nondisruptions. Only 15% of the children had attempted a fost-adopt placement prior to the study placement, with 3% having two prior fost-adopt placements. Disrupted children had no more fost-adopt placements.

Almost one-fifth of the children (18%) experienced a change in placement between the referral to adoption and the adoptive placement. Most of these changes in placement occurred because the foster family could not deal with the child's behavior (50%), or because they experienced a family crisis (13%). A change in placement at this time was not associated with disruption or difficulty, nor with the type of adoption.

The time between the last foster care entry and the adoptive placement of the child ranged from less than 1 month to 8 years, with an average time of 2 years. There was no difference between disruptions and nondisruptions on the length of time between the last foster care placement and the adoption—even for new adoptions.

The majority of children in the interviewed sample (58%) had at least one other sibling free for adoption, with most having one free sibling (58%), followed by three siblings (21%), two siblings (16%), and four siblings (5%). Almost one-half had other siblings not adopted by this family (47%). Having freed siblings was not associated with disruption or placement type. The most common reasons for placing siblings together were: that the children wanted to stay together (67%) and that the family had resources for more children (62%). The most common reasons for separating children were: that the siblings had a poor relationship (52%) and that one sibling was ready for adoption before the other (33%). Separating siblings and placing them in separate homes when they were available were associated with greater ease of the adoption ($r = .53$, $p < .01$).

The majority of social workers reported no difficulties (63%) in freeing the child for adoption. Those that did report difficulties (37%) most often attributed the difficulty to a search for the parents (15%) or parents contesting the petition (13%) or parents being indecisive about relinquishment (12%). Contrary to prior studies (e.g., Borgman, 1982), problems in freeing the child did not destabilize the placement.

BEHAVIOR PROBLEMS

The child is an active partner in an adoption, and the child's behavior is a strong determinant of the placement's viability. Adopted children, in general, use more professional mental health care (Brodzinsky, 1987b) and may be more likely to be hyperactive (Dalby, Fox, & Haslam, 1982) than nonadopted children. Studies cited by Brodzinsky and colleagues (1984) have shown adopted children to be at greater risk of aggression and acting out, low self-confidence, and learning difficulties. These may be artifacts of accidental sampling, residual effects of poor perinatal care, or negative ramifications of the confusion of adoption. We expect that all contribute to these differences. Although their behavior is still within the normal range, adopted boys are especially likely to exhibit uncommunicative behavior and hyperactivity, and adopted girls are likely to be depressed, hyperactive, and/or aggressive (Brodzinsky, 1987a). Findings that older adopted children are more likely to have external behavior problems are consistent with Offord et al.'s (1969) finding that, among referrals to a psychiatric clinic, adoptees did not differ in the severity of problems from matched nonadopted children, but only in the type. Adopted children manifested more antisocial behavior. Further, these differences were primarily a consequence of children older than 3 at the time of adoption. Fanshel and Borgatta (1965) and Menlove (1985) also reported more overt behavior problems rather than overinhibited behavior.

In addition to demographic and historical characteristics of the child, data were collected on the child's behavior during the first 3 months of the placement. Adoptive parents provided reports of the child's behavior using the Child Behavior Checklist (CBC) (Achenbach, 1978; Achenbach & Edelbrock, 1983), a well-established measure for assessing the children's behaviors that are associated with maladaptive outcomes. Separate editions of the Profile have been developed for boys and girls aged 4–5, 6–11, and 12–16. Norms have been constructed by computing normalized T scores

Table 8.1. High Behavior Items for All Children (n = 85)

Item	Mean[a]	SD
Can not concentrate	1.42	.78
Demands attention	1.37	.78
Acts too young for his/her age	1.28	.84
Impulsive, acts without thinking	1.19	.81
Stubborn, sullen, irritable	1.05	.83
Does not feel guilty after misbehaving	0.99	.84
Poor school work	0.99	.88
Temper tantrums	0.99	.89
Argues a lot	0.97	.87
Nervous, highstrung	0.97	.88
Does not get along with other children	0.95	.82
Lying, cheating	0.95	.87
Can not sit still, restless	0.95	.90
Disobedient at home	0.93	.77
Daydreams	0.93	.81
Easily jealous	0.93	.87
Clings, too dependent	0.92	.86
Prefers younger children	0.92	.88
Showing off, clowning	0.91	.84

[a]Scale: 0 = never true to 2 = often true

from Checklists completed by 1300 parents of normal children (Achenbach & Edelbrock, 1981). Procedures for classifying profiles of individual children have also been developed (Edelbrock & Achenbach, 1980).

For all children in the interview sample, the most common behavior items that parents checked were: cannot concentrate, demands attention, acts immature for his/her age, impulsive, stubborn, temper tantrums, poor school work, and does not feel guilty after misbehaving (see Table 8.1).

The behavioral items that significantly differentiated disrupting children from those in stable adoptions are shown in Table 8.2. Children that disrupted were significantly more likely to display these behaviors, except for "feels he has to be perfect," which was less likely among children in disruptions. The majority of distinguishing behaviors are interpersonal or external behaviors, including meanness (cruelty), fighting, and threatening and arguing.

Each child, according to his age and sex group, received scores on several behavioral dimensions appropriate to that group. These dimensional scores were transformed into T scores. As always, the mean of a T distribution is 50. According to Achenbach's classification (Achenbach & Edelbrock, 1983), a T score higher than 70 indicates that a child is in the clinical range for that dimension. Several of the children in this sample were in the clinical range

Table 8.2. Percentage of Children Demonstrating Troubled Behavior

Item	Disrupt ($n = 27$)		Nondisrupt ($n = 58$)		χ^2
	Often true	Some-times true	Often true	Some-times true	
Cruelty, meanness to others	33	41	14	21	11.71**
Gets in many fights	37	33	16	16	11.63**
Threatens people	15	30	9	5	11.45**
Argues a lot	56	30	26	24	10.69**
Hangs out with bad friends	19	37	12	12	9.05*
Disobedient at school	44	26	16	33	8.53*
Physically attacks people	22	33	10	14	8.12*
Vandalism	11	11	5	0	7.96*
Disobedient at home	44	37	17	43	7.93*
Feels he has to be perfect	15	4	22	24	7.21*
Trouble sleeping	22	0	5	7	7.14*
Prefers younger children	30	41	36	16	6.73*
Destroys others' belongings	30	30	14	17	6.24*
Swearing, obscene language	19	26	7	12	6.14*
Lying, cheating	41	37	33	19	5.89*

*$p < .05$ for differences between disrupt and nondisrupt.
**$p < .01$ for differences between disrupt and nondisrupt.

on a variety of dimensions. Table 8.3 shows the percentage of children in the interview sample who scored in the clinical range on the behavioral dimensions for their age and sex group.

In keeping with other findings, the older males in this sample seem to have the most behavioral problems. Their problems are more external than internal. The boys aged 6 to 11 and 12 to 18 score in the clinical range on many dimensions, with hyperactivity and delinquency very common. The older females were also likely to be withdrawn or depressed (see Table 8.3).

When behavioral dimensions are common across age and sex groups, T scores can be aggregated. Every child received internal and external T scores, as well as a summary T score (see Table 8.4). The following aggregate T scores were computed: internal, external, summary, aggressive,

BEHAVIOR PROBLEMS   135

Table 8.3. **Percentage of Children in the Clinical Range on Behavior Dimensions by Age**

	Males			Females		
Dimension	Ages 3–5 ($n = 18$)	Ages 6–11 ($n = 23$)	Ages 12–18 ($n = 6$)	Ages 3–5 ($n = 9$)	Ages 6–11 ($n = 22$)	Ages 12–18 ($n = 7$)
Aggressive	50	52	17	33	23	0
Schizoid	6	30	33	33	46	14
Social withdrawal	44	50	—	56	50	—
Immature	44	—	83	—	—	14
Depressed	44	30	—	44	68	0
Delinquent	39	52	67	—	36	29
Sex problems	17	—	—	44	41	—
Somatic complaints	6	22	0	22	27	0
Uncommunicative	—	33	17	—	—	—
Obsessive/ compulsive	—	65	50	—	—	—
Hyperactive	—	74	100	33	64	—
Hostile/cruel	—	—	83	—	23	43
Obesity	—	—	—	33	—	—
Anxious	—	—	—	—	—	14

delinquent, withdrawn, schizoid/anxious, somatic complaints, hyperactive, and depressed. The mean internal T score for the total sample was 65.57 ($SD = 11.12$) and the mean external T score was 66.55 ($SD = 13.35$). These scores indicate that the behavior of the average adopted child in our sample was rated as one and one-half standard deviations worse than the norm.

Previous examination of specific behavioral problems as well as t-tests indicated that external, rather than internal, behavioral problems would be associated with disruption. In fact, the mean external T score was significantly different between disruptions and nondisruptions ($T = 2.32$, $p < .05$), while the internal T scores were not distinct between groups (see Table 8.4). T scores on the dimensions of aggressive and delinquent (both external dimensions) were significantly different between disrupters and nondisrupters, with disruptions much more likely among aggressive and delinquent children.

Overall difficulty of adoptive placement (a composite mean score, discussed in an earlier chapter) was examined in association with behavioral items, as well as behavioral dimensions. The dimensions of aggressive ($r = .24$; $p < .01$) and delinquent ($r = .22$; $p < .05$) were associated with placement difficulty.

Table 8.4. T Scores of Disrupting and Nondisrupting Children ($n = 85$)

Dimension	Total	Disrupt	Nondisrupt	t
Summary	68.26	70.07	67.41	0.89
External	66.55	71.11	64.43	2.32**
Internal	65.57	64.41	66.12	0.61
Aggressive	68.20	72.41	66.24	2.18**
Delinquent	69.28	72.28	67.80	1.70*
Withdrawn	69.58	73.50	68.53	0.71
Schizoid/anxious	64.78	64.15	65.07	0.45
Somatic complaints	61.11	60.70	61.29	0.33
Hyperactive	75.42	76.04	75.03	0.31
Depressed	66.81	66.71	66.85	0.06

*$p < .05$
**$p < .10$

In terms of individual behaviors, overall difficulty is significantly ($p < .01$) correlated with destroying others' belongings, disobeying at home or school, cruelty, arguing, fighting, hanging around with bad friends, being disliked by other children, depression, physical attacks on others, swearing, and lying. Difficulty is negatively correlated ($p < .01$) with parental reports that the child feels he has to be perfect (see Table 8.5). Several parents made humorous notes (e.g., "Don't we wish") next to this item.

Behaviors that made the placement difficult, but were not as highly correlated with actual disruption included: does not seem to feel guilty after misbehaving, stealing at home or outside the home, impulsivity, truancy, teasing, and sleeping too much (see Table 8.5).

Behaviors that were negatively correlated with disruption ($p < .05$) but uncorrelated with the difficulty of the placement were: self-consciousness, shyness, fear of certain situations or places, and complaints of loneliness.

ATTACHMENT BETWEEN ADOPTIVE PARENTS AND THE CHILD

Attachment, or reciprocity between parent and child, cannot be adequately measured at one point in time, but must be assessed in relation to its development over time. There is no absolute level of attachment that is best for the child or parent, but changes in attachment are noteworthy. We predicted that attachment behaviors would increase among stable placements, and that disruptions would occur when attachment either did not increase or declined. Parents were asked about specific attachment behaviors regarding the first 3 months of the placement (Time 1) and then the 3 months preceding the finalization or disruption (Time 2). Attachment behaviors changed from Time 1 to Time 2, generally increasing (see Table 8.6). The most significant changes from time of placement to time of finalization or disruption were in the ability to be comforted by the parent when hurt, caring about the parent's feelings, showing curiosity in the world around him, and asking about the future. All of these behaviors increased over time. Asking about prior caretakers is the only attachment behavior that decreased over time. However, showing no preference for the parent, a negative attachment item, increased from Time 1 to Time 2.

Change scores between Time 1 (time of placement) ånd Time 2 (time of finalization or end of adoption) were computed by subtracting the Time 1 value from the Time 2 value. The change scores most closely associated with disruption were: curious about the world around him ($r = .33; p < .001$), needs for attention could be met ($r = .27; p < .01$), showing spontaneous affection ($r = .24; p < .01$), and caring about whether the parent approved ($r = .24; p < .01$). A decrease in these behaviors was associated with disruption.

The change scores most closely associated with placement difficulty were: showing spontaneous affection ($r = -.41; p < .001$), asking about the future ($r = -.35; p < .001$), could be comforted ($r = -.25; p < .01$), curious about world around him ($r = -.27; p < .01$), needs for attention could be met ($r = -.24; p < .01$), and has same abilities as peers ($r = -.24; p < .01$). A decrease in any of these was associated with greater difficulty in the placement.

Parents in disrupted placements reported that the placement made the spouses feel much farther apart (22%) or somewhat farther apart (35%) while those in intact placements often said they had become much closer (26%) or somewhat closer (60%; $\chi^2 = 13.60$, $p < .001$). Being driven further apart was associated with disruption, especially among new adoptions ($\chi^2 = 11.71$, $p < .01$). There was no significant difference between disruptions and non-disruptions regarding closeness between parents and other children except among new adoptions ($\chi^2 = 7.15$, $p < .10$). Almost one-half of all families said that the adoption brought them somewhat closer to their other children (48%), while another one-third (37%) said it drove them somewhat farther apart.

Prior Attachments

Our model of adjustment to adoption predicted that children who had developed an attachment to prior caretakers would fare better in adoption than children who had never developed an attachment. Indeed, a strong attachment between the child and his birth siblings at time of placement was related to placement stability (7% disruption rate vs. 42% for those not attached to siblings, $\chi^2 = 3.74$, $p < .05$). An attachment to siblings was mildly associated with having the same abilities as peers at time of placement

Table 8.5. Behavior Item Correlated with Adoption Difficulty, Disruption, or Both

	Difficulty	p	Disruption	p
Destroys others' belongings	.44	.000	.26	.008
Disobeys at home	.39	.000	.29	.003
Disobeys at school	.35	.001	.29	.003
Cruel to others	.34	.001	.35	.001
Argues	.31	.002	.35	.000
Gets in many fights	.30	.002	.35	.001
Hangs around with bad friends	.30	.003	.24	.013
Not liked by others	.28	.005	.23	.015
Sad, depressed	.27	.006	.18	.053
Physically attacks people	.27	.007	.28	.005
Swearing	.27	.007	.26	.008
Lies	.27	.007	.18	.047
Threatens people	.23	.018	.26	.008
Vandalism	.22	.019	.20	.033
Does not get along with others	.21	.026	.20	.036
Feels worthless	.21	.026	.19	.044
Excessive masturbation	.21	.028	.21	.029
Demands attention	.18	.048	.12	.034
Feels has to be perfect	$-.32$	.001	$-.21$	.029
Sex problems			.22	.022
Trouble sleeping			.20	.034
Alcohol or drug use			.19	.040
Thinks about sex too much			.18	.047

continued

($\chi^2 = 5.57$, $p < .10$) and asking about prior caretakers at time of placement ($\chi^2 = 5.16$, $p < .10$), as well as the ability to satisfy his needs for attention at the end or finalization of the placement ($\chi^2 = 4.86$, $p < .10$).

Children had a strong attachment to biological parents in foster parent adoptions (69%), but not in fost-adoptions (29%) or new adoptions (9%; $\chi^2 = 10.16$, $p < .006$). Attachment to biological parents was not associated with adoption stability overall, but was associated with showing preference for the adoptive parents at time of placement ($\chi^2 = 5.99$, $p < .05$), having the same abilities as peers at time of placement ($\chi^2 = 6.54$, $p < .05$), asking about prior caretakers at time of placement ($\chi^2 = 4.75$, $p < .10$), showing spontaneous affection at finalization ($\chi^2 = 5.22$, $p < .10$), and having the same abilities as peers at finalization ($\chi^2 = 7.27$, $p < .10$).

As expected, preplacement attachment to the foster family was significantly different by placement type, with attachment most commonly deep

Table 8.5. *Continued*

	Difficulty	p	Disruption	p
Self-conscious			−.21	.029
Shy			−.20	.031
Fears certain situations, places			−.18	.047
Complains of loneliness			.18	.049
Does not seem to feel guilty	.35	.001		
Steals at home	.35	.001		
Steals outside home	.34	.001		
Impulsive	.33	.001		
Truant	.30	.002		
Teases a lot	.27	.006		
Sleeps too much	.26	.009		
Poor school work	.25	.011		
Suspicious	.23	.016		
Runs away	.23	.016		
Overtired	.22	.023		
Prefers younger children	.21	.025		
Sulks	.21	.026		
Nervous, tense	.21	.026		
Daydreams	.20	.032		
Moody	.20	.033		
Wets the bed	.19	.038		
Brags	.19	.042		
Likes to be alone	.18	.046		

(79%) among foster parent adoptions, moderately deep (33%) or moderately weak (33%) among fost-adoptions, and very weak in all new adoptions (100%; $\chi^2 = 24.81$, $p < .001$). This attachment either did not change among foster parent adoptions (54%) and fost-adoptions (50%) or deepened (42% each), while it either did not change (55%) or weakened (41%) for new adoptions ($\chi^2 = 15.93$, $p < .01$).

Children had a strong attachment to other former caretakers in fost-adoptions (57%), but not in new adoptions (18%) or foster parent adoptions (0%; $\chi^2 = 10.94$, $p < .005$). Attachment to relatives was more common in foster parent adoptions (15%) than in new adoptions (4%) or fost-adoptions (0%; $\chi^2 = 4.52$, $p < .10$).

SUMMARY

Among the interviewed sample, there were many significant differences between disrupted and stable placements. Children who disrupted were

Table 8.6. Mean Scores for Attachment Behaviors Around Time at Beginning of Placement and Time Around Finalization/Disruption ($n = 88$)[a]

Attachment behavior	At placement	at final/end	t[b]
Cared about possessions more than love	1.22	1.25	−0.40
Showed spontaneous affection	1.06	1.35	−2.82**
Could be comforted when hurt	1.27	1.56	−3.44***
Care whether parent approved	1.38	1.42	−0.50
Showed no preference for parent	0.98	1.20	−2.32*
Cared about parent's feelings	0.79	1.14	−4.51***
Clung to parent	0.85	1.11	−2.84**
Curious about world around him	1.10	1.41	−3.50***
Needs for attention could be met	0.97	1.14	−2.19*
Same abilities as peers	1.22	1.42	−2.57**
Asked about prior caretakers	1.22	0.91	3.15**
Asked about future	0.48	0.97	−4.93***
Reacted negatively when left with someone new	1.06	1.16	−1.12
Overall reciprocity	1.05	1.16	−2.39*

[a]Scale: 0 = never true to 2 = often true.
[b]Difference from Time 1 to Time 2 is significant at *.05 level, **.01 level, ***.001 level.

significantly different than nondisrupting children in the following ways. As expected, disrupting children were older when placed for adoption and had more emotional or behavior problems and had more often been adopted before. They exhibited behaviors of cruelty, fighting, threatening, arguing, disobedience, and vandalism and showed high scores on tests of aggression and delinquency. They were less likely to increase attachment behaviors over time, specifically those regarding curiosity, showing affection, caring about parental approval, and satisfaction of need for attention.

Many child characteristics made no difference regarding disruption and are not high-risk indicators. The gender and ethnicity of the child were not strongly related to disruption, nor were the total time spent in foster care and the number of prior foster care placements. Long waits in foster care were, however, associated with more difficult adoptions after controlling for placement risk. That is, this relationship is not only an artifact of the reality that older higher risk children have spent more time in foster care. On the other hand, longer waits for adoptive families were not associated with disruption.

If broadly defined, open adoptions were the rule and they were no more likely to disrupt than were closed adoptions. A majority of adoptive parents felt that they had control over the openness of the adoption. Parents were about evenly split between those who felt the contact was helpful and those who did not. Social workers assessed that the contacts with former caregivers weakened the relationship between the adoptive parent(s) and child in many of the disruptions. Open adoption is discussed in more detail in Chap. 9.

The Achenbach CBC (Achenbach & Edelbrock, 1983) was used as a research tool in this report and can assist in the standardization of information. This checklist consists of 113 child behavior items and the parent indicates whether each behavior occurs never, sometimes, or often. In this study, the checklist significantly differentiated disruption and nondisruption children on several key child behaviors as well as some overall behavioral dimensions. Given its accuracy in identifying behaviors that are difficult in adoptive placements, this instrument would be quite helpful as an assessment tool.

One worthwhile use of the instrument involves foster parents filling out the checklist as a specific inventory of the child's current behavior. This gives potential adoptive parents a realistic and specific rundown of the child's problematic behaviors that the parents could then be prepared for prior to the actual placement. One such mechanism is the printout from the Achenbach clinical report (see Fig. 8.1). By obtaining a parent or foster parent report on the child, it is possible to generate a graphed clinical profile of the child that shows his or her strengths and weaknesses vis-á-vis other children of the same age and gender. The profile of one child in this study suggests areas of greatest strength (health symptoms) and weakness (aggression) and which scores are above the norm of 70. Under and along side the graph are lists of behaviors from the CBC. A "1" indicates the occurrence of a problem and a "2" indicates a serious problem. From this checklist, we learn that the child has some problem with clinging, sulking, crying, over-eating, arguing, and stubbornness (to list a few). She has serious problems with such behaviors as acting young, poor peer relationships, teasing, lying, and impulsivity.

Another use of the Checklist involves the adoptive parents responding to the checklist in terms of the behaviors that they would have difficulty in managing. This would provide the adoption worker with specific behavioral information about which kind of child would be best for the parents, as well

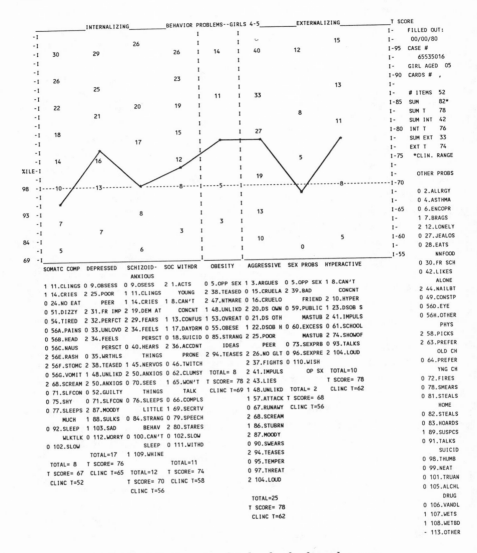

Figure 8.1. Sample of Achenbach clinical report.

as indicating behavioral information about areas in which the parents might need training or support. Last, collecting CBC information on a population of children in special-needs adoption would provide rich research data illustrating the normative behaviors of this group of children, which would guide training material for adoption workers and parents to meet the needs of these young people. Such data could be used for comparisons to a growing body of studies that use the CBC ("NIMH Sponsors Conference," 1987) and could, thereby, provide a strong basis for comparing children who are adopted, remain in foster care, or return home.

As evinced by the behavior checklist data, and in keeping with findings by Reid, Kagan, Kaminsky, and Helmer (1987), the children with the most trouble often lied, stole, set fires, and the like. Whereas a few families concluded that this was a result of adjustment to adoption, most did not believe that this was the cause. In only a few cases were disruptions a clear result of a child's confusion about his current placement, resentment of the adoption, or related to the complexities or differences of an adopted child role. Certainly these issues may have contributed to a diminished commitment to adapt to a new adoptive family, but they seem secondary to the family's and treatment community's inability to respond to often serious behavior problems. More often, the problem behaviors preceded the placement and were not known to the family or the family was not prepared to manage them.

From our experience and results, we would argue that an "adoption specialist" would, in great part, be a professional who helps families to care for and about children with serious academic, behavioral, and interpersonal shortcomings. An adoption specialist who is familiar with all the loyalty issues related to adoption would not have been especially useful to the families we interviewed unless they also knew how to help families with children who steal, run away, lie, set fires, eat peculiarly, and have difficulty executing the basic maneuvers of reciprocal interpersonal interaction related to attachment. We provide some guidance regarding these matters in Chapter 12.

9

Social Worker Characteristics and Services

The need for and limits of services to support older child adoptions are obvious, but not evident. That is, the question on what services help which families is unanswered. What is known was described in Chapter 4 and it is sketchy. This chapter considers the relationship between disruption and services to adoptive families following the placement of the child.

SOCIAL WORKER CHARACTERISTICS

Social worker's gender and race were not related to outcomes. Years of experience in child welfare was moderately associated ($p < .10$) with more stable placements (workers on the stable cases had a mean level of experience of 6.8 vs. 4.3 years for those handling disruptions) but the number of years in adoptions did not differ between the groups. Caseload sizes did not differ significantly and averaged about 30 cases. The number of workers a family experienced was modestly related to the degree of difficulty experienced by families, $r = .28$, $p < .05$, especially for new adoptive families, although no significant relationship between the number of workers and the occurrence of a disruption emerged. More experienced workers (with a mean of 10 years in adoptions) were somewhat more likely ($p < .15$) to handle cases that were predicted to disrupt but did not. The average adoption experience of workers handling cases that were predicted to disrupt and did was 7 years. (A similar effect held for workers with more child welfare experience.) These relationships between experience and disruption were almost nonexistent for foster parents who adopted—foster parents apparently become their own social workers after a while.

AGENCY CONTACT

Among families with stable adoptions, there was a strong positive relationship ($p < .001$) between the riskiness of the placement and the

145

length of continued agency contact with the family. Yet, there was no relationship between the level of contact and the parents' reported level of difficulty. Hence, agencies and families understood that continued contact was warranted, but such contact did not ease the adjustment to adoption.

Social workers reported that more than one-third (39%) of placements required a great deal of effort to maintain, 18% required moderate effort, 16% required slight effort, and only 18% required very little effort. The level of effort needed differed by placement type. New adoptions (64%) and fost-adoptions (79%) were far more likely than foster parent adoptions (33%) to require moderate or great agency effort. According to the prediction model, social workers allocated their time wisely. Overall, the amount of effort exerted by the agency was highly associated with risk. Social workers were significantly more likely to provide greater effort on behalf of placements that were predicted to disrupt than to those that were predicted to be stable. Only 19% of adoptions that we predicted to disrupt required very little effort. This finding can help agencies that compute disruption risk scores to plan for the likely resource allocation of workers according to level of risk.

The average number of contacts (including both telephone and face-to-face) between social workers and families was 21 with a range from 2 to 95. Phone contact was only twice as frequent as face-to-face. The difference between cases with different outcomes was striking as the group with stable outcomes had only an average of 13 contacts but the families that disrupted averaged 31 contacts [$t(50) = 2.80, p < .01$]. Agencies were heavily involved with these families as their adoptions deteriorated. Families who were predicted to disrupt had more ($M = 26$) contacts than families who were predicted to be stable ($M = 18$). There was no real difference in level of contact for families predicted to disrupt that were stable and those that were predicted to disrupt and did. The relationship between the amount of effort invested in strengthening the placement and the risk of the placement was strongly significant for fost-adopt and new adoptions but was weak and nonsignificant for foster parent adoptions. These placements may be the most difficult for adoption workers to assess. Or, perhaps foster parent adoption does not follow the rules of other adoptions.

SUBSIDIES

Dividing the annual incomes of these families by the number of children in the home yields an average amount of annual income available per child in these families: $13,342. The majority of adoptive families in the total sample of 120 received an adoption subsidy (61%), with a mean monthly award of $125, or $1500 a year. The median for families that did receive a subsidy was $229. Subsidy amounts ranged from $1 to $920 a month, and the majority were expected to extend 3 years or less. Only 11% of the grants were expected to extend until the child's majority.

For two-thirds (66%) of families in the interviewed sample, an adoption subsidy was discussed early in the placement preparation. This discussion usually covered subsidy availability (93%), eligibility requirements (73%), medical coverage (55%), and the amount (47%) and duration (43%) of the subsidy. The discussion seldom included coverage for the child's therapy (23%). Discussion of the subsidy award was not related to disruption or type of placement, although discussion of the duration was associated with stability of the placement (19% disruptions vs. 47% stable; $p < .05$), but not type of placement. Discussion of the amount of subsidy was more common among foster parent adoptions (68%) than among new adoptions (28%; $p < .01$), as was discussion of coverage for the child's medical problems (82% vs. 31%; $p < .001$). Parents reported that placements were more difficult when there was no discussion of subsidy availability ($r = -.26, p < .05$), eligibility ($r = -.32, p < .01$) or medical coverage ($r = -.21, p < .05$).

The award of a subsidy was not associated with stability of the placement, perhaps due to the large numbers of placements receiving subsidies. Foster parent adoptions were no more likely than new adoptions to receive subsidies. Among those who did not receive a subsidy ($n = 25$), 44% would have liked one. Eight respondents related the reasons they did not receive a subsidy: four did not qualify and four said they did not know about subsidies. For those adoptions that were not subsidized, social workers provided varied reasons, but one-half were judged ineligible due to income, even though this is not a condition of receiving subsidies under the law. Some (17%) were ineligible because the child was assessed to have no special needs (16%). Other families refused a subsidy prior to eligibility (17%) or after being deemed eligible (16%). Most social workers (83%) said that the question of a subsidy had no effect on the agency's relationship with the family, whereas others said it either moderately (9%) or greatly (6%) strengthened the relationship. Only 2% said it moderately weakened it and these were all foster parent adoptions.

Amont those who did receive a subsidy, most were offered it (85%), although some had to ask for (12%) or demand it (3%). Most of those who received a subsidy definitely (48%) or probably (41%) could have adopted without it. There is a strong ($p < .001$) negative relationship between the subsidy amount and the total family income. Yet, several families indicated that the amount was not at all (6%) or mostly not (11%) sufficient for the child's needs. Again, this perception was not associated with disruption or type of placement, but was related to the difficulty of the placement—with less sufficient subsidies reported by parents experiencing placements as more difficult ($r = .35$, $p < .002$). Among those not receiving a sufficient subsidy, the amount that would have been sufficient ranged from $100 to $1500, with a mean of $509 ($SD = 372). There was no difference in reports of sufficient amounts between disruptions and nondisruptions.

Adoption workers said that families were told about subsidies when they were first recruited (53%) or when presented with a specific child (38%). Only 1% said that families were not told about a subsidy. Disruptions were especially likely among placements where families knew about subsidies before contact with the agency (75% disruption rate) or found out when they were first recruited (53%). These differences do not hold for placements predicted to disrupt, indicating that these relationships may be an artifact of families who adopt the highest risk children being most likely to get subsidy information early on. Disruptions were much less likely if families were told about them at the time they were presented with the child (31%; $\chi^2 = 9.85$, $p < .05$).

Higher risk placements do not have higher subsidies. The risk of the placement and subsidy levels have a nonsignificant but somewhat negative relationship. This relationship is consistent across all three types of placements and suggests a less than efficient and equitable use of subsidies to support continuing placements. Among low-risk placements there was no difference in use of subsidies for those that did and did not disrupt.

When placements that were predicted to disrupt and did so ($n = 34$) were compared to those that were predicted to disrupt but did not ($n = 18$), several interesting differences emerge. Only 58% of predicted disruptions did disrupt when they had a subsidy, whereas 76% disrupted when there was none. The difference is not statistically significant, but is provocative. Of all placements that were predicted to disrupt, those which did not receive subsidies were reported as less difficult than those with a subsidy.

COPING WITH DIFFERENCES

Among the 11 families who reported specific concerns about the children being older than they had wanted, 46% were predicted to be stable and were stable and 27% were predicted to disrupt and did. Another 18% were predicted to be stable and disrupted, whereas only 9% were predicted to disrupt but did not. These percentages suggest that the preference related to age is not, in and of itself, sufficient to change the predicted outcomes. The proportion in each category of SURPRISE was no different than it was for placements in which the parents expressed no concern about age. Strong relationships existed between concern about the child being too old and disruption among new adoptive families and among foster parents who adopted children in their care. Among the seven adoptive families with this concern, there were five disruptions. Of three foster parents who reported this concern, two disruptions occurred. Among the three fost-adopt families with this concern, there were no disruptions.

Almost one-third of parents indicated concern about differences between the desired and actual child's emotional level. Parental worries about differences in the level of emotional disturbance they hoped for and the actual level of emotional disturbance in the child they adopted were significantly ($p < .05$) related to outcomes. Many of the parents who reported concern about this difference (44% of the concerned parents) had placements that were predicted to disrupt and did. When these worries existed, families performed about as expected. Among the 14 families with a predicted disruption that had concerns about emotional problems, 12 (86%) disrupted. This contrasts with a 13% disruption rate for parents who did not worry about this difference. Far more of the parents that reported not worrying about this difference had placements that were predicted to be stable and were.

There were no significant relationships between surprise outcomes and worries about gender of the child, worries about taking a sibling group or worrying about the child's race. Only two families worried about race and their placements both ended as predicted—one in disruption and one stable.

POSTPLACEMENT SERVICES

Participation in self-help or peer support groups was uncommon, but appeared to provide some buffering of risk. Reports by social workers or families indicate that 21 (18%) of the total sample of 120 families participated in support groups during the placement process. Several ($n = 6$) of the predicted and stable placements used groups whereas none of the predicted stable families that did disrupt used groups ($p < .10$). Groups may be as helpful for low- and medium-risk placements as for the higher risk placements.

Help-seeking patterns differed dramatically for stable and disrupted placements ($\chi^2 = 28.8$, $df = 4$, $p < .001$). Almost one-half of disrupted placements did not report seeking help from any source and 43% reported seeking professional services. The stable placements, on the other hand, rarely reported seeking no help (9%) and more often used professional assistance (60%). Only one-third of families that disrupted reported immediately contacting their social workers about their concerns. More than one-half never discussed their concerns and almost 10% began to discuss them more than 2 months after their initial concern. Families that disrupted waited longer than stable placements to talk to their workers about their concerns. Only 1 of the 63 families that were stable waited as long as 1–2 months to contact the agency about their difficulty. Among disrupting families, 5 of 50 waited that long. These findings suggest less contact with social workers than in Hornby's (1986) study in which the family requested help prior to the disruption (but most often less than 2 months before the disruption) in about two-thirds of the disruptions, and in only one-fifth the agency was not contacted until the disruption was occurring.

Social workers report that they referred or helped to arrange needed services for 25 of the 98 families. Among those families, only 22 disrupted. Referrals for treatment were apparently to resources that were not helpful or the referrals were too late, or both.

In our study, the mean time to disruption was 18 months. This is considerably longer than Cohen (1984) who reported a mean time of 4 months to the disruption. This lengthy time to disruption indicates that immediate pre- and postplacement services are not well timed. More lasting, postadoptive services are indicated.

Families primarily reported the use of five strategies to keep the adoption from ending. They often obtained therapy for themselves or family; placed their child in a special school or changed the special school; relied on temporary out-of-home care; changed their expectations; and set or changed limits with child. Agencies primarily responded to finalized adoptions that were at-risk of failing by referring children to therapy, encouraging placement in a special school, and refusing the relinquishment.

OPEN ADOPTIONS

As reviewed in earlier chapters, controversy governs whether contact with prior caretakers is beneficial for the adopted child and the adoption (Kraft et al., 1985; Borgman, 1982). Adoptive parents and workers were asked about the plans for contact between the child and birth parents, siblings and relatives, and former foster parents and siblings. Other questions about openness concerned actual people with whom the child was in contact, the frequency of these contacts, and the helpfulness of these contacts as perceived by both adoptive parents and adoption workers.

According to the adoptive parents, the majority of adoptions in this sample (n = 91) were open (79%), with 42% of all children having contacts with their foster parents, 27% with their birth parents, 27% with other relatives, and 32% with birth siblings. Many fewer had contacts with foster siblings (9%) or other people (3%). For all contacts, the majority occurred less than monthly: 79% of contact with birth siblings, 75% of foster sibling contacts, 66% of contacts with foster parents, 68% for relatives, 68% for birth parents.

The disruption rate was not significantly different between open and closed adoptions. Open adoptions disrupted at a rate of 30%, while closed adoptions disrupted at a rate of 47%. There was no difference between fost-adopt, foster parent, and new adoptions concerning whether they were open. Openness was also not related to the age of the child.

Of the open adoptions, the majority of adoptive parents (62%) felt they had complete control over the contacts. Only 21% felt they had very little control. Two-fifths (40%) of the parents in open adoptions said the contact was not helpful at all and another 17% said they were only slightly helpful. Control over contacts was related to perceiving the contacts as helpful ($\chi^2 = 15.22$, $p < .10$). Less than one-third of the open adoptive parents (31%) thought the contact was very helpful. Parental control over contacts or perceptions of helpfulness of contacts were also not related to stability of the placement. According to a substantial percentage (61%) of the 80 families who reported a substantial amount of contact with prior foster or birth families, the effects on the placement were generally negative. Few (28%) indicate that such contact contributed to improvements in the placement.

Contacts with relatives were seen as not helpful (67%) or slightly helpful (33%), but never moderately or very helpful. Contacts with birth parents were either seen as very helpful (46%) or not helpful at all (54%). Contacts with siblings were most often seen as very helpful (60%), although sometimes as not helpful at all (27%). Most contacts with former caretakers (75%) and other relatives (67%) were seen as not helpful at all.

Among open adoptions, there was no difference between disruptions and nondisruptions in terms of frequency of birth parents' visits. Few visits in any placement took place more than monthly. Social workers for disrupting families were slightly more likely to say that the visits with birth parents weakened the child's relationship with adoptive parents.

Some adoptive families complained that social workers did not supervise the birth parent visits. Fost-adopt families complained bitterly about the requirement to have birth parents visit in their home (which was not true of many counties, but was true of a few). They were concerned about their future safety and that of their adoptive child if the adoptive placement was completed. Several suggested the establishment of familylike visitation centers.

Workers planned contact for 54% of the open adoptions. Plans for contact made by the worker were very common among new adoptions (72%), but not as common for fost-adoptions (43%) and foster parent adoptions (42%).

Planned contact usually did not concern birth parents (0% of new adoptions, 50% of fost-adoptions, and 55% of foster parent adoptions; $\chi^2 = 14.61$, $p < .001$), but usually concerned siblings. Among those placements for which contact was arranged planned contact with birth parents (but not siblings, relatives, and previous caretakers) was associated with stability ($\chi^2 = 2.78$, $p < .01$). Workers usually arranged for contact with former caretakers for new adoptions (62%), but not for fost-adoptions (33%) or foster parent adoptions (18%; $\chi^2 = 5.96$, $p < .05$). Planned or not, when contacts occurred, workers reported that this contact weakened the relationship between the adoptive parents and child and contributed to disruption.

A composite score of openness was computed from family reports of the occurrence and frequency of contact with birth parents and siblings as well as foster parents and siblings and relatives. This openness variable ranged from 0 to 18, although no child scored higher than 10, and the mean score of openness was 2.08 ($SD = 1.99$). According to family reports, the degree of openness of the placement was negatively related with the amount of control the adoptive parents had over those contacts ($r = -.32$, $p = < .01$), but was not correlated with the helpfulness of the contact. That is, as the amount of contact increased, the feelings of control over that contact decreased but the helpfulness of those contacts did not. Less difficult placements were judged by the social worker to be improved because of openness and more difficult placements were judged to be more damaged by openness. Openness seems to be a desirable addition for an adoption that is progressing smoothly, but is a threat to risky placements.

POSTLEGALIZATION CONTACT

Respondents indicated that it was important for the agency to keep in touch after legalization. Whereas 36% indicated that it was not important or only slightly important, 65% indicated that it was moderately or very important with the latter category receiving the highest percentage (45%). The most common reason given by the 80 families agreeing that agencies should keep in touch with families after legalization was to address continuing problems and need for help (60%). The desire to continue to share information about the child and his or her birth or foster families was reported by 24% of families that agreed that agencies should maintain contact. Several ($n = 6$), but not a majority of, disruption families also indicated the importance of debriefing about the disruption.

SUMMARY

Social worker characteristics were generally not related to the outcome of the placement. Experience did seem to make a difference—especially for the highest risk cases. A higher number of workers on a case did, however, have an important negative influence on the placements. Whether they had high-risk placements that endured or disrupted, families reported that having more workers made the placements more difficult. The change in workers between pre- and postplacement services may undo careful planning and relationship building. The typical family had different social workers at the time of placement and the time of finalization or disruption. One adoptive parent reported a good preplacement experience but her worker left and she did not develop the rapport with the new worker. The parent failed to ask for the kind of consultation that she needed from the agency during a crisis. She never informed the new social worker of the crisis until after she had decided to return her adopted child to the agency. (Given our varied sampling strategies we could not assess agency characteristics associated with disruption.)

Postplacement services begin with good preplacement services. If the home study helps the family to feel less defensive they will consult more readily with the agency during the probationary period. Group home studies may have the greatest chance of generating helpful relationships that last beyond the change in workers. A significant percentage of families with high-risk placements indicated that they relied on other adoptive families for assistance—these were often families they met during group home studies. Indeed, families that used groups had somewhat more risky placements. Families that reported their concern that the adoption might end, also relied somewhat more heavily on members of an adoptive group or organization than did other families. Although the efficacy of this reliance for reducing disruption is not proved, it is suggested by the way that group participation mitigates the relationship between placement risk and perceived difficulty.

The adoption worker's role has become, in great part, that of an information resource. Adoptive families must be treated as consumers who need information in order to decide on a child to whom they might commit their resources. In order to be information brokers, adoption workers must learn about the child. The current organization of adoption services does not make this knowledge easy to obtain. Adoption workers for families are not usually workers for the children. With foster care adoptions becoming increasingly typical, most knowledge of adoptable children will lie with foster care workers. Efforts to standardize the exchange of information about children must be developed.

Postplacement services were few and generally inadequate to the task of preventing disruption. Families that disrupted sought the agency's help later than families that were stable. Social workers made significant efforts to save endangered placements, but had few or no adequate resources to call on. When agency social workers made referrals to postplacement therapy, families report that it was usually too little and too late—agreeing with those in Hornby's study (1986).

Standard postplacement services deserve reexamination. The purpose of postplacement services should be to offer help as needed and desired by the family and child, in both development of the parent–child relationship and in the resolution of problems inherent in adoption. Yet, the discrepancy between needed and desired help can be widely interpreted. Several families—especially those with busy work schedules and an "executive" upper middle class attitude about efficiency and the expenditure of time—complained that worker visits were not wanted and alienated them from the agency. In one case this alienation was so severe that the adoptive mother failed to discuss any of the more significant concerns she was having that finally led to the adoption disruption; instead, she merely chatted with the adoption worker while she prepared meals and did house cleaning. As such, the "as needed" role of the adoption worker is not always taken literally. A standard number of required postplacement visits works against this creed. The surveillance and placement strengthening functions of those visits are not evinced by our findings since adoption workers did not report any abuse from first-hand reports and since most disruptions were well after the visits ceased.

Overall, clients showed great variation in the way that they rated the importance of postlegalization services. Families with legalized adoptions maintained contact with the agency for an average of 22 months after the legalization and families with disruptions received 12 additional months of contact. Among clients who did receive such services—which lasted for an average of 18 months—after the finalization or the disruption, there was modest support for the importance of these services. Among stable families, one-third reported that it was very important to keep in touch whereas two-thirds of families that disrupted reported that it was very important. The relationship between the amount of postplacement services and adoptive family member's evaluation of the worth of those services was modest. Length of contact did ameliorate the relationship between difficulty and risk for stable adoptions. If the length of contact is statistically removed from the relationship, the relationship between risk and difficulty is a bit stronger. Families that were predicted to disrupt but that remained stable did not, however, differ from the other groups on the level of postplacement services.

10

Discriminating Disruptions from
Intact Placements

This and previous studies of disruption identify a variety of characteristics associated with adoption stability or disruption. These characteristics can be categorized as occurring in the three areas we previously specified as key to the adjustment to adoption: the child, the parents and household, and family interaction. Agency services and support that respond to these characteristics are a fourth part of this model. This chapter begins by reviewing the important variables in each of these areas to determine their relative importance within each area in contributing to adoption disruption or stability. The second part of this chapter considers the way these factors combine to influence adoption outcomes.

Toward this end, the data were analyzed in a series of discriminant analyses, which test the ability of several independent variables to discriminate between group membership for some dichotomous dependent variable. In our final analysis, we simultaneously tested the ability of child, family, family interaction, and service characteristics to discriminate between disrupted and stable placements. The results of the analyses informed us as to whether discrimination was possible, the degree of discrimination achieved, and which characteristics were the most powerful discriminators.

We discussed two of our previous analyses in Chapters 4 and 5. To reiterate, the first discriminant analysis was conducted using data from the intake records of 898 older child adoptive placements in California from 1980 to 1984. Four submodels were analyzed, concerning variables about the child, the placement, the "match" between parent and child, and services. The five key variables associated with disruption that resulted from an overall analysis were the following: a previous adoptive placement of the child, older age of the child, nonfoster parent adopters, special problems of the child, and higher education of the adoptive mother. This model correctly predicted 82% of the stable adoptions and 70% of the disrupted placements. The amount of variance explained above chance involved variables concerning subsidies, matching, or other demographic data, and did not contribute any more to the predictive success of the model.

Although it is convenient to predict with 82% certainty which placements will disrupt based on five key intake variables, we obviously do not recommend limiting preplacement assessment to these five variables. As we emphasized in our model of adjustment to adoption, there are many elements to consider in any placement, especially regarding the ongoing interaction between parent and child, and the support from the agency. Accordingly, we expanded our model from intake data to include the richer data from our interviews with adoptive families. This reduced our sample size from 898 to around 100. Since only 69 of the cases had data from both family and social worker interviews, all the characteristics were drawn from the family interviews, allowing the sample size to remain at 91 (or less, depending on cases with missing values on key variables).

Starting with the five key characteristics identified at intake, these discriminant analyses added further information from ongoing characteristics, in order to increase the discriminatory ability of the model. Again, we separated out the four submodels: child, parent and household, family interaction, and service characteristics. After the four submodels identified the key characteristics of each area, these variables were tested in a full model. The results will be discussed in that order.

CHILD CHARACTERISTICS

The key characteristics of children related to disruption were identified in Chapter 8 as having a bivariate relationship to disruption. These are listed in Table 10.1. The child characteristics associated with disruption are mostly demographic, but do include a behavioral index and an attitudinal rating of the child's desire to be adopted. Of these characteristics, three were found to be important discriminators between stable and disrupted adoptions (see Table 10.2). The characteristics concerning the child's desire to be adopted and the attachment to birth siblings were excluded because they were most difficult to reliably assess and because the low number of worker interviews made them unstable.

In order of importance, the discriminating variables were the child's externality score, the child's age, and whether the child was of minority race. The degree of external behavior problems was a better discriminator than was the child's older age, indicating that, when the two characteristics are analyzed together, it is the behavior and not the age that predicts disruption.

This submodel of three child characteristics, based on 82 cases, correctly predicted 61% of the stable placements and 80% of the disruptions. The

Table 10.1. Significant Variables from Bivariate Analyses

Child characteristics
  Older age
  Prior adoptive placement(s)
  External behavior score
  Minority ethnicity
  Not attached to birth siblings
  Not in favor of adoption

Parent and household characteristics
  Nonfoster parent adoption
  Higher education of adoptive mother
  Lower frequency of church attendance
  Higher number of other adopted children in the home
  Lower number of relatives within visiting distance
  Lower frequency of visits with relatives
  Family in opposition of adoption
  Do not know other adoptive or foster parents

Family interaction characteristics
  Less comfort with decision to adopt
  High expectations on part of parent
  Child's low reciprocity behavior score
  Negative impact of adoption on family

Service characteristics
  Longer parent wait for placement
  More information deficits about child
  Difference between family and worker reports of information provided
  More parent "stretching"
  Information about child was too positive

overall accuracy was 67%. Of all the submodels, this was the least accurate in predicting stable placements, indicating that the child alone is a weak indicator of stability. This model, however, is the most accurate predictor of disruption. This model overpredicted the disruptions, however, which, if used alone, would lead to the assumption that placements would disrupt when they would not.

PARENT AND HOUSEHOLD CHARACTERISTICS

Characteristics related to the parents and the household mostly concerned the placement type (foster parent vs. new adoptions); family

Table 10.2. Contribution of Child, Parent, Family Interaction, and Services to Disruption

	Standardized canonical discriminant function	Wilks Lamda	Correct classification of cases	Squared canonical correlation
Child characteristics ($n=82$)				
Externality	.76801	.87	67%	.13
Older age	.41849			
Minority ethnicity	.35694			
Parent and household characteristics ($n=81$)				
Nonfoster parent adoption	.57246	.72	77%	.28
Higher number of adopted children	.64800			
Fewer relatives in area	.38781			
Know fewer fosters/ adopters	.27316			
Lower frequency of church attendance	.23844			
Higher education	.25306			
Family interaction characteristics ($n=90$)				
Negative impact on family	.63436	.89	67%	.11
Less comfort with decision	.35701			
Child's lower reciprocity	.55340			
Service characteristics ($n=62$)				
Information was too positive	.54199	.91	68%	.09
More stretching	.44420			
Shorter parent wait	.42614			
More information deficits	.27425			

continued

constellation (specifically concerning the presence of other adopted children in the home); and informal social support. Eight such variables (see Table 10.1) were identified as having a bivariate association with disruption. Due to a low response rate, the variable concerning the frequency of relative's

Table 10.2. *Continued*

	Standardized canonical discriminant function	Wilks Lamda	Correct classification of cases	Squared canonical correlation
Complete model (*n* = 57)				
Fewer relatives in area	.51310	.68	77%	.32
Higher number of adopted children	.50196			
Nonfoster parent adoption	.45471			
Lower frequency of church attendance	.37695			
Child's external behavior score	.37526			
Child's older age	.30932			
Child's lower reciprocity	.25223			
Child's minority ethnicity	.22213			
Information was too positive	.18757			
Know fewer fosters/ adopters	.14087			
More information deficits	.09232			
Negative impact on family	.08624			
Less comfort with decision	.07740			
More stretching	.04863			
Higher education	.03708			
Longer parent wait	.00374			

visits was omitted, leaving seven variables. These were analyzed via discriminant analysis, and most were found to have an important contribution to discrimination (see Table 10.2).

The single most important variable in the group of family characteristics indicates that families with other adopted children in the home are at high risk (see Table 10.2). This was closely followed by nonfoster parent adoptions, demonstrating the value of adoptions by foster parents. Moving down in order of importance, disruptions were discriminated from stable adoptions by the fewer relatives in visiting distance, the fewer adoptive and/or foster parents known by the adopting parents, the higher education of the adoptive mother, and the lower frequency of church attendance. Opposition to the adoption by family members was not a good discriminator between stable and disrupted placements. This analysis indicates that, of family characteristics, the most important items to consider are the in-home dynamics that may contribute to tension around the adoption, and the informal social support available to the family.

This submodel, based on 81 cases, correctly predicted 77% of the stable placements and 75% of the disruptions, qualifying as the submodel with the highest overall accuracy of prediction (77%). This model predicted that more placements would be stable than actually were.

FAMILY INTERACTION CHARACTERISTICS

The variables pertinent to family interaction were few. They concerned how comfortable the family was with the decision to adopt, the impact of the adoption on the family (a summary score of several questions concerning the impact of the placement and adoption on the closeness between the respondent and his or her spouse and children), and the reciprocity shown by the child toward the parents after a substantial adjustment period in the placement.

The family interaction analysis is presented in Table 10.2. It shows us that the best discriminator of disruption and stability was the impact on the family, with a less positive impact indicating disruption. Following this, the child's less reciprocal behavior was also associated with disruption. The family's comfort with the decision to adopt was a less significant, although important, discriminator.

This submodel, based on 90 cases and containing three key discriminators, correctly predicted the outcome for 68% of the stable adoptions, 65% of the disruptions, and 67% of all placements. It overpredicted the stable placements. Therefore, predictions based on this submodel alone were least accurate.

SERVICE CHARACTERISTICS

There were four service characteristics associated with disruption (see Table 10.1), most of which were summary scores of a group of related questions to the families. For instance, the "no information" score was a computed variable, based on the difference between family and the worker reports on a range of specific items concerning information about the child (discussed in Chapter 6). Of these service characteristics, all were important discriminators between disrupted and stable placements (see Table 10.2). The most important discriminator was whether the information provided about the child was too positive or not, indicating the importance of realistic information about the child. The next most important discriminator was the stretch required by the parents to adjust to differences between what they expected in the child they adopted and the reality, indicating that the more parents had to stretch, the higher the probability of disruption. The more information deficits the parents reported, the higher the probability of disruption, and the shorter the parent's wait between application and placement, the higher the probability of disruption. Parents and workers used the waiting period to prepare.

This model, based on 62 cases, correctly predicted 70% of the stable placements, 60% of the disruptions, 68% of all placements, and overpredicted the stable placements.

COMPLETE MODEL OF ALL CHARACTERISTICS

The characteristics of the child or parent or agency do not occur in isolation, but interact to produce an outcome. Based on the key discriminators identified in the preceding submodels, a full model was analyzed to ascertain the relative importance of all these characteristics in a placement.

The top four discriminating variables concerned the household and family characteristics of the adoptive placement: the number of relatives within visiting distance, the number of other adopted children in the home, if the foster parents adopted the child, and the frequency of church attendance by the family. Following these household characteristics, the child's external behavior score and older age were also important discriminators between stable and disrupted placements. The interaction and service variables, while providing some discriminating ability, were not the most important discriminators between success and disruption. Of the interaction variables, the child's reciprocity was the best discriminator in this overall model, while, of the service characteristics, the accuracy of the information was the most important variable.

This ordering of predictors when all are analyzed simultaneously indicates that, as has been found in studies of foster care stability, household characteristics and not child characteristics are the key associates of success.

This model, based on 57 cases, correctly predicted 75% of the intact placements, 85% of the disruptions, and 77% of cases overall. The kappa is .48, indicating a 48% gain in prediction accuracy that means that 48% fewer errors of classification would be made using this model than would be made by chance. This is 50% superior to that of the intake model described in Chapter 5, demonstrating the utility of including factors concerning the family environment and interaction.

DISCUSSION

This discriminant analysis confirms that the resources of the parents and the impact of the adoption on the larger family system contribute to the stability of the adoption. The family submodel was the most powerful of the submodels, with a correct classification of 77% of the cases. Our model of adjustment to adoption identified these factors as contributing to placement stability, and indeed, foster parent adoptions were the best predictor of success, followed by several social support indicators including having relatives in the area, friends who are foster or adoptive parents, and church affiliation.

In the complete model, the top four discriminating characteristics related to the household: foster parent adoptions, other adopted children in the household, and the two social support indicators of relative and church support. Following these, the characteristics of the child were important, including age, behavior, and reciprocity. This model shows us that the characteristics of the child are important to assess, but only in relation to parent and household characteristics.

The characteristics concerning services were not as powerful in predicting disruption. This lends support to our conclusion that agencies can generally be less intrusive and more peripheral in their support of adoptions, but when they intervene they should provide some intensive services. Indeed, since social support is a much better predictor of stability, agencies would do well to build in home study and postplacement service elements that increase their strengthening of the family's natural support network, an implication suggested in our theoretical model and described further in later chapters.

RESEARCH LIMITS

Since this concludes the reporting of study results, acknowledgment of research shortcomings is warranted. The results of this study must be interpreted with recognition of research limitations. The interview portion of the study was not prospective nor did it entirely involve randomly selected families who had not disrupted. In the early parts of the study, we did randomly select families in stable placements for participation in the study. Our ability to achieve this random sample was compromised by our low return rate. We clearly obtained families in both the disruption and stable subsamples who were particularly interested in the study. With a low interview rate, questions about the representativeness of the sample naturally arise. Fortunately, our analysis of differences between the larger prediction sample and our interview sample suggest that the biases do not appear significant.

In the latter parts of the interview substudy we sought to find more higher risk families that were stable in order to better determine which characteristics of families that we predicted to disrupt were associated with their unexpected stability. Although these sampling strategies would both yield many of the same families, their emphasis was different. This may have resulted in less focus on the characteristics of stable and disrupted families that were most striking (e.g., age of the child and prior disruptions). The nonrandomness of both samples is frustrating but consistent with most adoption research. We believe that our sample size and randomness of the first part of the stable sample contribute a measure of confidence that we can generalize our findings to other older child adoptions. Most of our sample came from public adoption agencies and all were in California.

This study suggests additional areas of investigation. Open adoption and its limitations are still largely not understood. The overstated claims that open adoption is the procedure of choice for infant adoptions is based on virtually no evidence that such a procedure provides lasting benefits to most children. The most significant benefit may be that it encourages the placement of children for adoption. The evidence for the benefits to children of open older child adoptions is no more clear or impressive. We do not now know what kind of open adoption is good for which children at what ages and with what kind of birth and adoptive families. Our study raises some concerns about open adoption but is insufficient to answer them.

At a more basic level, we need to know more about which children who are not being adopted because they are judged to be "unadoptable" fit the profile of children at high risk of disruption. Some of the children who are considered unadoptable may be low risks for disruption. If so, they should be given more consideration for placement.

The Future of Adoption Research

Prospective studies of older child adoptions remain to be done. Most studies like ours are retrospective (cf. Boyne et al., 1984; Boneh, 1979). The findings of retrospective studies are, by necessity, clouded in that memories of disrupted adoptions may be distorted by the experience of the disruption itself. A longitudinal study of adoptions would allow examination of the child and family prior to placement, in the beginning stages of integration, and, if disrupting, during the disruption. A comparative longitudinal study of the transitional tasks of adoption and foster care would assess when adoption of adolescents is a feasible and desirable alternative to foster care. Such a study would also identify the process of adoption, and disruption, as it occurs, not in retrospect. Follow-up studies on adults who were adopted as older children will clarify the extent to which adoption is corrective for young lives headed in troubling directions.

III

Implications of the Study

11

The Path to Disruption

The previously described statistical model addresses static characteristics of children, parents, and services associated with disruption. No one ever involved with an adoption disruption would call it static. Disruptions occur in time—sometimes a very short time and sometimes over years. A model of disruption is not complete without a discussion of the process by which decisions and practices beginning with recruitment finally result in disruption. Partridge, Hornby, and McDonald (1986) inspired this endeavor with their inaugural efforts to describe the stages of disruption. These stages focused on the experience within the family from a time of diminishing pleasures with the adoption through to the decision to disrupt. While saluting their work, our results convince us that disruptions begin well before the period of diminishing pleasures, last until after the removal of the child, and involve the agency as much as the family.

The remainder of this chapter identifies twelve issues or steps in the process of adopting an older child. The resolution of each of these issues explains the final outcome of a stable or disrupted placement. For each step, some differences between disrupted and nondisrupted placements will be discussed. The steps are delineated in Table 11.1 The process for a given family and child may stop at any of the above steps, may skip any step, and may reverse the order of steps. Disguised case histories from our study illustrate stages to adoption disruption or stability. Most were "surprise" cases that strikingly under- or outperformed the model. We attribute part of that performance to their success or failure at resolving these stages.

MISMATCHING OF ADOPTIVE
FAMILY AND CHILD

Matching has no menus. Neither this study nor any other has clearly identified compelling indicators of good matches on the basis of parent or child personality. Overall, we believe that the way agencies contribute to

Table 11.1. Issues Explaining Adoption Outcomes

1. Mismatching of adoptive family and child
2. Inadequate preparation of adoptive parent
3. Poor preparation of the child
4. Fragmented postplacement visits
5. Expectations of change in the child's behavior
6. Child and parent fail to develop reciprocally positive personal exchanges
7. Uncovering of previously unknown characteristic of child
8. Ineffective problem solving with persons outside the family
9. Delayed or no contact with agency
10. Failure to find an appropriate interventive service
11. The choice of disruption to cope with the adoption crisis
12. The aftermath of disruption

the matching process has been overestimated as a contributor to disruption or stability. Some specific contraindicators were, however, evident. The usual types of matching (concerning race, religion, or intellect) did not contribute to stability in our sample. The adoptive parents' education level did have some bearing on disruption, as more highly educated parents tended to have less stable adoptions. This tendency however, did not seem related to the intellect of the child, which would have confirmed the value of conventional matching, but seems related to expectations, which confirms our view that matching involves identifying compatabilities between parents' strengths and resources and children's vulnerabilities and needs. This type of matching and mismatching influenced adoption outcomes. For example, families with high expectations for a loving child and sibling who adopted children with low reciprocity were especially prone to disruption, a "mismatch" predicted by our model. Disruptions occurred when one family was selected because of their background as educators but without full recognition that their major intent was to find a playmate for their single child—a risky premise for an adoption. The child was returned to the agency within 4 months and with 1 week's notice.

More often, careful selection of families seemed to forestall disruptions. We found, as have others, that families without birth children have a better record with more demanding placements. We found dramatic examples of well-matched placements. Amos Watson is one child placed into such a setting. Despite the model's prediction that this placement would disrupt, an astute choice of a home apparently saved it. Amos was 11 years old, aphasic, encopretic, and effectively mute. He was placed into a new adoption with a single mother after 4 years in foster care. The mother was a special education teacher and speech therapist with a mild neurological condition, and no previous full-time parenting experience (she had provided respite foster care). The mother knew a great amount about Amos prior to the placement and had much contact with the child's former foster mother. Because of the beautiful match between the mother's abilities and the child's needs, the placement did not take a great agency effort to maintain.

INADEQUATE PREPARATION OF
ADOPTIVE PARENT

"Stretching" and other failures to provide families with accurate information about children's characteristics were powerful contributors to disruption. As we discussed in Chapter 3, information is a potent resource. Families who have been adequately informed are not as surprised and stressed by the child's behavior. Families who are not well-informed face the burden of unraveling the mysteries of their child's behavior, which compounds the stress of adoption. Of course, information about a child's difficulty is not sufficient. Parents need preparation about ways to manage challenging child behaviors, how long the family integration process might take, and the likelihood that there may be unpleasant surprises and how to manage them. Several of the surprise disruptions resulted from inadequate preparation. Jay Johnston was a 7-year-old in a fost-adopt placement of siblings—the siblings had already had a disruption together when their previous adoptive parents separated and returned the children to the agency. The family had two other older children and originally wanted to add only a girl but took the brother along as part of a "package" deal. The placement was an emergency; the agency started preplacement preparation but the foster parents wanted the children removed immediately. All parties were poorly prepared for the transition. Jay did not even know that he had been adopted by the prior family. In turn, the family did not know that Jay wet his bed and had a learning disability. The worker and mother agreed to end the adoption when the worker realized that the mother had a drinking problem and that she continued to belittle Jay. The children were successfully adopted by a third family.

The more successful placements involved group preparation that promoted support networks among families on whom they could rely and to get a clearer sense of what was ahead. These families were able to obtain needed information and consultation even if their relationship with the social worker who made the placement was strained or had ceased. One couple adopted a troubled 6- and 8-year-old sibling pair into a home with two other children— a difficult arrangement at best. The couple divorced within 9 months of the placement and the children stayed with the mother. (She was emphatic that the adoption was not a contributor to the divorce.) She was a participant in a pilot project to support high-risk older child and minority adoptions. This project offered group preparation and continued support services with such features as child care during support meetings and outings. She indicated that the group preparation was particularly valuable in helping her develop a structure for managing the behavior of her children from the outset. From one other adoptive parent, she learned several concrete strategies for containing a child's shoplifting and stealing in the home, which she instituted in the first weeks of placement as she witnessed her kids engaging in these behaviors. For example, the group gave her permission to put a deadbolt on her bedroom door after her daughter stole some family jewels. The placement was very stable 4 years later. Certainly the continued support was also a contributor to the better than predicted outcome of this adoption, and that support, in great part, derived from the group preparation.

The emphasis on group preparation does not minimize the role of the social worker in preparing the adoptive parent. The adoption of Billy Sanders reflects the extensive information provided by some social workers to preempt disruption. Billy was placed in a new adoptive family at age 14 after nine foster placements. Between the referral to the adoption unit and the placement, Billy was moved to his ninth foster home because of complaints about his behavior. The adoptive family received a subsidy and the full case information. The social worker was an MSW with 26 years of experience. Billy was described as a psychotic youth who was destructive, self-abusive, and hyperactive. His external behavior score was in the clinical range ($T = 72$) and he had been in a residential treatment facility for 4 years. The single adoptive father (who described himself as difficult to upset) was able to tolerate the child's reportedly bizarre behavior. The concerns of the worker included the existence of pets in the home (since Billy had previously killed animals), limited informal resources, and the father's suspected homosexuality. Billy was also separated from two siblings because he was ready for adoption sooner and their relationship was not strong. The adopting father was provided with extensive information, met Billy, attended preadoption counseling, and met with the child's former caretakers. The placement required a great amount of services from the agency and the previous treatment center. The adoption was legalized 2 1/2 years after the placement.

POOR PREPARATION OF THE CHILD

Children should be routinely provided with preparation for adoption. Few are. When birth parents fight parental rights termination or the agency has not prepared the children and parents by fully testing the possibility of reunification, this ambivalence is heightened. Such is the case of Joanna Shimley. Joanna, the Barrell's adopted daughter, had slept with a boy while in the adoptive home and had experimented with drugs. She ran away after 11 months of adoptive placement to return and live with her birth mother. Mr. and Mrs. Barrell felt that Joanna should have been reunified with the birth mother earlier and never placed for adoption. Their grievance, then, was that the agency was only trying to answer the question "in which new family should this child be placed?" From their perspective, the agency failed to correctly answer the more fundamental question, "can this child be returned home?"

Many disrupted families complained that their children were not sure that they wanted to be adopted and that has often been considered a telltale sign. This is a difficult judgment to make before (or after) the adoption. Parents who explain the disruption in that way may not grasp the full complexity of adoption disruption and may have settled on this convenient explanation. Several parents of children in stable placements also reported that it took a long time for the youths to really begin to act as if they were home. One mother said that she had adopted two older children (ages 12 and 13 at the time of adoption) who had become independent and still did not treat her like their "mom."

Another family with a disruption had a placement that our prediction model gave very high risk scores. The chances of outperforming the model would have been stronger with better preparation of the child. The adoptive parents of Dean McNiel, a 13-year-old boy with an external behavior T score of 69, believed that the agency failed to support the child's attachment to them by telling Dean that the worker could find another family if this one did not work out. They argue that workers need to believe in the placements they make and not consider placements to be "shopping trips" in which they support a policy of "let's try this and see what happens; if you don't like it you can always take it back." The disruption incident also involved Dean's repeated running away.

Older children have multiple attachments. When they are adopted, they struggle with the significance of that event for the continuity of other attachments. If those attachments are positive but not strong, children and adoptive families may be able to incorporate them with little effect on their own relationship. Open adoption provides such opportunities. If the attachment to birth or prior foster parents is more intense, then efforts to facilitate disengagement may be necessary. We previously described a situation wherein the child had to communicate in writing to his birth mother that he no longer wanted any contact. More common is the need to help a child disengage from previous caregivers. This may involve an intermediate or "bridging" placement that lasts a few months between adoptions (Kirgan, 1983). Several social workers in our study reported that they believed the replacement of a child into a second adoption was orchestrated too quickly. Other kinds of disengagement work can occur during the placement including getting permission and encouragement from earlier caregivers to whom the child is attached to join a new family and to give and get love in that home. This effort involves identifying various attachment figures in the child's life, deciding on the most powerful and most amenable attachment figures, gaining the cooperation of that person, and determining a way for that person to signal his or her permission to the adopted child. This signal need not be in a face-to-face meeting and, preferably, will be recorded in writing or on tape.

FRAGMENTED POSTPLACEMENT VISITS

Postplacement visits were generally innocuous and probably unrelated to adoption outcomes as they occurred before significant concerns arose. In a few cases, however, early concerns were not addressed or were misinterpreted because the social worker did not know or understand the family. In one such case, the mother of a 10-year-old adopted boy was irritated that the private agency was sending out an unknown social worker to make the eight visits they require. The mother ignored the social worker and went about her housework during the visits. She resented that the "agency did not think enough of me or my time to keep that hired gun out of my house. I'm Black, sure, but that doesn't mean that I just love to socialize. I've got things to do at home like everybody else who works." Partly due to her resentment, she did not call the agency to make alternative plans for her son when she had 3 months notice that she would have to have major surgery. Instead, she called to inform the agency that they had to find another home for the child.

David Grover was in an adoptive placement that ended contrary to our prediction that it would last. He had previously been in an adoptive placement that disrupted and had also been sexually molested prior to that in a foster home. David was 6 years old, white, and placed with a slightly younger brother at the time of this placement with a family who had planned to adopt siblings. There was one other child in the household. The family had some experience working in residential care for children. By their account, the adoptive family received good preparation. They met with the boys' former caretakers who were not being allowed to adopt the boys. The family met weekly with professionals to help them learn new disciplining techniques for these children. The adoption lasted 5 months until a social worker at the agency who was not involved in the placement investigated and removed the boys because of reported physical abuse. The family knew that the report was coming—because it had been threatened by a babysitter who had become very attached to one of the boys—and they reported that to the agency themselves. Police removed the boys but did not investigate—neither did the agency. The boys did not even have a chance to say goodbye to the adoptive father who was overseas—they still believed him dead years later. The family appealed the removal of the child for an additional 3 months. Following a hearing, the family was exonerated of abuse but the agency director went against the recommendation of the hearing officer and did not return the children. The boys were replaced in an adoptive placement that has lasted.

On the other hand, although postplacement therapy seemed to have little overall relationship to placement outcomes, good and continuous postplacement services from adoption workers seemed to have positive effects on several placements that were expected to disrupt. One of those involved over 100 contacts to stabilize a very high-risk placement.

EXPECTATIONS OF CHANGE IN THE CHILD'S BEHAVIOR

Adoptive parents risk their smoothly functioning family and work lives when they adopt older children. They expect any serious threat to be temporary or, at least, diminishing. They strive, through their love, example, and ingenuity to help the child understand all that they offer and change in accordance with this reevaluation of their home. The findings of Howard and Smith (1987) most clearly demonstrate that disruption is associated with stable but serious behavior problems of children. Stable placements were characterized by improved behavior. Their conclusions and ours differ slightly from those of Partridge, Hornby, and McDonald (1986) on this account, as the latter suggest that disruptions are usually accompanied by deteriorating behavior. Naturally, the family may perceive behavior that is not improving as getting worse. When behavior fails to improve, as was the case for most disruptions, expectations for a happy family future are abandoned.

One family which continues to maintain a stable placement came close to disrupting when their 14-year-old son—whom they had adopted at age 9—broke into their house with a friend at lunchtime and trashed the living room. They experienced this as a very personal attack and called their social worker to express their bitter disappointment and to learn whether they could still set aside the adoption. They were concerned that the 5-year statute of limitations was almost up and that they would have to act soon.

The social worker told them that she would permit them to have an extension on their set aside time frame and helped them to explore alternatives. Family therapy and a private special education school for their son apparently made a difference, gave them an expectation of change, and helped to stabilize the placement.

CHILD AND PARENT FAIL TO DEVELOP RECIPROCALLY POSITIVE PERSONAL EXCHANGES

In the early stages of an adoption, the rewards of parenting may be mere punctuation marks in a complex and trying sentence. Parents can tolerate delayed rewards for only so long. After a time, their failure to develop loving exchanges with their children is experienced as a deep loss. The child's reciprocity after an adjustment period in the placement was a moderately good predictor of success in our overall discriminant analysis. The development of reciprocity, or positive exchanges, is an indicator to the family that the adoption is working out, and provides a resource that the family can draw on during inevitable trying times. Some exchange of affection, smiles, or affirming experiences buffers other difficulties and helps to maintain the adoption. One family adopted 8-year-old Myra who had been severely sexually abused and was a chronic thief. She required a private special education placement because of her eroticized behavior. She embarrassed and frustrated the family by pulling down her underpants and pulling up her dress, rubbing herself against other children and adults, and by inserting a wide range of objects in her vagina. She also seemed to have expressive aphasia and very repetitive and stereotyped behavior. Despite the difficulties she presented, she was a bright-eyed, beautiful, and affectionate child. She would abandon her overtly sexual behavior for opportunities to sit on a parent's lap and hear a story. This was used as a reward for periods of "good friend" behavior. She also enjoyed learning: and after learning something new would exclaim, "how did I learn that?" and show her new ability to her parents with great delight. Her family's patience, her educational resources, and her ability to give and take cemented the placement.

Robert James was in a fost-adopt placement. This 6-year-old white boy had no prior foster placements but had to leave home when his grandmother died and the grandfather (who was pretending to be his birth father) began to physically abuse the boy. The adoptive parents were both professionals in the corrections field and had a birth child about this boy's age. The child was concerned about why he was given up. He was placed over a one-weekend period. The family had no experience as foster parents. The worker was concerned that the birth child seemed undisciplined and the parents were not affectionate with him, but did not address these issues directly. The agency provided little supervision because all seemed smooth. The family did not communicate that they were struggling and there was no development of a bond between Robert and his parents. The family moved and courtesy supervision was provided in a limited way by the receiving county. Robert had a habit of bingeing and vomiting and the family did not know how to handle this. The child was removed from the home after two severe incidences of abuse and returned to the county of origin. One of the parents was incarcerated. Robert was placed with another fost-adopt family for 2 months before disrupting—he was violent toward his siblings and rejecting of his adoptive parents. He is now living with another adoptive family.

UNCOVERING OF A PREVIOUSLY UNKNOWN CHARACTERISTIC OF CHILD

All parents are surprised by what they learn about themselves and their children. The greater the surprises, the greater the difficulty. As shown in Chapter 3, part of the path to disruption passes through the family's style of coping with the child's differences and difficulties. Whereas families cope differentially with differences, they handle them better when they have preparation. Lansing Wood (1987) writes that adopting families will

> have surprises, or rather shocks, as the getting acquainted process happens. And all of this with a child who may look beautiful and act charming initially, tempting us to believe that he will be just like most of the other seven-, ten-, or fifteen-year-olds we know. As soon as he settles in and gets over the initial adjustment to a new family, school and neighborhood, we feel, he will somehow be released from that history and those past experiences. Teachers, friends and social workers tell us how well he's adjusting and how lucky he is. Perhaps, but his experiences still separate him from the neighborhood kids and make him different, in spite of his "normal" external package. As the reality of this begins to take shape in concrete ways, it can be quite terrifying. The reality may confront us as smeared feces on a bathroom wall, the $40 missing from a father's drawer, Fuck You spray-painted on a neighbor's fence, a young girl molested by an older sibling. Or reality may come as the $1340 per week paid to the therapist, the gamble on a year of residential treatment, the frantic search for the right special education setting. Perhaps part of the reality is the strain on a marriage as thoughts of who initiated all of this begin to form and longings to escape from it all become resentment or depression (pp. 7–8).

Other families find surprises but, given adequate resources, view the adoptive arrangement as a rewarding challenge. Steve Vestille was an 8-year-old boy adopted by a single father in the boy's second adoptive placement. He was the second child adopted into the family—the older adopted brother was 9 at the time of Steve's adoption and needed special education services. At the time of placement, but unknown to the father, this boy had an external behavior T score of 81 and was involved in satanic worship that included slicing his penis open to draw blood for his daily ceremonies. The father adopted Steve because he claims, and our study generally bears him out, as a single parent he had no choice but to adopt the most difficult, older kids. He had a subsidy. He did not adopt Steve's half-sister who was placed with her birth father. They had only one meeting—the boy was picked up for dinner and told the father that "I want to stay here;" the father knew virtually nothing about the child and later found out about the child's history of sexual abuse, emotional problems, and self-injurious behavior. The agency indicated that if they could not find an adoptive home they would institutionalize the boy. Steve had frequent contact with his former foster mother, which was a significant asset to the father. For the first year of the placement, the social worker and father had contact twice a week! The placement is now 5 years old.

INEFFECTIVE PROBLEM SOLVING WITH PERSONS OUTSIDE THE FAMILY

People in trouble generally turn to friends and clergy for help before enlisting professionals. In some of our disruption cases, families were uncommunicative with workers about their contemplation of a disruption even though they discussed other day-to-day matters of child management with their worker. Families that could turn to knowledgeable friends— usually developed during a group home study or during a tenure as a foster parent—frequently overcame this split between the agency and themselves. Indeed, one of the functions of such peer support was to help families decide when they should discuss concerns of disruption.

Angela Ramos was placed in a fost-adopt home that disrupted before finalization. This 9-year-old Latino girl had been in five foster placements across 3 1/2 years. She had previously been placed in a fost-adopt family, but that foster family's own children were having problems and they abandoned the idea of adoption. The adopting family was also Latino and wanted a child exactly like her—they somewhat begrudgingly agreed to the fost-adopt status. Two siblings who were considered unadoptable because of behavior problems were not considered for placement with this family. Angela had a history of sexual and physical abuse. Contact between Angela and her birth parents reportedly greatly weakened the placement. There were two other birth children in the adoptive home and the family was increasingly divided about her growing truancy and defiance. The father sided with her and the mother sided with the birth children. The worker made 20 contacts during the 21-month placement. When the adoptive family learned that the birth mother was again interested in taking Angela back, they contacted their neighbors and their priest. The neighbors knew Angela and were familiar with some of the crises in which she had embroiled the family. The neighbors were not able to provide much assistance and their lack of enthusiasm for Angela was obvious. The Ramos' priest was concerned for the family welfare and believed that Angela should be with her mother if that was a possibility. The priest asked the family to pray for guidance. They gathered together that night when Angela did not return home for supper and asked for guidance. They relinquished Angela back to the agency the next day. She went to Texas to live with the birth mother.

Scotty Jeffers was placed with a new adoptive parent at age 6 after 5 years in foster care (where he had been placed just after birth by his parents who were told that he had no brain tissue and needed complete care). This white boy was congenitally hydrocephalic, legally blind, assaultive, oppositional, developmentally disabled, and manipulative. The family reported not knowing the degree of his developmental disability and found out later that the child had also been sexually abused. The family had adopted two severely disabled children previously. The worker was, naturally, concerned that this child would overburden the family. The worker and parents needed more information about how children who have been institutionalized behave—the parents reported wishing that they had parenting skills training. The family reported that it took 3 years for the child to feel at home. They attended more than 100 self-help or parenting meetings related to adoption or parenting a developmentally disabled child. In this case, the same worker placed all of their children. The adoption is intact.

DELAYED OR NO CONTACT WITH THE AGENCY

Disruptions were rarely precipitous. Most involved at least a year of difficulty; some lasted many years before deteriorating to the point of disruption. The typical family gave the agency little notice that the placement was heating up until the water was about to boil over. One family had a 9-year-old boy and wanted a younger sister. Their great hopes for the perfect daughter were affronted when their adoptive daughter lied about her activities and was viewed by them as seductive with her brother. After only 2 1/2 months, with no preparation for the worker, the mother called and said that the child had to be removed that week. She refused to have subsequent contact with the agency or the child. The child was later adopted as a middle child—the most difficult position according to Festinger's (1986) study—into a family with other adopted children.

Families that did not disrupt more often reported that they thought the adoption might end than did their social workers; about (15%) of the families that did not disrupt had serious concerns that they might. Of the families that reported a concern that the placement would disrupt, none reported that the agency was helpful in maintaining the placement. Yet during the time of concern, most families reported receiving much more frequent contact with the agency. Apparently, the families did not typically perceive contact with the social worker alone as an effective intervention.

Jane Daniels was a 14-year-old white child in her second placement, but her first with a single parent. This mother had 50 friends and relatives to call on. Jane also had siblings who were adopted by other families—she was the last to be adopted. The information provided was excellent and thorough and the mother reported that there were no surprises. She was encouraged to use private special education for Jane and provided with the needed adoption subsidy. The mother reported having had complete control over contacts with Jane's birth family. The agency provided the standard four home visits. Jane is now a senior in high school—the agency maintained contact with the family for 4 years after legalization. The mother reported that the continuity of the social worker was very important. She still felt that agencies should try to improve the family selection and matching process by making it more objective.

A few families sought help from their agency and received none. One family called our research project to seek professional assistance when the agency failed to provide it. Their daughter who was adopted several years earlier was frequently running away and disobedient. Four years after the placement they attempted to obtain assistance from the placing agency but were told that the case record was closed and in another building and that they would have to re-enter the service system via children's protective services; that is, they could receive services if they had abused their daughter or were at risk of so doing. The placement subsequently disrupted.

The failure to contact the agency does not always portend a disruption. Betty Rhodes, age 10, had previously been promised adoption by a foster family and was reluctant and withdrawn with her new adoptive family. She had been sexually molested in her prior foster home, increasing her wariness. The adoption came close to ending when Betty called her adoption worker and told her she did not want to be adopted. The parents did not report their concern that the placement would end to the agency although they admit that they went through unexpectedly difficult times. Betty eventually changed her mind because she knew that the family was committed to her.

The family did criticize the agency because they too readily considered failure as an option. They felt that "you do not get off the bike in the middle of the hill" and were determined to reach the child. This family, like a handful of others who maintained stable placements against the odds, placed their child in a private or special education program because the public school could not provide the structure and personal appeal that the child needed.

Some families succeeded without agency assistance. The adoptive mother of Debra Winston–who was predicted to disrupt but did not—attributed her parenting problems to her own expectations. Soon after the adoption, she was taxed by a move to another state and her 6-year-old child's crying, bedwetting, and soiling. She was not provided with any services. She reports her coping strategy as "I prayed a lot and kept on trying—I was expecting too much too soon. I knew I wouldn't give her up. We've always come through bad times." Although considerable evidence indicates the difficulties of such passive coping styles (Barth & Schinke, 1983; Pearlin & Schooler, 1978), this placement lasted. Under these less than ideal circumstances, this may have been the best she could do.

The placement of Louis Williams epitomizes the route to a stable adoption. Louis was placed into a new adoption in a intercounty placement at age 11. [Note that Nelson (1985) found such placements to be at unusually high risk.] He had been in foster care for 30 months and had a prior disruption and a fost-adopt breakdown. Louis had a severe learning disability, was withdrawn and nonresponsive, and hoarded and stole food and other items. His external *T*-score was 81, but his adoptive family reported him as being generally well-mannered. The family was religious and had a strong informal support network. The family was chosen because they were willing to take an older black child with developmental delays. The marriage was biracial. Louis was separated from three siblings also awaiting adoption. The family was provided with all case information, met with former caretakers, Louis, his therapist, and special education personnel. There was no contact with the birth family. The agency had 28 contacts with the family during the adoptive period to strengthen the adoption—especially related to behavior management. Louis was expected to always need help and was still receiving therapy 2 years after the legalization.

FAILURE TO FIND AN APPROPRIATE INTERVENTIVE SERVICE

As discussed in our model, external support for adoptive families is a much needed resource. Adoption workers may routinely refer troubled families to therapists or support groups without ensuring that the referral agency is capable of addressing the special needs of adoptive families or the challenges they face. Adoption workers would also do well to assess whether family troubles are a reflection of family integration problems, or perhaps, simply a result of the child's need for special education or the parent's need for concrete behavior management training. In preceding chapters we described the frustration of families experiencing adoption crises without recourse to adequate intervention services. Perhaps it is this failure that lowers the expectations of change in the child's relationship to the family and that finally destroys the binding thread and provokes the final call to the agency.

The Sansomes received little assistance from the agency regarding their boy's sexual acting out. William Sansome had an Achenbach external score of 74 and no prior adoptions. He frequently masturbated and urinated wherever he wished. The social worker was unable to provide a suitable referral to help the mother cope with this difficulty and she subsequently ended the placement.

Our model predicted that the placement of 9-year-old Julie Francis would disrupt and it did. Her adoptive parents were denied access her agency and juvenile justice record. The extent of the information was not given until the child was arrested for breaking and entering. The family's greatest complaint involved the agency's requirement that they assist the child in maintaining contact with her foster family (with whom Julie had resided for 7 years). They protested this activity, but were overruled by the agency on the basis of a recommendation by the agency's consulting psychologist. This advice underscores the need for professional mental health consultation by persons who are familiar with adoptions. The psychologist appears to have followed a model which has been adopted by professionals in divorce custody mediations—that the child is better off with equal access to all interested parental parties—without evidence or experience to justify the application in older child adoption. After a child has been adopted by a family that objects to an open adoption approach, it is too late to insist.

A few families received expert help. The adoptive family of 8-year-old Jack Frizza considered returning him to the agency 1 month after placement when they recognized Jack's problems in learning and impulse control. Jack persuaded his mentally retarded 5-year-old adopted sibling to perform masturbation on him. An experienced adoptive family (Jack was their fourth adopted child), they immediately talked to their worker and developed a plan to receive counseling for themselves and Jack and to obtain a more appropriate educational program for Jack. They were not satisfied with the counseling and recontacted their social worker for another referral. (In this case, even the counselor agreed that she could not help this family.) They subsequently joined a foster parent's group and were referred to a clinic that provided parent skills training for parents of emotionally disturbed and mentally retarded children. They acquired special expertise in the sexual behavior and developmental disabilities. The sex play terminated and the placement continued.

The Manganos adopted 11-year-old Martin who had six prior foster placements and a prior adoption disruption. The boy was verbally and physically abusive and fervently opposed attending school. After he threatened their birth child with a knife after residing with the family for 1 year, Martin was hospitalized in a local facility, which was paid for by their private insurance. When the hospitalization became too expensive, the family informed the placing county that they needed to place Martin in foster care until his behavior was under control. The county was willing to comply and agreed that Martin could go home on weekends only if his behavior improved. After 6 months, the child returned home full time and remained in the placement.

The Choice of Disruption to Cope with the Adoption Crisis

Many adoptive families contemplate how life used to be and how it would be if the adoption ended. While most families only contemplate change, a small portion of these families request agency assistance and also decide to discontinue the placement. This choice of disruption as a coping alternative will arise in a variety of families, but will be most likely when the child's behavior has been consistently problematic and/or the parents' management of that behavior has been consistently ineffective and neither party expects the future to bring change.

The most common precipitants to disruption were repeated running away and assault on a parent or sibling. These incidents were not troubling incidents in an otherwise happy home, but were, rather, the last straw for consistently stressed parents. For example, one child slept with a boy while in the adoptive home (she sneaked him into her room) and experimented with drugs. The placement lasted until she repeatedly ran away to return to her birth mother. Another family with a similar experience of a child returning to live with her birth mother, however, continues to keep her on their insurance and to welcome her home. The child provides enough love and affection when she is in her adoptive home to provide her parents with the reassurance that her running is a stressor worth tolerating. In other families, singular stresses can still be too much to bear. One mother collapsed and was hospitalized after her adopted child jumped on her birth son's arm and broke it. The child was returned to the agency the next day.

In another family in which the youth assaulted his adoptive mother, the worker encouraged continued efforts to maintain the adoption including temporary foster care. The worker said the agency would refuse the relinquishment. The adoption worker thought the family was overreacting to the child's behavior. After a psychiatrist recommended therapeutic placement, the agency accepted relinquishment and placed the child in foster care.

Sexual abuse and acting out also precipitated disruption. One precipitating incident was an accusation by an adopted daughter (who had been in the home for almost 3 years) of physical abuse by the father. The report was unfounded, but the embarrassment for the family and the recognition that this child continued to want to fight the family rules and undermine their notion of her as a family member was too much for them to bear. After consulting with the agency, they ended the adoption.

Only two children of 120 (2%) in our sample—as compared to 9% in Festinger (1986)—suffered a disruption because the agency chose to remove the child. In the first case, the agency alleged sexual abuse by the adoptive father. The mother did not believe the claims but talked with the worker and agreed to abrogate the adoption. In the second case, the mother was charged with physical abuse and the children were removed with no notice. The latter report was subsequently unfounded.

Most descriptive of disruption incidents is the family's report that they had run out of alternatives. They typically, but not always, attributed this to the agency or child's shortcomings and unwillingness to work to make the adoption succeed. "Disruption" has become the new description for adoptions that end because the old descriptors "adoption failure" or "breakdown" suggested that all was lost and unsuccessful when the adoption ended. The social and cognitive model of adjustment to adoption argues otherwise. For some families and children, the best coping strategy is to withdraw from the adoption. If well-handled, disruptions can facilitate further growth. Many children who disrupt are placed again. The more they understand about the contributors to the stress and the difficulties that their coping styles created for the adoptive family, the more ready they will be for a lasting placement. Such information cannot always guide a successful new placement, but it may help.

THE AFTERMATH OF DISRUPTION

Older child adoption—more than infant adoption—concentrates on the child rather than the adopting family as the client. As a consequence, the significance of the aftermath of disruption for adoptive families can be underestimated. As Donna Holmes (1979) writes

Sometimes when I read or hear about the happy experiences of adoptive families, I get that warm 'goose-pimply' feeling. Words like great, wonderful, fantastic, superb dance through my mind. Then I begin to wonder about those glowing reports. Are these people real? Does anyone else have problems and heartaches because of adoption? Does anyone understand what it is like not to live happily ever after? (p. 37).

Responses to our interviews, and notes scrawled on reply cards by families that experienced disruptions but did not want to discuss them, offer poignant evidence of the trauma of disruption. One mother who had adopted nine children ages 8 and older and had been a local "Adoptive Parent of the Year" was so embittered by the two postlegal disruptions her family experienced that she said "If I had to do it all over again, I would not have adopted a single one of them." Sweet and collegial relationships with agencies turned sour and hierarchical following disruptions in families with longstanding commitments to adoption. Our interview sample included no divorces among families experiencing disruptions, but reply cards from several respondents who refused interviews and interviews with social workers indicate their view that the disruption had terminal effects on their marriage. We cannot know, of course, if any causal relationship exists between these two events. Yet our interviews inform us that families with disruption report worsening relationships between spouses and between parents and their birth children.

One family described the conflict caused by the contradiction between the adulation and praise they received from friends, co-workers, and family for their magnanimous concern toward their adoptive daughter and their final decision to return her to the agency after 2 years. They described it as "like a death in the family; you feel so helpless and so much loss because you realize that you couldn't help yourself or them." Families had some difficulty calling on the community to assist with the problems of parenting an adoptive child after so recently calling on them to welcome and accept the child as they were. We did not assess the impact of the disruptions on the extensive networks of friends and relatives often engaged in the initial promise and glory of adoptions, but expect that disillusionment with older child adoption might follow. This might have negative ripple effects on recruitment of additional adoptive homes. Some parents who had birth children and then tried to adopt to provide their birth children with siblings report the bitterness and hurt of their children when the adoption ended. The impact on the adopted children may also be quite painful, although we know that many children recover sufficiently to complete subsequent adoptions.

Disruption conferences provide a structure for promoting subsequent success for the family and child (Fitzgerald, 1983; Elbow & Knight, 1987). These conferences are held soon after the family has concluded that they will disrupt and include social workers, therapists, administrators or supervisors, current caregivers, and, if willing, the parent(s). The intent is to explore what occurred and plan for the future of the family and child—particularly, is the child a good candidate for another adoption and should the family be considered again? Few such meetings were held following the disruptions in our study. Most of the children were routinely restaffed at the agency with little direct discussion of the adoptive family's experience. The family was interviewed separately. Such a procedure may also provide needed information for increasing the likelihood of successful future placements, but seems less instructive than a conference.

Adoption disruptions are considered by most child welfare professionals to be a "necessary risk" (Festinger, 1986). Recognition of points along the way to a stable adoption helps practitioners identify the most significant contributors to risk, to identify the level of risk in a placement, and to know how to reduce that risk through the choice of an alternative placement or the use of ameliorative services along the pot-holed route from placement to permanence. However accurately the risk that a placement will disrupt can be assessed, and we still cannot assess this very well, this risk is only one of several considerations in making a placement. The cost of a false positive— that is, not placing a child who might disrupt—is a still more serious concern. Although this and preceding chapters suggests that adoptions of older children are uniformly fraught with hidden peril, that is not the intent. Most adoptions result in lifelong gratitude that families and children assumed the necessary risk.

12

Practice Implications

Adoption workers, parents, researchers, administrators, and policymakers all know and respect the complexity of adoption. Few are naive enough to believe that adoption outcomes hinge on single characteristics or practices, no matter how significant they may seem. Years of placing older children for adoption tell us that there are exceptions to every rule and almost every reader will be able to think of a placement that prevailed in the face of many poor practice decisions or in which the odds for a successful placement seemed unforgivingly slim. We had in our own study a successful placement of a 12-year-old boy with three prior adoption disruptions, 19 prior placements, no preplacement visit, and in which the family rejected the bulk of postplacement services; that placement is intact 6 years later. Whereas we reported single relationships between family, child, and service characteristics and disruption, we are more comfortable with the analyses that include information combined from multiple factors. We also encourage adoption workers to assume this position. We listened to too many social workers who had drawn fast conclusions based on a single disruption and a sole characteristic (e.g., "I'll never place another sibling pair with a single mother" or "I'll never place another child across county lines"). Such conclusions are a disservice to children. Our use of discriminant analysis and our discussion of the path to disruption respect adoption's complexity.

Although there often seems to be an inverse relationship between the complexity of the researcher's models and the clarity of implications for practice, this is not necessarily the case. We believe that researchers have the opportunity and responsibility to systematically describe some of the myriad conditions on which successful adoptions depend and provide suggestions for small but significant improvements in adoption practices. This chapter draws on key findings and hammers out implications for practice. We consider the decisions to refer older foster children for adoption planning, the home study and preplacement preparation, postplacement services, and postlegalization services.

ADOPTION PLANNING

While permanency planning legislation has freed many children for adoption, agencies in California (and we expect elsewhere) have been slow to implement the specifics of legislation (State of California Auditor General, 1983). Whereas more has probably changed than remained the same, many barriers to placement and permanence remain. Eligibility for adoption continues to be a confused mixture of answers to three questions. Is the child: (1) easily interested in adoption; (2) likely to be adopted; (3) likely to remain adopted? Social workers with limited ideas about "adoptability" may reject some children as too severely handicapped or too old to be adopted. Adjusting practice to the needs of these older children includes recognizing that some disruption is inevitable. As Betsy Cole has commented, "The only failed adoption is the one you didn't try." Workers who recognize and accept the possibility of disruption in adoption will find creative ways to facilitate adoptions for all waiting children, and will support the placement in accordance with the risk involved.

Proof that a child will be better off adopted than in long-term foster care or guardianship is unattainable. The best any social worker, foster parent, and child can do is try to make the best prediction that a placement will work out for the best. In general, the value of adoption and the relatively modest disruption rates shown in our and other studies makes adoption the clear and convincingly superior plan over foster care. Yet children are routinely resigned to foster care, given little encouragement toward adoption, and their promising tomorrows routinely swapped for a manageable placement today. Nationwide, the percentage of children with permanent plans who were adopted in 1985 were only marginally higher than those adopted at the beginning of permanency planning (Barth & Berry, 1988).

Practitioners need the tools and the support to work with foster children and parents toward adoption. Agencies neglect latency-age children in care. Younger children are likely to get referrals to adoption units and older foster children are increasingly referred for emancipation services. Life planning services (McDermott, 1987) are needed for the 5- to 12-year-old group of children. These should be more than a clarification of values, and deserve the best presentations of the available alternatives. Interactive reading books and interactive videodisc presentations that allow youth to choose different endings for their lives depending on their choices are a new innovation in health education that can be applied here. Video tapes of panel discussions of youth who have chosen to be adopted and foster parents who choose to adopt are also needed. These should focus on the process of thinking through the adoption decision (e.g., looking at myths about adoption) as well as the outcome. All the panel presentations and high tech equipment will not matter if social workers do not help the children in their caseloads personalize the evidence of the superiority of adoption to foster care.

HOME STUDIES AND PREPLACEMENT PREPARATION

Conventional home studies and selections of adoptive families double as preplacement preparation. In the name of efficiency, this is a sensible approach, however, the requirements of the two activities are not singular. Many adoptive parents are still interviewed under a format which has survived the change in agency practice from a concentration on infant adoptions to the current day. As such, a worker may interview couples together, then each member of the couple alone, and then, again, the couple together. The honorable intent is to understand if either member of the couple has views which they cannot express in front of his or her partner and that reflect on uncertainty about adopting. The peculiarity of assuming that a spouse would tell a nearly complete stranger of concerns that they would not tell their spouse is only one flaw in this approach. To the contrary, most couples have discussed their differences together and with friends who play a role very much like the social worker. They have typically managed to combine their truths and myths into a rather seamless garment that they will wear regardless of individual discussions with social workers.

Couples or individuals that meet with others in a like situation can more effectively challenge their false expectations. The most developed group model is that developed by Barbara Tremetiere (1979). The nine-session group format includes: (1) informing the 5 to 7 couples or single applicants of the purpose of the group and what will follow; (2) exposure to panels of adoptive parents who present the challenges (and threats) of adoptive parenting; (3) clarification of family and individual values about adoption; (4) visits with a family that has adopted a child with characteristics similar to the child of interest to the adoptive parent(s); and (5) completing the writing of the home study which is a joint effort by the applicant and social worker. This approach to preplacement endeavors provides opportunities for ongoing support. Adoptive families in our study who began the process in such multifamily groups often maintained contact with one or more families— many times well beyond their time of contact with their social worker. Many agencies still do not use such a model. Our evidence argues strongly for its consideration and testing in all agencies.

The use of interim placements between discharge from institutional care or group care and placement in adoptive or fost-adopt family care is often advisable according to workers and families. Fost-adopt parents (who have no prior foster parent experience) may be particularly unprepared for children's food hoarding, lying, and stealing. These behaviors may be better addressed in more intensive forms of care. Programs like Children's Garden's Placement Evaluation Program provides a thorough assessment of the best placement for the child (Kirgan, 1983). A temporary nonadoptive placement following a disruption may also provide some perspective. In one agency the workers refer to several foster families as "fix-it" families because of their ability to help young people resolve the difficulties of disruptions and prepare for subsequent placements.

Information Sharing

Agency protocols that detail systematic ways for social workers to obtain and communicate information about the child and his or her prior experience are needed. Adoption workers increasingly provide assessments of the adoptive family or of the child, but not of both. Because of inevitable coordination problems, much valuable information that is gathered on each of the parties is not told to the others. This inefficiency is not necessary and could be redressed by rethinking the type of information that is collected and how it is summarized and transmitted to the families.

The strong confirmation in this study of the inadequacy and importance of information sharing cited in other studies calls for prompt action. One of our families adopted a boy with a history of sexual assaults who molested their adopted son who had Down's Syndrome. They argued that "every social worker that knowingly denied available information to an adoptive applicant should be suspended from their job and reviewed for dismissal." We share their sentiment although not their policy recommendation. Other families also share their sentiment. One family recently won an out-of-court settlement in Orange County, California, claiming that the agency withheld information that their adopted boy had Fetal Alcohol Syndrome and had abused animals and other children and the agency assured the family that the boy's behavior was normal for a newly adopted child ("Couple wins $70,000." San Francisco Examiner, January 5, 1988). The family suggests that people considering adoption should get a court order to force the agency to release all documents on the child. Guidelines and procedures for candid and complete sharing are overdue in any agency without them.

We offer a beginning to agencies by providing an information-sharing checklist for use by social workers and adoptive parents (See Fig. 12.1). The sheet would be included in every case record and would allow for each party to initial information provided about a given child. Information that is not available can be duly noted. This should reduce the confusion about whether information was known but not shared or was not available. We expect that

Child's First Name _____ Case ID _____

Adoptive Applicant _____ Social Worker _____

Social worker initials column (A) or (B) to indicate the availability of information and parent(s) initial column (C) to indicate that you did discuss or receive a written report on the following:

	(A) Info Not Available	(B) Info Available	(C) Info Provided
Child History			
Characteristics of birth family	_____	_____	_____
History of physical abuse	_____	_____	_____
History of sexual abuse	_____	_____	_____
History of neglect	_____	_____	_____
History of multiple placements	_____	_____	_____
Child Problems			
Physical or medical disability	_____	_____	_____
Developmental disability	_____	_____	_____
Learning disability	_____	_____	_____
Emotional or behavioral problems	_____	_____	_____
Subsidy			
Eligibility			_____
Amount			_____
Duration			_____
Other			
Availability of post-placement services			_____
Legalization			_____
Postlegalization services			_____
Risk of disruption			_____
Laws regarding set aside			_____
Discuss disruption			_____

Worker: Please describe plans to obtain additional information on items initialed as not available_____

_____

_____

Figure 12.1. Information checklist.

189

this simple device may lead to better placements and less stretching of families in a way that is now followed by disruptions.

We believe that the possibility of disruption should be addressed in all adoptions. Discussion of disruption provides the opportunity to offer families pertinent information about the chances of disruption given the case characteristics (such data can be cautiously drawn from the prediction study). Such discussions also offer the chance to consider the fate of children who do suffer disruptions and review family options should they begin to consider ending the adoption. Discussing disruption will not any more encourage such an idea than does discussing suicide encourage suicide attempts. It helps the worker and family prepare for thoughts and reactions that are common and to clarify their pre- and postlegalization service agreement. Indeed, the home study should include questions about what experiences (e.g., sexual molestation of a birth child or assault on a parent or founded or unfounded allegations of abuse by the child) would make it unacceptable from the parents and agencies' viewpoint for a child to continue living there. Such information can help placement workers to plan aid and for a family to see that they are approaching a point of great risk. These discussions may also prompt more active searching on the part of social workers into the child's past to see what the past foretells about the likelihood of future behavior.

POSTPLACEMENT SERVICES

While matching of compatible children and families has been identified as important to adoption success, the assurance of proper matching before placement is not the only requirement for a successful placement. Agency support after placement is also crucial. Any placement will have challenges. The goal is to be close enough to the family to remain aware of these problems and guide the family to resources to aid in their resolution.

The importance of providing lasting and intensive supportive services rather than focusing on preplacement services is heightened by the explosion of foster-parent adoptions. These have become the typical adoptions. They often begin as emergency placements without much choice about placement and matching. Indeed, some of these adoptions occur despite serious agency misgivings as foster parents have an entitlement to adopt children in their care who are free. At the time of the adoption, the child has been in the home for some time. Immediate postadoption services are inappropriate. If the placement will disrupt, that will usually come later when the difficulties arising from mismatches between the child and family are more manifest.

Fitzgerald and his colleagues (1982) begin with the assumption that both the child and the parents have needs in postplacement services. The agency maintains close contact with the family during the first 3 months to reassure the child of continuity with his past and to enable the family to explore uncertainties without feeling lost (Fitzgerald, Murcer, & Murcer, 1982). The goal is to catch problems early in the placement before they escalate into unsalvageable disasters. The evidence is clear from our study that 3 months is far too brief a time. Mechanisms must be established in agencies to provide services for high-risk placements throughout the adolescent years. This is not simply a call for more postlegalization services. These are also needed but are typically not pitched at preserving placements on the verge of disruption.

Development of community resources can help make the promise of treatment for an adopted child more than just a prayer. Community-based service providers should be recruited and trained by participating in the home study process and during explicit agency training. Part of that training should involve participation in in-house reviews of each disruption. Adoption workers and the therapists to whom social workers refer adoptive families need to have a far better understanding and greater commitment to working with educational systems—particularly special education. Numerous families in our study identified the attainment of an appropriate public or private special or regular education program as a turning point away from a disruption. Typical postplacement services that are limited to office or kitchen counseling and fail to fully explore the child's broader work suggests that many social workers do not recognize or know how to respond to the importance of schools in the lives of parents and children. Collaborative training with educators, school social workers, and school psychologists would benefit adopted children.

The Failure of Psychotherapy to Prevent Disruption

Adoption workers either have great faith in psychotherapy or have few alternative resources to provide families when problems arise. Whichever is the case, many families experiencing difficulties in the adoption are encouraged to bring their children to therapy despite the general lack of evidence that conventional psychotherapy for children is effective (Levitt, 1971; Barrett, Hampe, & Miller, 1978). Most therapy involved the referral of only the child instead of the whole family. Parents interpret this as yet another indication of the secondary status of adoptive parents with little control over the treatment of their child. Hornby (1986) also reports that disrupting parents complained that they received no tangible assistance from agencies—many times they were given nothing more than an interpretation of the child's behavior. Few therapists were knowledgeable about adoptions or foster care. Therapists did very little to promote the understanding of parents about therapy or to involve them in the process of altering their interactions with the child or the child's environment to support more acceptable and competent behavior. Families that did not receive such support for the family—and consideration of what the family system could or could not do to accommodate the children—left therapy. Families also became concerned and terminated therapy when there was no change in the presenting problem. It is not sufficient to inform families that "sometimes things get worse before they get better"; families will often not be around for the latter part (and they probably should not be, since there is not particular evidence to support the necessity for a worsening of behavior before it improves). Reitnauer and Grabe's (n.d.) study of therapy provided to adoptive and foster families indicates that the families go for help because of "behavior-centered problems" (p. 17). The type of therapy most often used was, however, child or play therapy even with children ages 9, 12, and 15. A large portion of the children were exposed to nondirective counseling which was evaluated by parents as of little use. According to Reitnauer and Grabe (n.d.), and we agree, "the non-directive approach is not useful in most situations with foster/adoptive children" (p. 19).

The grossly imperfect choice between conventional therapists can be glibly categorized as: (1) arcane psychodynamic play therapists; (2) adoption specialists who work primarily or exclusively with families who adopted infants; (3) family therapists who know little or nothing about adoption; and (4) child and family behavior therapists who know nothing much about adoption. We did not ask our families which therapists would be most useful, but from our interviews we would venture that they would rank them in ascending order of desirability. The frustrations with individual passive therapists were nearly universal. On the whole, the most satisfied were those who received help with behavior management from therapists even though the families were left to rely on themselves and their social workers to address specific issues related to issues of adoption. With a few exceptions—when youth had not disengaged from birth parents, for example—families did not see the unresolved issue of adoption as the key contributor to the problem behavior. Rather, the problem behavior was seen as the key barrier to resolving ambivalence about the adoption. Adoption specialists often view unresolved issues about the adoption as causing the problem. This has some truth, but ours and other studies suggest that children's difficult behavior typically preceded the adoption.

Referrals

Social workers will not often have the time or skill to help families who are struggling with their child's difficult behavior. Referral is often indicated.

This is more difficult than it appears and requires a fundamental grasp of the characteristics of successful treatment (Barth, 1986b; Reid & Hanrahan, 1982). Briefly described, the best treatment approaches are those that offer: (1) available models of competent behavior (like groups); (2) the least restrictive necessary service (the program treatment structure must be all that the child needs but should not rule out social integration with successful peers); (3) assistance in enhancing the information, material aid, and social support of the child caring system (family treatment rather than individual treatment); (4) help with between-setting coordination (treatment that facilitates information sharing between relevant services and family members); and (5) service standards based on current information about effective practice (therapists should have recent training in behavior management). A treatment service or therapist should combine people and environment changing and have plans to enhance the functioning of the family, social service system, and school context.

Social workers typically have few referral resources. Grabe and Schreiber (n.d.), illustrate the typically frustrating characteristics of two families seeking treatment for their adoption crisis. In search of information about their children, the first family was told, "confidentiality policies do not permit us to disclose anything about our sessions" (p. 3). Given this typical but still inexcusable view, this therapist is clearly unable to work with the child caring system. The second family referred their son because they were concerned about disrupted sleep patterns and nightmares. They were told "We can't talk about it, if Paul won't bring it up." No referral was made for an evaluation at a sleep clinic, suggesting the therapist's failure to foster between-setting coordination. The complaints of our families were similar and sometimes more egregious.

Alternatives to Conventional Treatment

What alternative to referrals to conventional child therapy might preempt disruptions? The first is to prevent the need for referral to therapy. Tremitiere (1984) argues that "the use of a realistic educational process prior to placement" can markedly reduce the need to refer to psychotherapy—less than 5% of families in her agency attend therapy. The more typical recourse of these families is to contact other families with whom they participated in a group home study. Families in our study who had a group home study seemed to continue to rely on contacts developed during this period for a range of consultative, recreational, and legal resources during their placements. The likelihood of a useful referral to therapy for placements that could benefit from such a resource can be increased by inviting therapists and special education personnel to participate in group home studies. They learn about adoption and the concerns of families and families learn about the availability of these resources.

A second alternative is to rely on therapeutic resources that emphasize the importance of the child's current family and educational experiences and not just the child's past or the child's personal experience (Barth, 1986b). The importance of obtaining appropriate regular or special education resources for children was consistently identified as a pivotal point in determining the outcome of the placement. As a starting point for helping agencies decide which therapist a family should see, we recommend that the agency or family ascertain whether the therapist will have direct contact with the school. This is a strong indicator of the therapist's willingness and ability to obtain a complete picture of the child. If the therapist indicates that he or she does not have the time or talent or that such contact violates his or her therapeutic notions, then another resource should be found.

Therapists who are knowledgeable about adoptions and family and behavior management are scarce and valuable gems. Partly because of our own experiences and partly because of our review of the literature and data from this study, we argue that families come to therapy to look for specific strategies for reducing the most difficult behaviors of children. The origins of these behaviors can be better understood with knowledge of the many stressors suffered by children who come to be adopted, but the most fundamental knowledge needed by social workers and therapists has to do with strategies for changing difficult behavior. Even if they have never heard of adoption, experienced social and cognitively oriented child therapists can help families to find positive incentives for improved behavior, help families improve on their nonaversive strategies for reducing problem behaviors (e.g., by clarifying how time out and naturally occurring consequences might be used more effectively), and support a gradual and focused change effort.

Social and Cognitive Treatments

Generally, social workers have traded their clinical roles for case management responsibilities. At times, however, adoption workers seem to be in a time warp that allows them to provide direct services. We were astounded at the number of contacts social workers had with families. Although we do not expect that this is the rule, we provide examples of social and cognitive approaches toward handling two common problems in older child adoptions: lying and stealing (see Barth, 1986b for discussion of other problems). When social workers are unable to provide direct services, they can help families determine whether the families' behavior seems to be generally helpful and whether the interventions proposed by other service providers are promising or inert.

LYING.   Lying is as endemic to childhood as dirt. Chronic lying is a strong contributor to difficult and disrupted adoptions. Parents hope that lying will end by the time a child enters elementary school; however, lying peaks at age 6, drops off for 2 years, and then rebounds at about age 8 before dropping sharply after age 10 (Macfarlane, Allen, & Honzik, 1954). Many children (and especially children with inconsistent parenting) continue to lie thereafter. At around age 8, children typically change their ideas of lying and no longer say that lying is bad because you might get punished for it. Instead, they begin to report such cognitive reasons for not lying as guilt and destroying trust (Peterson, Peterson, & Seeto, 1983). The timing of this transition varies greatly according to the child's developmental level, experience with lying, and their belief about what is lying and what is an acceptable "mistake" or "white lie." Many older children who are adopted have not reached this transition and lie if they won't get caught. These children can learn to internalize the notion that telling the truth is best, although that may follow consistent and clear external incentives to be trustworthy. Adoptive families should recognize, however, that white lies, lies of convenience, and lies of omission typically continue until life's end.

Parents tolerate lying to vastly different extents. Lying upsets adoptive parents for many reasons including: fear that the child will grow up and think he or she can get away with deception and crime, worry that the lying habit will infect other children in the home, or that lying may be an assault on moral or religious beliefs and may result in embarrassment or inconvenience with teachers, neighbors, or family members. One family who successfully adopted a 12-year-old boy who had been in 19 prior placements indicated that they specifically asked if the boy was a liar. They understood that, given their own dispositions, they could tolerate a child who was aggressive or rejecting or who ran away but not a child who lied.

Children who have learned to be honest are less likely to engage in other problematic childhood behaviors (Patterson, 1982). Still, lying does not in itself predict criminal activity. Children lie to protect themselves in the face of an angry—or expected to be angry—parent. Adopted children will also lie to protect themselves from possible rejection by other children. For example, a foster-adopt child might say that their birth father is famous. Children need help to master a truthful and simple story about who they are and how they came to be adopted: that is, a cover story (Donley, 1978). A well-crafted and rehearsed cover story will help a child resist embroidering the truth and becoming tangled in the web of deception. (Donley notes that this cover story is not the same as a "cover-up story" and is more similar to a cover letter—short and to the point.) Construction of the cover story follows three steps. First, imagining the potential questions about the wherefores, wherefroms, and whys of the placement from neighbors, teachers, relatives, and classmates. Second, reviewing the information to be shared. Children often need to know that they do not have to provide information that violates their sense of privacy or makes them uncomfortable. This is the time to construct simple responses like, "I'm being adopted because my other family could not take care of me and this family wants me to live with them." Responses to predictable questions about what went wrong in prior placements can be handled just as succinctly, "My mother just couldn't get it together" or "It's hard to describe why, but we all know that this is a better place for me to live." Third, the family (or social worker) and child rehearse using these declarative statements in response to a range of questions.

Most often, the focus on intervention can be on the problem behavior rather than the lying. That is, if a child smashes the neighbor's toy cars and lies about it, the penalties should be addressed primarily at the destructive behavior (e.g., having to give the offended child something of greater value than was destroyed and having a time out). In the future, telling the truth about such misbehavior can be afforded praise and a more lenient penalty (e.g., restitution of destroyed property but no time out).

At times, children will lie for little apparent reason and not to disguise a larger transgression. For example, one adoptive parent complained that her child lied after she had watched him kick his sister and after she had reprimanded him. His frequent "I didn't do it" drove her wild. It took 2 years of using time outs following such lying, praise when he did not lie, and the use of "the truth is . . ." statements to teach him to respond to reprimands with a simple, "OK." When children who tend to lie have committed misdeeds, they should not, at first, be asked to admit to the misdeed, but only to accept the consequences for their error.

Conventional wisdom about lying says to minimize its development by modeling and praising honesty. This is not especially valuable advice to adoptive parents, even though they can begin by correctly labeling lies for what they are. Since adoptive parents seek to build a trusting relationship, they are often more concerned about incorrectly labeling their child's honesty as a lie than they are about incorrectly failing to call a lie what it is. The adoptive parent is certainly at a disadvantage with regard to past events that a child describes—e.g., my foster mother always let me stay up and watch Saturday Night Live. Responses to such claims need not be confrontational, nor need they show acceptance of the lie; a simple, "Well, in our home 9:30 is the bedtime every night" will do. Yet, little has been written about lying and adoption. Ryan's (1978) training manual for foster parents is one resource and focuses on why children lie (or steal), why this bothers foster parents, the consequences of stealing for the child, and some suggestions for addressing lying.

Millar (1985) reports on a four-step procedure for working with children who continue to lie beyond developmental appropriateness. First "catch him" by developing a high index of suspicion and checking up on him. When your 7-year-old child tells you that his friend's mom was home when he went down to the street to play, ask him if that is the truth. That gives him a chance to tell the truth about his prior untruth. In either case, call and talk to her. If she was there, praise him for his good judgment and for telling the truth and if she was not, then move to step two: keeping score. Develop some way of vividly recording when a lie occurs. Millar recommends putting an item in a jar for each lie. When there are three items in the jar then the child is punished by removing one of his or her privileges. The third step is to persist and continue to employ this system and encourage the child to practice the truth.

STEALING.   The rewards of stealing—excitement, a sense of mastery, and material new belongings—must be counteracted with consequences for stealing. This is not easy for adoptive parents who are known to be lenient and understanding. Assessment must consider the key elements of family and school management: rules, monitoring, and consequences (Barth, 1987). Many birth families do not have articulated or understood rules for children. These families are more likely to raise children who steal (Patterson, 1982). Birth families' definitions of stealing may vary sharply from those of foster-adopt or adoptive families. Families' ways of recognizing and rewarding adherence to rules against stealing also need to be known. If rules are developed but not used, they soon become meaningless and children become inoculated against taking rules seriously. That is the starting point for many children entering foster care.

Rules cannot be used unless caregivers observe children's behavior. Monitoring requires that parents know where the child should be according to the rules, whether his or her responsibilities have been fulfilled, and whether he or she has unfamiliar possessions. Rules without consequences do not shape lives. Since more than one-half of children that steal are also socially aggressive (Patterson, 1982), parents often do not provide the negative consequences that should follow stealing because it becomes such a dreadful chore. Because reprimands and removal of privileges will typically result in hostile outbursts, parents must have considerable instruction, encouragement, and monitoring to build skills in child management. When possible, the adoptive family should assess the response of children to past efforts to reduce stealing. The service provider should identify the adoptive parent's ability to: stick with his or her definition of stealing, reprimand, use time out, and withdraw privileges as needed.

Children learn that their behavior is stealing and that it is serious when parents repeatedly tell them and show them by providing consequences for telling the truth and lying. Good definitions of stealing and adherence to those definitions help parents to stop arguing with their children about whether they were stealing and to begin helping children to label their stealing behavior more accurately. Children's slang that blurs the interpretation of the act of stealing—"borrowed", or "souvenired", for example—should be corrected. Strict interpretation of stealing definitions and applying predetermined consequences for *all* stealing should lessen or end possession of items (1) that "my friend did not want anymore"; (2) that "I found on the way home from school"; (3) that "the lady at the store gave me because I did some errands for her and she likes me; and (4) that "my friend left over here when he stopped over (and you weren't home) and I'll be sure to try to return to him (but he doesn't go to my school anymore so I'm not sure I can)".

Children who lose privileges for stealing—even if parents are not certain that the child is guilty of stealing—may complain bitterly. Adoptive parents are particularly likely to sympathize and, in respect for the child's rights, drop or reduce the charges and consequences. Adler (1981) in his otherwise fine book on group care, argues that "when there is a stealing incident and the culprit is identified *beyond a reasonable doubt,* disciplinary action is necessary" (p. 165; emphasis added). This conclusion is mistaken and reliance on this guideline will severely curtail opportunities to help children who steal. Knowing beyond a reasonable doubt that stealing occurred requires catching a child with an item of known origin and for which the accused child provides no other reasonable explanation for the article's appearance in his possession. In practice, this rarely happens. To help children who steal, adoptive families will do well to operate on their convictions when they have a "preponderance of evidence" rather than "clear and convincing evidence" or evidence that goes "beyond a reasonable doubt." The suspicion of stealing is all the proof that is needed. The result may be some unfairness, but that is a lesser evil than the ineffectiveness that results from using other standards. Parents must dare to be wrong. The child is responsible to avoid giving them reason to err.

Extra chores and loss of privileges are feasible and appropriate consequences for stealing. For each stealing event (and depending on the age of the child), 2 hours of work (e.g., chores, writing or arithmetic practice, or reading assignments) is fitting. All basic privileges—that is, telephone, television, and snacks—should be suspended until the work is completed. Other special privileges—movies and going out to play with friends, for example—should not be reinstated until after the next weekend. If the theft occurs on a weekend, full privileges can be earned back for the following weekend days. Restrictions may be required for no longer than the end of the next weekend. This procedure is compatible with Toughlove's general approach, but adoptive families should realize that some Toughlove groups may encourage families to move very quickly to a confrontive, "lock-out" strategy. Such an approach should not be tried too soon—especially in adoption—as the parent-child relationship is often too tenuous to serve as the magnet to pull the child back into line.

The Bible suggests restitution of 5 oxen for every one stolen and 4 sheep for every sheep stolen, and if the thief has nothing then he shall be sold! Although the penalties are rather harsh, the concept is sound. Restitution is still used often—at least in a partial way—with youth who steal. Group care facilities surveyed by Russo and Shyne (1980) reported using "reparations" in 54% of their facilities in response to "usual" stealing. Some form of restitution for stealing is always possible—even when the child consumes the stolen item. Aside from the previously described consequences for stealing, the child should be required to meet the person who was victimized (e.g., the store owner or neighbor), apologize, and either return the object or provide whole or partial remuneration for it. If the child has stolen from a classroom, the parent should ask if the child can speak to the class to apologize to the other children and school administrator. In a face-to-face meeting the child should apologize and return the merchandise or, if it has been consumed, damaged, or lost, ask how he can repay the theft (e.g., by returning the item, working at the store, or staying out of the store for some fixed amount of time). If a child steals from another family member, then an overcorrection of the cost of the goods plus 100% of their cost is appropriate. The overcorrection payment should be made over time to be sure that the child who stole is not prevented from participating in all social events that require some money. Children should also have the opportunity to earn income from chores that exceed what is typically expected. Washing the car, digging out a stump, or cutting down a yard full of weeds are appropriate.

These are not foolproof solutions—none are. But they offer the best available interventions for stealing. Preventing stealing by removing or locking away valuables offers the best prevention. Implementing these solutions requires the adoptive parent to allow some hardness and a high suspicion index into their family life while still maintaining a softness and openness to their child. It is a necessary challenge.

Supportive Services

In addition to referral and treatment, agencies are developing supportive services. We found sporadic efforts to do so in our study and describe such programs as a spur to renewing efforts to develop supportive services in all agencies. Many agencies have introduced support groups of adoptive

families for parents and children (Cordell, Nathan, & Krymow, 1985; Tremitiere, 1979; Gill, 1978). It is often helpful for new adoptive parents and
children to talk to fellow adopters and adoptees, to know what is normal in
adoption, and to share realistic expectations and feelings about the process.
These groups also facilitate supportive relationships that parents and children can fall back on in individual need. We suspect that these groups
operate best when started during the home study, but have seen successful
versions developed to support high-risk placements.

Developed by the North American Council on Adoptable Children
(NACAC), the Buddy System is a cooperative effort between adoption
agencies and adoptive parents that pairs experienced adoptive parents with
those new to adoption (Boersdorfer, Kaser, & Tremitiere, 1986). Bringing
these families together provides opportunities for preadoptive families to
learn what to expect in their own adoption, enables them to develop lasting
supportive relationships, and helps the more experienced (but still in
progress) adoptive families to benefit from the review of their adoptive
accomplishments. Buddies are often drawn from an adoptive parent organization, but this is not necessary. Families known to the adoption unit can be
solicited for participation as buddies. Foster parents can also make good
buddies and can be recruited through their association (which are more
numerous than adoptive parent organizations). Buddies are assigned according to the type of adoption anticipated. For instance, a family planning to
adopt a sibling group of three children might be assigned to another family
that adopted a large sibling group and fost-adopt parents would be paired.
Ideally, the buddy will participate in parts of the parent participation and
home study process since this is a time when families are deciding what
kinds of children they want to and can parent. Supportive postplacement
activities include occasional telephone calls, cards, invitations for a cook-out,
sharing books and articles, and referrals to other resources, and explaining
the many mysteries of the agency.

Another strategy for providing support to adoptive families is via an
adoption warmline or, as Tressler-Lutheran calls it, a Listening Ear. The
model is designed to help families reach out to needed resources without
calling the social worker who they may perceive as a threat to their
placement. This requires recruiting and training adoptive parents to be good
listeners and to know when to refer the family back to their agency or on to
other resources. The logistics of centralized vs. decentralized reception of
these calls must be developed locally.

When workers recognize that several families are experiencing running
away, extensive sexual exploration, or school problems, groups to address
those issues that include experienced and inexperienced parents can be very

useful. These groups can combine most or all of the ingredients of the effective interventions delineated above.

Adoptive and foster parent associations are beginning to develop respite care arrangements. Families agree that they would be willing to provide care for a child in their home for a time—some families designate 3 weeks and some designate 3 hours. Arrangements are made for reimbursement of meals and other expenses. (For children in foster-adopt programs, agency guidelines about the use of respite must be clarified.)

Intensive Adoption Preservation Services

With so much riding on the outcome of an adoption crisis, reliance on kitchen counseling or office-based psychotherapy is foolhardy. At times, intensive in-home adoption preservation services may be needed. Over the last decade, such services have emerged in most of our states but have been primarily reserved for preventing entrance into the child welfare or mental health systems. Programs like Homebuilders (in Washington and New York) have had remarkable success in preventing the placement of children who are at "imminent risk." The contributors to their success are not fully understood, but involve a crisis time-limited orientation, use of social and cognitive methods of intervention, intensive work that occurs in the home (sometimes exceeding 15 hours per week per family), and linkage to other resources. Adoption agencies have generally not called on these services to help preserve adoptive placements.

Recently, Medina Children's Services, the Seattle-based agency specializing in adoption of older and special-needs children and the Behavioral Sciences Institute (parent of Homebuilders) have begun collaborating to develop and evaluate intensive adoption preservation services and provide training in its use. As in all Homebuilders interventions, each full time therapist in the project has a caseload of two families, the intervention consists of 4 weeks of in-home therapy, and the therapist sees the family as often as needed—typically, three to five sessions of 2 hours or more. To date, 89% of adoptive families indicating that they are experiencing an adoption crisis and are at-risk of a disruption have been helped to maintain the placements. (A similar intensive family preservation services program operated by Oregon's Children's Services Division found that the 50 adoptive families provided with family preservation services had the highest success rates of any other types of families they served; Showell, 1988.)

The synopsis of a case (Johnson, 1987) from the Homebuilders-Medina adoption preservation project illustrates the way that intensive adoption preservation services transcend conventional postplacement services. The intervention with the Averys lasted 4 weeks and included approximately 40 hours of contact time. Darlene, Abe, and their children Pam (now 17 but adopted at age 10) and Daniel (5) were referred to the Homebuilders Adoption Services Project after Pam ran away and stated that the situation at home was so bad that she wanted to cut her wrists. A neighbor reported hearing the father tell Pam that he wished she was dead: she was in a receiving home at case opening, but the family agreed not to relinquish her if she would participate in counseling.

The night the therapist brought Pam home from the Receiving Home, Abe was so mad at her that he broke down in tears and did not look at her. The intervention addressed the goal of improved communication among family members. Parent training promoted Abe and Darlene's ability to praise and be positive with Pam. With role playing and homework assignments, Pam learned ways to refrain from lying and to build better social relationships with peers. The therapist encouraged the family to find activities to do and worked with them until they formed specific plans. As a result of the intervention the parents and Pam renewed their commitment to a permanent relationship. Abe and Darlene changed their view from "the adoption didn't work and we made a mistake," to "we are having trouble parenting our child but are learning to do so." By the end of the intervention, all family members reported enjoying each other more and using improved communication. Abe changed from reporting that he was not bonded to Pam and that she was never part of the family to reporting that she was more a member of the family than ever before.

What is remarkable about the intervention is not the activities—with the exception of logs and role plays, many therapists would have proceeded in a similar manner. More critical was the timing and intensity of the efforts. Pam was home before the family could solidify their decision to relinquish her and the therapist worked with them nearly every day for a month to take advantage of this crisis time to make significant changes. A more typical 90-minute per week family therapy session would be unlikely to provide such facilitative timing and intensity.

OPEN ADOPTION

As reviewed in Chapter 1, the practice of open adoption, or the continuance of contact of the adopted child with birth parents, seems especially applicable among older children who still have ties to their parents, siblings, and extended family. Yet, our findings are mixed about the use of open adoption with older child placements. Whether the family had control over these contacts or not, they seemed to disturb the higher risk placements. The benefits to the lower risk placements are in keeping with those witnessed in open adoptions—they provide a resource for coping with the typical transitions of the adopted infant as he or she marches across time to adulthood. Certainly, the practice of some mental health consultants to social service agencies of insisting on maintaining contact with birth parents or former caregivers is outrageous. Our sample included several families who had this experience. This may be especially common in states like California where the presumption in divorce custody proceedings—a far more common event than adoptions—is toward joint custody. The situations are comparable, but more different than similar insofar as the divorced child is not attempting to develop a bond to the family, he or she is trying to maintain bonds to her or his parent(s). The adoptive child and parent are endeavoring to become a family and need a structure to do so. The older a child, the less detrimental and more natural it should be to retain ties to former caretakers. This is not strictly so because older children also have a more difficult time developing ties to their new family—since they are also pushing toward independence—and this may be preempted by contact with birth families. Whereas Sorich and Siebert (1982) recommend matching adoptive and birth families partly on the basis of their choice of open, semi-open, or closed adoptions, this is more applicable to infant than older child adoptions where there are usually few families to choose from. At best, adoptive parents should not participate in fost-adopt programs if they are unduly cautious about the possibility of contact with the birth family. Also, open adoption should be viewed as an enrichment to a stable placement, not a palliative of a troubled one. Still we are not in agreement with Kraft, Palombo, Mitchell, Woods, & Schmidt (1985) that open adoptions of infants necessarily interfere with the process of bonding between the adoptive parent and child. We restrict our concerns to the older child who has not been able to detach from his or her birth parent.

SUBSIDIES

Subsidies were not as common or as substantial as we expected. Adoption subsidies averaged about one-third the level of foster care rates. Parental reports of the absence of a discussion of the availability of subsidies, the eligibility criteria, or the coverage of medical and therapeutic procedures was associated with reports of more difficulty in the placement. The sufficiency of the subsidy, but not the mere award of a subsidy, was also related to reported difficulty. Higher risk placements did not have higher subsidies. Among these higher risk placements, the difficulty of the placement reported by parents was significantly higher when there was no subsidy. Among placements that were predicted to disrupt, somewhat more did disrupt when there was no subsidy.

The equitable and efficient delivery of subsidies is hindered by the varied use of subsidies within and between agencies. In some agencies, subsidies are considered to be a lasting entitlement and in some a short-term special favor. In one agency, workers commented that families should not become dependent on subsidies and some families were told that their subsidies would be cut back after 5 years. In another agency a mother had to win a Fair Hearing to obtain a subsidy for her special-needs adoption. The following year her subsidy was reviewed and terminated by an agency administrator. Agencies should be sure that social workers support the rights of families to receive subsidies. Most social workers do, but some have not heeded the guidance of Ruess: "The state which denies the child its birthright of a home, with due physical, mental and moral care, must pay with compound interest, as in California, for its sins of omission against the child. Nothing that a child receives can justly be termed a charity; the world owes the child a chance" (Ruess, pers. correspondence to W. H. Slingerland, October, 1911; quoted in Slingerland, 1916; p. 203).

Federal law requires a formal written agreement that constitutes a binding contract between the state and the adoptive parents that ensures the continuity of the subsidy. The agreement must specify the amount of the assistance payment, the types of services or other assistance to be provided to the child and his family, and the duration of the agreement. The agreement must also stipulate that the subsidy will remain in effect if the family leaves the state. Other significant provisions of the agreement should include procedures for recertification of eligibility, the bases and mechanism for future benefit adjustments, and the parents' right to a fair hearing in the event of disagreements with the agency about the subsidy. Every adoptive parent should have a copy of such an agreement in their possession (Segal, 1985). (California passed a law, effective January 1, 1988, that requires that every family involved with special-needs adoption receive a written explanation of the difference between adoption subsidies and foster care benefits.) Yet, the families we interviewed were often confused and even misled by social workers. As many as one-third of the states violate the express intent of the Federal Act by indicating that subsidies are conditional on the continued availability of state or federal funds. This denies adopting families and children financial security. Practitioners should work to see that state subsidy laws are carefully described to families and the barriers of mystification and misrepresentation are destroyed.

POSTPLACEMENT AND POSTLEGAL SERVICES

Professionals in adoption are beginning to stress the need for postlegal as well as postplacement services for adopted children and their families.

Postlegal services would include education, counseling, and crisis intervention (Cole, 1986). The current emphasis of older child adoptions focuses on the recognition that the adopted older child is different than other children (implicit in the "special-needs" distinction) and needs special services. These special needs do not last only during the trial period and magically disappear after legalization. We continue to see families rush to legalization, as described in Holmes (1979), to "strengthen" their adoption. This unhelpful action stems from a misconception that the sense of "permanency" is the most important contributor to a child's welfare. Instead, the sense of permanency follows from a successful adjustment to adoption and the resolution or diminuation of family conflict. Families with high-risk placements need far more than such symbolic gestures. They often need concrete educational and crisis intervention services.

Adoption affects the child and his family all their lives, in some way or another. Adolescence, for example, is a time of heightened awareness and concern about identity, and the need for counseling may be acute during this time. Postlegal counseling services with sensitivity to the developmental tasks of adolescence for the adopted individual and his family are evolving. Counseling and other noncrisis services continue to be primarily aimed at families with children. A recent committee on postlegal services (North American Post-Legal Adoption Committee, 1984) offered this list of methods for the provision of postlegal services: (1) individual and family counseling, (2) intermediary in legal matters, (3) workshops on topics such as transracial and intercountry adoption, (4) support groups, (5) classes, (6) retreats, (7) social events, (8) intermediary in "adoption triad" matters, such as specifics of visitation, (9) professional consultation, (10) information, (11) films and other materials for distribution, and (12) research on evaluation of services as well as other postlegal concerns. Searching for birth families is another key component in those agencies which do provide postlegal services. While laudatory and helpful to facilitate adjustment to adoption, this is only a small part of the spectrum of services needed by families in crisis. Intensive adoption preservation services and respite care must also be expanded.

Postlegalization case reviews may also help preserve adoptions. While the child in foster care usually has a case review every 6 months, the child in an adoptive placement has no further case reviews, and only four required visits from the social worker prior to finalization. Postlegalization contact with the agency is not currently required by law, and thus varies from agency to agency, usually at a minimum amount. The usual reason for a case review in adoption is the threat of disruption, and disruption conferences are highly recommended to promote future success in a subsequent adoptive placement (Fitzgerald, 1983). Disruption conferences are intended to identify the problems and process of the problematic placement, to resolve these problems if possible, and to gather as much information as possible about the child and the placement from all important parties in any case.

Except for home studies prior to placement, intact adoptive families, including the adoptive child, seldom experience such intensive review of the placement as in a disruption conference. If voluntary yearly adoption case reviews were instituted, before and after finalization, the child, family, and agency would be able to share important information prior to a disastrous crisis state. These reviews would need to be voluntary, if the family felt they would be helpful, in order to assure adoptive families that they will not be under scrutiny for the rest of their lives. These reviews might save the agency the costs of returning a child to foster care and subsequent adoption.

Adoption practices are changing fast. Use of the evidence presented in prior chapters and its translation into practice will contribute to social workers' growing commitment to practices informed by research. Assessment of adoption outcomes as a part of routine adoption agency practices could also add immeasurably to this process. Given the increasing availability of computerized placement data and adoption workers' knowledge of most placement outcomes, agencies can assess the outcomes of their own high-risk placements and determine which agency practices increase the odds for a stable adoption. One adoption unit secretary had a log of all the adoptions and disruptions and key placement characteristics organized on dBase III which she could use to generate frequencies or to send data files to SPSS-PC to look at relationships in the data. Agencies can cross-check our conclusions about preplacement preparation, case characteristics, and subsidies against their current practices.

13

Policy and Program Implications

If in some localities child placing (adoption) has been in bad repute, the probability is that the reason may be found in the unsystematic methods employed. The fault is not in the plan itself, but in the imperfect working of it. Poor placing-out gives uncertain, often exceedingly bad results. Good placing-out gives almost uniformly excellent results.

Slingerland, 1916, p. 184.

Whereas the best practices, programs, and policies cannot eliminate disruptions—which are inherent in the necessary risk of older child adoption—they can be minimized. Our findings, along with others, indicate that about 90% of older child adoptions will endure. We would not want to see the disruption rate fall below 10%, although we believe it could be somewhat less with more effective policies and practices. We would rather that more high-risk adoptive placements are made. Even a figure of 20% disruptions would be satisfactory if accompanied by the knowledge that we were providing intensive services and overall, the number of lasting placements increased. The value of stable adoptions is worth the strategic risk of disruption.

RECRUITMENT AND PLACEMENT

Preservation of family life is the accepted goal of child welfare services. Recruitment policies often have the contrary effect of prohibiting lasting family life. Most succinctly, these contrary policies are the continued failure to adequately recruit adoptive homes and to adequately reimburse private adoption agencies for making and maintaining the placements of high-risk children.

This study has said little about the recruitment of families—clearly the most vital part of an effective adoption program. If government was serious about capitalizing on the exceptionally generous in-kind provisions of adopting families shown in Chapter 2, they would offer a flat cash payment of, say, $10,000 to churches, civic organizations, or private agencies that develop placements of high-risk older children. This would double current payments to private placement agencies and provide an additional incentive to other organizations to find homes. (To be sure that the placements were not contrived only for the welfare of the agency or organization they would, of course, require oversight by public child welfare services.) The benefits to the state would far exceed the costs. Whether or not this cash payment seems abhorrent or appealing to any reader, they must recognize that the current rate structure for home finding is grossly inadequate given the value of adoptive homes to children and society.

Speedy efforts to place children while they are young and more able to adapt to an adoptive family's home are the starting point for reducing disruption. Efforts to more quickly terminate parental rights when reunification is improbable, to move children into fost-adopt situations, and to pursue speedier termination of parental rights when reunification is not likely deserves full support and dissemination. Those anachronistic states that require an evidentiary hearing in family or juvenile court to determine that the child should be freed for adoption, and then a separate civil court hearing to terminate parental rights, should abandon this practice. This is virtually triple jeopardy for children. The first jeopardy is that the family court will return them to a situation that is least likely to promote their well-being and allow them to grow unharmed. This is the jeopardy which we condone in our public policy that is so protective of parental rights. If they avoid that jeopardy, the second jeopardy is that the civil court—in its inexperience in these manners—will, after much delay, overturn the family court decision. The third jeopardy is that the child will grow without a plan, without the right to join a family, and without the freedom of permanence.

ORGANIZING POSTPLACEMENT SERVICES

There is a clamor for the development of postplacement and postlegalization services that are up to the task of supporting older child adoptions. The clarion call is for something far more than mandatory visits soon after the adoption. Our agreement with this principle includes a few concerns. First, these postadoption services should not be staffed at the expense of recruitment and home study efforts. We surmise that dollars spent on conventional postplacement services are not as valuable to agencies and families as dollars spent on recruitment. Second, whereas referral to services is often useful, our study suggests that social workers involved with the family should be primarily available to assess the situation and coordinate postplacement services from other providers. We also have concerns about emerging pressures to create special postplacement service units within the adoption unit. The impetus mounts as more workers are involved with foster-adopt cases and their draining legal procedures. As a result, these workers conduct fewer home studies. In some counties, families wait 3 months for a home study. One agency is considering a remedy which includes four adoption subunits. One would be responsible for. recruitment. A second subunit would conduct orientations, home studies, and initial placements. A third unit would pick up the families after the placement and take them through to the postlegal services. Finally, a fourth subunit would be responsible for obtaining needed evidence for the parental right terminations.

We find this seemingly sensible plan unappealing and contraindicated. Our families argued loudly that they were less likely to request assistance from the agency when they lost contact with the worker who did their home study. The home study is a poignant process that builds strong bonds between the workers and family. The organization of services should facilitate a continuous relationship between the family and social worker. In addition, to appropriately study and orient families, adoption workers need to know about the legal delays and challenges that await families. Increasing the number of workers in adoption units is similar to increasing workers in an Internal Revenue Services unit—the returns outweigh the costs. Whether or not such increases are achievable, resources now devoted to routine postplacement visits should be minimized in order to ensure that resources are available for recruitment and home studies. Services should not be further fragmented.

The length of the probationary period between the initiation of the adoption and its legalization deserves rethinking. The trend now is to reduce or waive visits for fost-adopt placements. For that reason and since the average time to disruption was 18 months, the 6-month probationary and service period appears inadequate and unneeded. Postplacement visits should be redistributed. Since disruptions occur well after the first 6 months and often after legalization, the current structure seems ill-suited. Agency resources should be spent on more intensive preplacement preparation or reallocated to provide one intensive postplacement visit or lasting post-adoption services as needed.

DEVELOPMENT OF INTENSIVE ADOPTION PRESERVATION SERVICES

Once placements are made, we typically provide fewer services to adoptive families than we provide to birth families with a lesser chance of providing adequate developmental resources to a special-needs child. Adoptive families are given equivalent statutory rights to birth families, but not equivalent services.

As the ages and troubles of adoptive children rise, so does the need for supportive in- and out-of-home care. According to parents, several disruptions may have been prevented by the use of out-of-home care. A few interviewees indicated that temporary out-of-home care led to significant improvements in the behavior of their suicidal, assaultive, or manic children and their subsequent return home. In some cases, those placements were at a significant financial cost to the agency. For the most part, however, these costs were incurred before legalization and were, therefore, reimbursable by Title IV-E funds. In other cases, counties paid for out-of-home care for children in legalized adoptions with adoption subsidy monies. In at least one case, the agencies assumed responsibility for arranging and paying for those placements. In other cases, agencies paid for placements that were arranged by adoptive parents. More often, families were left to arrange and pay for placements for their children. Families decried the lack of agency commitment to postplacement services.

No families had the benefit of intensive home-based, family-preservation services which have a striking success rate at preventing family breakdown (Sudia, 1986; Pecora, Fraser, Haapala, & Bartlome, 1987). For those families undergoing crisis, such brief interventions reduce the likelihood of alienation that can occur during out-of-home care. The specific presenting problems that precipitated disruptions are those that signal the breakdown of other families, especially, assault, running away, and noncompliance of latency and teenage children. Whereas such intensive services are costly, they can be favorably weighed against the benefits that follow adoption.

We previously considered the value of adoption to the child and family. The costs of disruption to the agency are also substantial. Estimating the savings from making and maintaining an older child adoption is feasible but not easy given the limits of cost-effectiveness analysis. To do such, the projected cost savings of a stable adoption above foster or group care are adjusted by the present value of those savings (to account for other ways the agency could have invested the money) and compared to the net investment. The amount that the cost savings exceed the net invested is the financial value of disruption prevention services to the agency. To capture the probabilities of certain life courses for adopted children who may disrupt, we begin with 2000 such youth. This is about 14% of all the older child adoptions each year. Our findings indicate that at least that number are at high risk of disruption.

Table 13.1. Cost ($) of Conventional Postplacement Services for 2000 Children at Risk of Disruption

Adoption worker time on each placement	2,400,000
Replacement of 720 children in adoptions	
Home study and placement costs (@ $3,748)	2,698,560
6 Months of group care costs (@ $7,500)	5,400,000
Subsidies to 720 continued placements for 8 years	
(@ $3,264 per year)[a]	12,537,677
Subsidies to 400 continued placements for 10 years[a]	
(@ $3,264 per year)	8,022,912
8 Years of specialized foster or group care	
for 880 children (@ $7,500/year)[a]	36,517,800
Total costs of conventional disruption prevention	$67,576,949

[a]Discounted to present values at 10% per year.

Costs of Conventional Services

Conventional child welfare services to prevent disruption witnessed in our study and others seem to have minimal success. Many families fail to contact their agency until the decision to end the placement is past and services are reportedly delivered "too little, too late." Social workers make many visits and phone calls—our disrupting families received an average of 31 contacts—but this is not all that is needed. Social worker time for these contacts must be borrowed from recruitment and home studies.

Given conventional adoption services, about 1500 of the 14,400 adoptive placements each year will disrupt. At least 2000 of these children will be at risk of disruption but many of their families will find an alternative to this action. In some cases, they will call on the agency for assistance. Our findings indicate, however, that families that recovered from the brink of disruption rarely credited conventional social services and referral to therapy as a significant contributor to the stability of their adoption. We estimate that only 20% of families that consider disruption and contact the agency will not later disrupt. Agency costs for these 400 that are averted would include subsidies of $8,016,384 and social worker efforts to stabilize the placements—as workers made an average of 12 face-to-face contacts and 19 phone calls to the highest risk and disrupting families (see Table 13.1). At $70 per face-to-face contact and about $15 per call (which includes salary, administrative, and clerical time) this amounts to $2,400,000. Thus, for stable placements, the additional social service cost is $1,200 per child. Of the 1800 children that disrupt, about 45% will be adopted again. This percentage is one used by Young and Allen in their 1977 work on adoption costs and is consistent with the findings of 61% replacement by Festinger (60%), 50% by Kadushin and Seidl (1971), and 15% in our study. Each of these placements will require home study and placements costs of about $3,748 (according to Young and Allen, 1977). This assumes that there were no additional court costs (although there would often be). Additional subsidies of about $3,264 per year will also be accrued. These disruptions and the 480 replacements will typically occur about 2 years after the placement and include a stint of at least 6 months in residential, group, or specialized foster care at about $7,500 or $3,600,000 for the sample. The cost of the 8 years of subsidies (discounted at 10% per year) for those 480 placements is $8,022,912. [Even though between one-half to two-thirds of these placements will again fail—acording to Donley (1983) and Kagan and Reid (1984)—we have not added these additional costs.] Youth who are not again adopted are likely to reside in specialized foster care or group care at $7,500 per year or $36,517,000. When the total costs are calculated, the expense of conventional services to prevent disruption is $67,576,949.

Intensive Adoption Preservation Services

Let us assume that an agency is committed to the most intensive adoption preservation services needed. Depending on the needs of the case, they can provide a disruption prevention package of 1 month of respite group home care or 1 month of intensive home-based services to stabilize an adoption. Further, we estimate that 2 of 10 such placements will still disrupt despite these efforts. This is a conservative estimate from preliminary reports from Homebuilder's and Oregon Children's Services. In their work with families on the verge of adoption disruption, they project that disruption was prevented in 89 and 88%, respectively, of cases—this is in keeping with their previously described success rates in preserving families at risk of dissolution (Shelley Leavitt, pers. commun., December 21, 1987; William Showell, pers. commun., February 29, 1988).

The cost of intensive adoption preservation services, additional adoption worker services, and adoption subsidies comprise the net investment amount. For the purposes of this illustration, we will assume the most conservative (i.e., expensive) case that the subsidies would have been incurred for the full 10 years (since these are more difficult children with greater needs) until the child would have emancipated from the child welfare system. Savings in foster, group, or residential care and additional agency administrative costs comprise the cost savings. Although we have shown in Chapter 2 that many other benefits would be received by the child that could be added to the cost saving side of the equation, we will not include those in this discussion. This, then, is a comparison of the agency

Table 13.2. Adoption Disruption Costs ($) to Agency and Funding Sources with Intensive Adoption Preservation Services for 2000 Children at Risk of Disruption

Intensive in-home adoption preservation services (@ $2,600 per child)	5,200,000
Adoption worker time on placement	1,400,000
Replacement of 180 children in adoptions	
Home study and placement costs (@ $3,748)	674,640
6-Months of Group Care Costs (@ $7,500)	1,350,000
Subsidies for new placements for 8 years (@ $3,264 per year)	3,250,748
8 Years of specialized foster or group care for 220 children (@ $7,500/year)[a]	9,129,450
Subsidies to 1600 continued placements for 10 years (@ $3,264 per Year)[a]	32,091,648
Total costs of intensive disruption prevention	$53,096,486

[a]Discounted to present value at 10% per year.

costs of services to maintain a high-risk older child adoption vs. the cost of not maintaining the placement (see Table 13.2).

The cost of intensive in-home services if provided by an agency like Homebuilders is roughly $2,600 per family according to 1986 figures. We expect that social workers would make about one-half the number of face-to-face and telephone contacts to arrange these services as would be made with conventional services: that is, $600 per case. The total average 3-month disruption prevention package would total $3,200 per child or $2,000 more per child than conventional services—in the short run. For 2000 children the cost is $5,200,000.

Of the 400 children who disrupt despite intensive intervention, 220 (55%) will not be readopted or will disrupt again. Using an 8-year period for foster or group care at $7,500 per year and a 10% per year discount rate (chosen as the high end of what an agency could yield if the money was otherwise invested), the costs of the 220 children whose placements would disrupt and who would stay in long-term foster or group care is $9,129,450. We assume that 45% (180) of the 400 children who disrupted despite intensive services and who the agency attempted to replace for adoption were, in fact, readopted and that each placement cost $3,748 for a total of $674,640 and subsequent subsidies cost of $3,250,748. For intact placements, the agency will bear 10 years of ongoing costs of adoption subsidies (at $3,264 per year) for 1600 children ($32,091,648); the overall cost is $53,096,486—a $14,506,575 savings from conventional services. (Even though we expect from our study that many families do not keep the subsidy for the full 10 years.)

Table 13.3. Summary of Adoption and Disruption Costs ($) and Benefits (2000 Children)

Total cost of conventional services	67,576,949
Total cost of adoption preservation services	53,070,374
Total agency savings	14,506,575
Total agency savings per child	7,254
Total value of lasting adoption per child	607,612,000
Total child and agency benefits from adoption preservation	622,125,828
Total agency and child benefits per child	311,062

Using intensive adoption preservation services, the average cost to agencies of each special-needs adoptive placement is $20,948, if every adopted child needed intensive services. Long-term foster or group care is a far more expensive solution. If none of these children were adopted, the total cost would be $92,175,000 or $46,088 per child. The costs of conventional adoption services to agencies is $20 million less than the cost if none of these 8 year olds were adopted. Implementation of adoption preservation services would save an additional $13 million. This ignores the additional family benefits to the children whose placements last. Nor do our estimates of agency savings include any additional long-term costs from providing foster care services to a disproportionate number of the children of previous foster children [if the findings of Jones and Moses (1984) are basically true]. Long-term social and economic gains from adoption are not included.

Previous financial analyses have also shown that adoptions are undervalued by policymakers. Young and Allen (1977) demonstrated that the costs and benefits of efforts to place older children have traditionally been misconstrued and undervalued. They conclude that the investment in the home study, placement, and supervision of the adoptions had a payback period of about 1 month. They report that "this period would be acceptable to almost any profit-seeking firm, even for investments with extremely high risks" (p. 255). We expect that this rate of return of 65% per year would also be quite attractive to almost any loan shark.

We recognize that we have not adequately addressed the source of funds for disruption prevention. All of the savings that we have identified as "agency" savings—especially reduced foster care costs—do not really accrue to the agency. The costs of postadoptive services are typically restricted to those covered by Medicaid for families with subsidies. Intensive in-home services and voluntary placements can be covered under Title IV-B, but these monies are capped. Legislation to fund uncapped postlegalization adoption preservation services is needed. Such legalization can accompany (but should take precedence over) other efforts to fund conventional postlegalization counseling services. Services would be paid for under this authorization only if there is imminent risk of disruption. Whereas these services should be supplemented by other postadoption services, the limits on the legislation should clarify its intent and allow evaluation of its effectiveness at preventing disruption.

Given that adoptions provide a nearly total environmental intervention, the value of each dollar spent to make or maintain a placement may comprise one of government's greatest returns. The risks of wounding the spirit and hopes of young people are only a few of the costs of disrupted adoptions or the decision not to try to place a child for adoption. These children are also kept from obtaining a substantial dowry from permanent membership in a family. Agencies incur considerable expense when they fail to make or maintain adoptive placements. Since intensive interventions seem to be effective in preventing disruptions, agencies should see that they nurture family preservation services for use by families at risk of breaking up at every point in their child-serving system. A growing number of agencies have standing arrangements to provide such intensive in-home services to families just entering the child welfare system but have no mechanism for using them to prevent the disruption of existing adoptions. This should be remedied in every agency.

We do not know what effects failed adoptions have on children. The personal significance of the disruption rate is currently impossible to assess. Further, the success of adoptions cannot be evaluated only on the basis of placement stability. While this provides a basis for estimating the quality of the adoption, other indicators of success in child welfare include protection from reabuse, achievement of developmental outcomes, and child satisfaction. The outcomes of adoptions, whether disrupted or not, must be compared to long-term foster care, guardianship, or residential care on these criteria. Fortunately, the evidence suggests that adoptions do have advantages over other permanency planning options and appear worth the calculated risk that they might disrupt (Barth & Berry, 1987).

The financial, personal, and professional commitments of agencies, social workers, and adoptive parents who pursue older child adoptions can be illustrated by the previously introduced notion of differing expectations. The laborers in the field of older child adoptions are the social worker, adoptive parent, and child. They are not just breaking rocks, nor earning a living, but are building a cathedral. Policies should provide more than just a sketch of a building. They must provide the materials that enable the adoption laborers' success.

The study provides important findings about older child adoptions and offers a framework for policymakers and program planners. We now know enough about the characteristics of high-risk placements to develop profiles of youth whose placements are in greatest jeopardy. Our analysis provides some early clues. Agencies can approximate this analysis by rating their placements on the risk factors provided in Chapter 5 and developing risk scores for youth. (These can be done more accurately by using the Child Behavior Checklist.) These scores should not be used as a basis for deciding whether or not a child will be placed, but instead for determining what services result in what outcomes for children in the top and bottom risk quartiles. Researchers can use this strategy with more agencies and continue to develop their picture of how agencies can most effectively support adoptive placements and increase the surprise successes in their adoption case loads.

UNCONVENTIONAL ADOPTIONS

Single-parent and transracial adoptions fared well in our study. Our findings do nothing to contradict the consistent findings that transracial adoptions have outcomes very much like same-race adoptions and are generally successful. Numerous investigators (e.g., Grow & Shapiro, 1972; Shireman & Johnson, 1986; Silverman & Feigelman, 1987; Simon & Alstein, 1987) have suggested that the differences in racial identity between black children in same and transracial adoptions are minimal. Our study did not address this issue, but the evidence of adoption's considerable benefits must be weighed against the unknown implications of undemonstrated identity confusion. It is past time that adoption agencies incorporate these findings in their policies and practices and give transracial adoption a fresh look. The same holds true for single-parent adoptions. The maintenance of these barriers to adoption in the face of evidence to the contrary should not be tolerated. The burden of proof has clearly shifted to the opponents of greater flexibility in racial matching and to those who believe single-parent adoptions should be a last resort. The burden of proof is on those who limit rather than expand children's right to a family.

SUBSIDIES

The benefits of subsidies are evident from our findings. The significant difference in disruption rate between children with special problems and those without does not hold among subsidized children. The higher disruption rate for older than younger children is more profound for unsubsidized children than for subsidized children. The interview substudy also suggests that subsidies mitigate risk. Since children with prior disruptions are at great risk of subsequent disruption, more uniform provision of subsidies seems warranted.

Adoption subsidies should not be limited to the foster care rate, but should be set no higher than the group care rate as older child adoptions have a value much greater than foster care and their stability is a means to prevent the use of group and residential care. Perhaps the subsidy could be divided by general use (up to the foster care rate) and justified use (up to the residential care board rate) according to means testing and specifically documented costs (e.g., for private special education). We should consider potential adoptive families as our allies and expect that they will use the money well. When they were conceived more than a decade ago, adoption subsidies were a risky and refreshing departure from concerns that adoption would become a racket and that subsidies would open the door for the entrance of deceitful and disturbed families. This could not be farther from what has happened. Hage (1987) adopted a three-sibling (4, 6, and 8 years old) group, after previously adopting four children, with the aid of subsidies; she writes: "One thing is certain: without the prospects of a subsidy, we would not have considered adopting the last time. We would have had to change the standard of living of the children we already had in order to meet the expenses of three more children with problems. And we simply would not have done it. We would have lived comfortably with six children instead of extending our resources to cover nine. In all likelihood, Jamie, Jesse, and Amber would have been split up" (pp. 18–19). As Waterman (1987) documents in the *Renewal Factor,* when leadership involves anticipating responsible behavior on the part of employees they typically live up to that respect. Our years of distrust of adoptive families should become part of our chagrined past.

Reforms to make subsidies available to families that adopt special-needs children were passed over the still warm and kicking bodies of legislators who believe that sentiment should be the only consideration in adoption. The notion is that subsidies can facilitate the adoption of special-needs foster children and promote new adoptions. Title IV-E adoption assistance is now provided in all states and state adoption subsidy programs operate in 49. Since the provision of state subsidies is only two decades old and of federal subsidies is only one decade new, policy and practice in this area are formative. The penny wise and dollar foolish approach to subsidies that had been promulgated is not so shortsighted as to do no good, but is unnecessarily onerous to families and agencies. For example, the law insists that "a reasonable but unsuccessful search has been made to place the child with appropriate adoptive parents without providing adoption assistance . . ." [42 USC 673 (c) (2) (B)]. Agencies, concerned about making speedy and culturally consistent placements, and at least generally aware of the value of adoption, do not always pay this requirement of reasonable search great heed. Yet, this requirement can work against the continuity for children when foster parents of small children will only adopt with a subsidy and other families would adopt a child without one.

Still, the attitude that a placement without a subsidy is better than a placement with a subsidy is also held by adoption workers and local and state policy setters. Social workers told us that they "try to wean families off subsidies within a few years." This notion that the award depends on families' "means" rather than on the child's needs in the context of families' resources is also expressed in policy. For example, some states have begun to use fixed schedules of payment levels based principally upon family income. This fails to consider the expenses that are associated with adequate care of children with different needs. Further, this ignores the point that the subsidies are designed to minimize disincentives to adoption and to help children tap into the vast pools of emotional and material resources that adoptive families provide across life's very long haul. Given the value of adoption, reasonable search requirements should be eliminated in future revisions of subsidy law.

There is also little justification for requiring that families receive Title IV-E adoption assitance cash payments for room and board before they are entitled to receive Medicaid. Even though awarding token (e.g., $5.00) subsidies is a way around the law, this is burdensome and deceitful. Some families only need medical subsidies; every family that adopts a special-needs child should have the right to request commencement or increases in IV-E assistance at any time during their adoption. Future law should allow families the flexibility they deserve.

Ironically, the same law that stipulates that adoption is preferable to long-term foster care requires that foster parents should get absolutely no more money and might get less money if they adopt children in their care. One county has a policy that the adoption subsidy will be set at the level of the foster care payment less $20. Agencies have much discretion in determining whether adoptions qualify as special needs and families are eligible for subsidies. Still, at least there is no means test for determining eligibility for a subsidy, although the wealth of the family may be considered when determining the amount received. Evidence from California suggests that there is a strong inverse relationship between family income and the subsidy rate. This is probably due to refusal of subsidies by some families and outlaw of means testing by some agencies. The subsidy is designed to encourage and support adoptions of difficult children, and since there was no obvious relationship between the difficulty of the child and family income, subsidy size should not be related to family income. Also, as many as one-third of the states violate the express intent of the Federal Act by indicating that subsidies are conditional on the continued availability of state or federal funds (Segal, 1985). This denies adopting families and children financial security.

Agency administrators and local and state policy makers can ensure that families understand the availability of adoption assistance. Certainly, adoptive families should know more about this program than those in our study. Wisconsin requires that every prospective adoptive parent be told about subsidies. Information about subsidy amounts should be promptly given— some of our families waited 2–3 months to learn the subsidy amount. Other families should also be informed by a vigorous plan of community outreach (Segal, 1985). At a minimum, every foster family should know about each child eligible for a subsidy. Several states (including New York) have meritorious laws or regulations to require the publication of information about adoption subsidies.

Adoption services to maintain placements should be reimbursed for the life of the adoption. Preservation of many more adoptions can be achieved at a small fraction of the adoption's value. Expenditures on adoptions that ultimately do disrupt are easily absorbed and overall savings accrued from success with those that last. And this cost model is the most skeletal. Our concerns about the sanctity of family life are not added to the model: nor are the benefits that result from the adopting families' lasting investment in adopted children. We estimated that the educational opportunities provided adopted children would translate into an average increase of $208,452 in lifetime earnings over a comparable foster child. The return in taxes at a 25% rate would be about $50,000—a tidy return to the state for their effort to find and keep a forever family. Of course, no multiplier has been used to account for the value of the investment of those dollars in a child's life satisfaction and health nor for lowered social, mental health, and justice costs.

The bulk of evidence on adoption outcomes informs us that older child adoptions far outdo the most heralded and successful of our early intervention programs like Headstart. Adoption is a total intervention. Adoptive families can have a great and lasting influence on children. The success of intensive preschool educational programs like the Perry Preschool Program and Headstart, is in much part attributable to enhanced family involvement (Berreuta-Clement, Schweinhart, Barnett, Epstein, & Werkhart, 1984). Older child adoption exceeds even Headstart on that account.

Arguing—indeed demonstrating in great detail—that adoption is of great value may seem like preaching to the converted. We think not. Many social workers we interviewed or know are not so convinced of adoption's superiority to long-term foster care or guardianship in such a way that they should try to make a compelling case about its value to foster families and children. Consistent with this, California recently modified its laws to give children veto power over an adoption at the age of 10. Whereas good sense always calls for engaging children in choices of placements, the implication of this change is to indicate that adoption is just one of basically equal alternatives and, given this equivalence, even a 10 year old cannot fail to make the right decision. Estimating and developing the lifetime value of adoptions is not child's play.

At an entirely different level, the Reagan Administration proposed to fund the Adoption Opportunities Title of the Child Abuse Prevention and Treatment Act at 28% of the authorized level of 5 million. They failed to recognize that adoption is the ultimate 1980's government program. For a government contribution of a home study subsidy, and intensive postplacement services that tallies only $27,960 for the highest risk children who need intensive services, the family contributes $286,409 and the return in taxes is $50,000. Administration officials might do well to reflect on an observation of a California child welfare administrator 70 years ago: "Each child is born with the right to a home, which is paramount to the parents' right to the child, when they do not provide a fit home. . . . The same money now spent in too many institutions, were it invested in child placing, in sifting through investigation, and in aftercare, would bring to the kind-hearted and generous ten times as much real satisfaction, and to the children and the state ten-fold as much good" (Slingerland, 1916; p. 201).

About 14,400 older child adoptions result in about 1500 disruptions yearly. The average costs of replacement in foster care and subsequent readoption or long-term care costs for a child who disrupts is $36,621. The overall cost of these disruptions to agencies is, then, approximately $55 million per year. The lost value to children is far greater. Adoptive families suffer, too, although we cannot put an economic value on their loss of a loved one and the damage to their belief in the power of caring to make life observably better. Concentration on the economics of adoption may seem unfeeling and crass. Families are established every day with a fitting disregard for the economics of their union. Many survive and flourish. They show that the argument for family strengthening is an argument for love. The government's conventional stance is to stand back and not interfere with love. For families remade through older child adoption, the government must step forward on behalf of families and love. There may be no more worthy step to take.

References

126 Congressional Record §6942, June 13, 1980.

Achenbach, T. (1978). The child behavior profile: I. Boys aged 6–11. *Journal of Consulting and Clinical Psychology*, **46**, 478–488.

Achenbach, T. M. and Edelbrock, C. S. (1981). *Behavioral problems and competencies reported by parents of normal and disturbed children aged four through sixteen*. Monographs of the Society for Research in Child Development. Berkeley, CA: University of California.

Achenbach, T. M. and Edelbrock, C. S. (1983). *Manual for the child behavior checklist and revised child behavior profile*. Burlington, VT: Department of Psychiatry, University of Vermont.

Adler, J. (1981). *Fundamentals of group child care: A textbook and instructional guide for child care workers*. Cambridge, MA: Ballinger.

Alpert, G. P. and Dunham, R. G. (1986). Keeping academically marginal youths in school: A prediction model. *Youth and Society*, **17**, 346–361.

Ashman, A. and Rubenstein, L. (1985). *American Bar Association Journal*, **71**, 116–117.

Bachrach, C. A. (1983). Children in families: Characteristics of biological, step- and adopted children. *Journal of Marriage and the Family*, **45**, 171–179.

Bain, A. (1978). The capacity of families to cope with transitions: A theoretical essay. *Human Relations*, **31**, 675–688.

Baran, A., Pannor, R., and Sarosky, A. (1976). Open adoption. *Social Work*, **21**, 97–100.

Barrett, C. L., Hamp, I. E., and Miller, L. C. (1978). Research on child psychotherapy. *In* S. L. Garfield and A. E. Bergin (Eds.), *Handbook of psychotherapy and behavior change* (2nd ed.) (pp. 411–435). NY: Wiley.

Barth, R. P. (1985). Collaboration between child welfare and school social work services. *Social Work in Education*, **8**, 32–47.

Barth, R. P. (1986a). Emancipation services for adolescents in foster care. *Social Work*, **31**, 165–171.

Barth, R. P. (1986b). *Social and cognitive treatment of children and adolescents*. San Francisco, CA: Jossey-Bass.

Barth, R. P. (1987). Assessment and treatment of stealing. In B. Lahey and A. Kazdin (Eds.), *Advances in clinical child psychology*, Vol. 10 (pp. 137–170). NY: Plenum Press.

Barth, R. P. and Berry, M. (1987). Outcomes of child welfare services since permanency planning. *Social Services Review*, **61**, 71–90.

Barth, R. P. and Berry, M. (1988). Child abuse and child welfare services. In M. Kirst (Ed.), *The conditions of children in California*. Stanford, CA: Policy Analysis for California Education.

Barth, R. P. and Schinke, S. P. (1983). Coping with daily strain among pregnant and parenting adolescents. *Journal of Social Service Research*, **7**, 51–63.

Barth, R. P., Berry, M., Carson, M. L., Goodfield, R., and Feinberg, B. (1986). Contributors to disruption of older-child adoptions. *Child Welfare*, **65**, 359–371.

Barth, R. P., Berry, M., Yoshikami, R., Goodfield, R., and Carson, M. L. (1988). Predicting adoption disruption. *Social Work*, **33**, 227–233.

Bass, C. (1975). Matchmaker-matchmaker: Older child adoption failures. *Child Welfare*, **54**, 505–512.

Bell, V. (1959). Special considerations in the adoption of the older child. *Social Casework*, **40**, 327–334.

Berns v. Pan American World Airways, Inc., 667 F2d 826 (CA9, 1982). Damages for wrongful deaths of mother and father. In J. J. Kennelly (Ed.), *Annual Trial Lawyer's Guide*. Willamette, IL: Callaghan & Co.

Berrueta-Clement, J. R., Schweinhart, L. J., Barnett, W. S., Epstein, A. S., and Weikart, D. P. (1984). *Changed lives: The effects of the Perry preschool program on youths through age 19*. (Monographs of the High/Scope Educational Research Foundation, No. 8). Ypsilanti, MI: High/Scope Press.

Block, N. M. (1981). Toward reducing recidivism in foster care. *Child Welfare*, **60**, 597–610.

Block, N. M. and Libowitz, A. S. (1983). *Recidivism in foster care*. NY: Child Welfare League of America.

Boas, F. (1888). The central Eskimo. *6th Annual Report*, Bureau of Ethnology (#6, 1884–85). Washington, D. C.: U.S. Government Printing Office, pp. 399–669.

Boersdorfer, R. K., Kaser, J. S., and Tremitiere, W. C. (1986). *Guide to local TEAM programs*. York, PA: Tressler-Lutheran Service Associates.

Bohannon, P. (1970). Divorce chains, households of remarriage, and multiple divorces. In P. Bohannon (Ed.), *Divorce and after*. NY: Doubleday.

Bohman, M. and Sigvardsson, S. (1980). Negative social heritage. *Adoption and fostering*, **3**, 25–34.

Bolton, F. G., Laner, R. H., and Gai, D. S. (1981). For better or worse?: Foster parents and foster children in an officially reported child maltreatment population. *Children and Youth Services Review*, **3**, 37–53.

Boneh, C. (1979). Disruptions in adoptive placements: A research study. Massachusetts Department of Public Welfare. Unpublished manuscript.

Borgman, R. (1981). Antecedents and consequences of parental rights termination for abused and neglected children. *Child Welfare*, **60**, 391–403.

Borgman, R. (1982). The consequences of open and closed adoption for older children. *Child Welfare*, **61**, 217–226.

Bowlby, J. (1969). *Attachment and loss. Vol. 1: Attachment.* NY: Basic Books.

Bowlby, J. (1973). *Attachment and loss. Vol. 2: Separation.* NY: Basic Books.

Boyne, J., Denby, L., Kettenring, J. R., and Wheeler, W. (1984). *The shadow of success: A statistical analysis of outcomes of adoptions of hard-to-place children.* Westfield, New Jersey: Spaulding for Children.

Brace, C. L. (1859). *The best method of disposing of our pauper and vagrant children.* NY: Wynkook, Hallenbeck & Thomas.

Brace, C. L. (1872). *The dangerous classes of New York and twenty years among them.* NY: Wynkoop & Hellenbeck.

Branham, E. (1970). One parent adoptions. Children, **17**(3), 103–107.

Breckenridge, S. P. (1934). *The family and the state.* Chicago, IL: University of Chicago.

Brinich, P. M. and Brinich, E. B. (1982). Adoption and adaptation. *The Journal of Nervous and Mental Disease*, **170**, 489–493.

Brodzinsky, D. M. (1987a). Adjustment to adoption: A psychosocial perspective. *Clinical Psychology Review*, **7**, 25–47.

Brodzinsky, D. M. (1987b). Looking at adoption through rose-colored glasses: A critique of Marquis and Detweiler's 'does adoption mean different?' An attributional analysis, *Journal of Personality and Social Psychology*, **52**, 394–398.

Brodzinsky, D. M., Schechter, D. E., Braff, A. M., and Singer, L. M. (1984a). Psychological and academic adjustment in adopted children. *Journal of Consulting and Clinical Psychology*, **52**, 582–590.

Brodzinsky, D. M., Singer, L. M., and Braff, A. M. (1984b). Children's understanding of adoption. *Child Development*, **55**, 869–878.

Brodzinsky, D. M., Schechter, D., and Brodzinsky, A. B. (1986). Children's knowledge of adoption: Developmental changes and implications for adjustment. *In* R. D. Ashmore and D. M. Brodzinsky (Eds.), *Thinking about the family: Views of parents and children.* Hillsdale, NJ: Erlbaum.

Bronfenbrenner, U. (1979). *The ecology of human development: Experiments by nature and design.* Cambridge, MA: Harvard University Press.

Bush, M. A. (1980). Institutions for dependent and neglected children: Therapeutic option of choice of last resort? *American Journal of Orthopsychiatry*, **50**, 239–255.

Bush, M. and Gordon, A. C. (1982). The case for involving children in child welfare decisions. *Social Work*, **27**, 309–314.

CDF (Children's Defense Fund) (1987). Youths without college education face earnings crunch. *CDF Reports*, **9**, 1–4.

Carney, A. (1976). *No more here and there: Adopting the older child.* Chapel Hill, NC: University of North Carolina Press.

Chambers, D. E. (1970). Willingness to adopt atypical children. *Child Welfare*, **49**, 275–279.

Cherlin, A. (1978). Remarriages as an incomplete institution. *American Journal of Sociology*, **84**, 634–650.

Chestang, L. and Hyemann, I. (1976). Preparing older children for adoption. *Public Welfare*, **34**, 35–40.

Child Welfare League of America. (1973). *Standards for adoption Services.* NY: Author.

Child Welfare League of America. (1978). *Adoption guidelines.* NY: Author.

Child Welfare Task Force. (1985). *New beginnings: A report on the fost/opt program of the San Francisco Department of Social Services.* San Francisco, CA: Zellerbach Family Fund.

Children's Home Society of California. (1984). *The changing picture of adoption.* Los Angeles, CA: Author.

Clement, P. F. (1979). Families and foster care: Philadelphia in the late nineteenth century. *Social Service Review*, **53**, 407–420.

Cochran, M. M. and Brassard, J. A. (1979). Child development and personal social networks. *Child Development*, **50**, 601–616.

Cohen, J. (1981). *Adoption breakdown with older children.* Toronto: University of Toronto Faculty of Social work.

Cohen, J. S. (1984). Adoption breakdown with older children. *In* P. Sachdev (Ed.), *Adoption: Current issues and trends.* Toronto: Butterworths.

Cole, D. (1987). The cost of entering the baby chase. *The New York Times*, 9 August, p. 9 (Section 3).

Cole, E. S. (1986). Post-legal adoption services: A time for decision. *Permanency Report*, **4**(1), 1.

Cole, E. S. (1984). Societal influences on adoption. *In* P. Sachdev (Ed.), *Adoption: Current issues and trends.* Toronto: Butterworths.

Cordell, A. S., Nathan, C., and Krymow, V. P. (1985). Group counseling for children adopted at older ages. *Child Welfare*, **64**, 113–124.

Coyle, N. and Lyle, I. (1983). The risks in adoption. *In* D. Powers (Ed.), *Adoption for troubled children: Prevention and repair of adoptive failures through residential treatment* (pp. 17–27). NY: Haworth Press.

Coyne, A. and Brown, M. E. (1986). Agency practices in successful adoption of developmentally disabled children. *Child Welfare*, **65**, 45–62.

Coyne, N. and Lyle, I. (1983). The risks of adoption. *Residential Group Care and Treatment*, **2**, 17–28.

Dalby, J. T., Fox, S. L., and Haslam, R. H. A. (1982). Adoption and foster care rates in pediatric disorders. *Developmental and Behavioral Pediatrics*, **3**, 61–64.

Demchak, T. (1985). Out of foster care; into the streets: Services ordered for homeless youth. *Youth Law News*, **6**(5), 12–15.

Deykin, E. Y., Campbell, L., and Patti, P. (1984). The postadoption experience of surrendering parents. *American Journal of Orthopsychiatry*, **54**, 271–280.

Dodson, D. (1984). Comparative study of state case review systems phase II—Dispositional hearings. *Legal Issues and State Statutory Survey* (Vol. 3). Rockville, MA: Westat and American Bar Association.

Donley, K. S. (1978). The cover story: Helping children explain their placement. Unpublished manuscript. NY: Spaulding for Children.

Donley, K. S. (1983). Further observations on disruption. Presentation at "think-tank" symposium: Adoption disruptions before and after legalization, April, 1983. Cornell University Cooperative Extension, New York.

Dumaret, A. (translated by J. Stewart). (1985). IQ, scholastic performance and behavior of sibs raised in contrasting environments. *Child Psychology*, **26**, 553–580.

Edelbrock, C. and Achenbach, T. M. (1980). A typology of child behavior profile patterns: Distribution and correlates for disturbed children aged 6–16. *Journal of Abnormal Child Psychology*, **8**, 441–470.

Elbow, M. (1986). From caregiving to parenting: Family formation with adopted older children. *Social Work*, **31**, 366–370.

Elbow, M. and Knight, M. (1987). Adoption disruption: Losses, transitions, and tasks. *Social Casework*, **68**, 546–552.

Epenshade, T. J. (1984). *Investing in children: New estimates of parental expenditures*. Washington, D.C.: Urban Institute Press.

Fahlberg, V. (1979). *Attachment and separation*. Dearborn, MI: Michigan Department of Social Services.

Fales, M. J. (1985). Adoption assistance—How well is it working? *Permanency Report*, **3**, 3.

Fanshel, D. (1962). Approaches to measuring adjustment in adoptive parents. *Quantitative approaches to parent selection*. NY: Child Welfare League of America.

Fanshel, D. (1972). *Far from the reservation: The transracial adoption of American Indian children*. Metuchen, NJ: Scarecrow Press.

Fanshel, D. (1982). *On the road to permanency: An expanded data base for service to children in foster care*. NY: Child Welfare League of America, Inc. & Columbia University School of Social work.

Fanshel, D. and Borgatta, E. F. (1965). *Behavioral characteristics of children known to psychiatric outpatient clinics*. NY: Child Welfare League of America.

Fanshel, D. and Shinn, E. B. (1978). *Children in foster care: A longitudinal investigation*. NY: Columbia University Press.

Feigelman, W. and Silverman, A. R. (1979). Preferential adoption: A new mode of family formation. *Social Casework*, **60**, 296–305.

Feigelman, W. and Silverman, A. R. (1983). *Chosen children: New patterns of adoptive relationships*. NY: Praeger.

Feigelman, W. and Silverman, A. R. (1984). The long-term effects of transracial adoption. *Social Service Review*, **58**, 588–602.

Fein, E. and Maluccio, A. (1984a). Permanency planning and adoption. *In* P. Sachdev (Ed.), *Adoption: Current issues and trends*. Toronto: Butterworths.

Fein, E. and Maluccio, A. (1984b). Children leaving foster care: Outcomes of permanency planning. *Child Abuse and Neglect*, **8**, 425–431.

Fein, E., Davies, L. J., and Knight, G. (1979). Placement stability in foster care. *Social Work*, **24**, 156–157.

Fein, E., Maluccio, A. N., Hamilton, J. V., and Ward, D. E. (1983). After foster care: Outcomes of permanent planning for children. *Child Welfare*, **62**, 485–562.

Felner, R. D. (1984). Vulnerability in childhood: A preventive framework for understanding children's efforts to cope with life stress and transitions. *In* M. C. Roberts and L. Peterson (Eds.), *Prevention of problems in childhood*. NY: Wiley.

Festinger, T. (1983). *No one ever asked us*. NY: Columbia University.

Festinger, T. (1986). *Necessary risk: A study of adoptions and disrupted adoptive placements*. Washington, D.C.: Child Welfare League of America.

Figley, C. R. (1983). Catastrophes: An overview of family reactions. *In* C. R. Figley and H. I. McCubbin (Eds.), *Stress and the family, Volume II: Coping with catastrophe*. NY: Brunner/Mazel.

Fitzgerald, J. (1983). *Understanding disruption*. London: British Agencies for Adoption and Fostering.

Fitzgerald, J., Murcer, B., and Murcer, B. (1982). *Building new families through adoption and fostering*. Oxford: Basil Blackwell.

Fitzharris, T. L. (1985). *The foster children of California: Profiles of 10,000 children in residential care*. Sacramento, CA: Children's Services Foundation.

Folks, H. (1894). Family life for dependent children. *In* A. G. Spencer and C. W. Birtwell (Eds.). *The care of dependent, neglected and wayward children*. Baltimore, MD: Johns Hopkins Press.

Folkman, S. (1984). Personal control and stress and coping processes: A theoretical analysis. *Journal of Personality and Social Psychology*, **46**, 839–852.

Folkman, S. and Lazarus, R. S. (1985). If it changes it must be a process: Study of emotion and coping during three stages of a college examination. *Journal of Personality and Social Psychology*, **48**, 150–170.

Funaro, L. K. (1984). "Disruption meetings" can aid permanence. *Permanency Report*, **2**(3), 3.

Gill, M. (1978). Adoption of older children: The problem faced. *Social Casework*, **59**, 272–278.

Gill, M. M. and Amadio, C. M. (1983). Social work and law in a foster care/adoption program. *Child Welfare*, **62**, 455–467.

Gollub, S. L. (1974). A critical look at religious movements in adoption. *Public Welfare, 32,* 23–28.

Goodfield, R. K. and Carson, M. L. (1986). *The Children's Garden attachment model.* Unpublished manuscript. San Rafael, CA.

Goodwin, J., Cauthorne, C. G., and Rada, R. T. (1980). Cinderella syndrome: Children who simulate neglect. *American Journal of Psychiatry, 137,* 1223–1225.

Grabe, P. and Schreiber, C. (N.D.). *A common sense approach to therapy options for families.* Webster, PA: Parents of Adopted Children.

Grow, L. J. and Shapiro, D. (1972). *Black children, white parents: A study of transracial adoption.* NY: Child Welfare League of America.

Groze, V. (1985). Special needs adoption. *Children and Youth Services Review, 8,* 363–373.

Hage, D. (1987). Love those subsidies. *OURS,* March–April, 18–19.

Harrari, T. (1980). *Teenagers exiting from foster family care: A retrospective look.* Unpublished doctoral dissertation, University of California at Berkeley.

Heisterman, C. A. (1935). A summary of legislation on adoption. *Social Service Review, 9,* 269–293.

Hepworth, P. H. (1980). *Foster care and adoption in Canada.* Ottowa: Canadian Council on Social Development.

Holmes, D. (1979). Adopting older children. *Children Today, 8,* 6–9.

Holmes, T. H. and Rahe, R. H. (1967). The social readjustment rating scale. *Journal of Psychosomatic Research, 11,* 213–218.

Hoopes, J. L. (1982). *Prediction in child development: A longitudinal study of adoptive and nonadoptive families.* NY: Child Welfare League.

Hornby, H. C. (1986). Why adoptions disrupt . . . and what agencies can do to prevent it. *Children Today, 15*(4), 7–11.

Howard, J. and Smith, S. (1987). Adoption disruption in Illinois. Presented at the National Association of Social Workers Annual Conference, New Orleans, September 9–11.

Immigration and Naturalization Service, Statistical Analysis Branch. (1987). *Statistical year books.* Washington, D.C.: U. S. Government Printing Office.

Jackson, D. D. (1965a). The study of the family. *Family Process, 4,* 1–20.

Jackson, D. D. (1965b). Family rules: Marital quid pro quo. *Archives of General Psychiatry, 12,* 589–594.

Jacobson, D. S. (1979). Stepfamilies: Myths and realities. *Social Work, 24,* 202–207.

Jarrett, J. M. and Copher, M. W. (1980). Five couples look at adoption. *Children Today, 9,* 12–15.

Jewett, C. (1978). *Adopting the older child.* Harvard, MA: Harvard Common Press.

Johnson, E. S. (1987). Special needs adoption—case summary #9. Tacoma,

WA: Behavioral Sciences Institute, Homebuilders Division, unpublished mimeo.

Jones, M. (1979). Preparing the school age child for adoption. *Child Welfare*, **58**, 27–34.

Jones, M. A. and Moses, B. (1984). *West Virginia's former foster children: Their experience in care and their lives as young adults*. NY: Child Welfare League of America.

Kadushin, A. (1970). *Adopting older children*. NY: Columbia University Press.

Kadushin, A. (1984). Principles, values and assumptions underlying adoption practice. *In* P. Sachdev (Ed.), *Adoption: Current issues and trends*. Toronto: Butterworths.

Kadushin, A. and Seidl, F. W. (1971). Adoption failure: A social work postmortem. *Social Work*, **16**, 32–38.

Kagan, R. M. and Reid, W. J. (1984). Critical factors in the adoption of emotionally disturbed youth. Paper presented at the 61st Annual Meeting of the American Orthopsychiatric Association, Toronto, April.

Kagan, R. M. and Reid, W. J. (1986). Critical factors in the adoption of emotionally disturbed youth. *Child Welfare*, **65**, 63–74.

Katz, L. (1977). Older child adoptive placement: A time of family crisis. *Child Welfare*, **56**, 165–171.

Kenelly, J. J. (Ed.). (1982). *Annual Trial Lawyer's Guide*. Willamette, IL: Callaghan & Co.

Kirgan, D. A. (1983). Meeting children's needs through placement: The placement evaluation program. *Child Welfare*, **63**, 157–166.

Kirgan, D., Goodfield, G., and Campana, E. (1982). *Attachment impairment*. San Rafael, CA: Mimeo.

Kirk, H. D. (1964). *Shared fate: A theory of adoption and mental health*. NY: The Free Press.

Kirk, H. D. (1981). *Adoptive kinship: A modern institution in need of reform*. Toronto: Butterworths.

Kowal, K. A. and Schilling, K. M. (1985). Adoption through the eyes of adult adoptees. *American Journal of Orthopsychiatry*, **55**(3), 354–362.

Kraft, A. D., Palombo, J., Woods, P. K., Mitchell, D., and Schmidt, A. W. (1985). Some theoretical considerations on confidential adoptions. Part I: The birth mother. Part II: The adoptive parent. *Child and Adolescent Social Work*, **2**, 13–21, 69–82.

Kraus, J. (1981). Foster children grown up: Parameters of care and adult delinquency. *Children and Youth Services Review*, **3**, 99–114.

Lahti, J. (1982). A follow-up study of foster children in permanent placements. *Social Service Review*, **56**, 556–571.

Lahti, J., Green, K., Emlen, A., Zadny, J., Clarkson, Q. D., Kuehnel, M., and Casciato, J. M. (1978). *A follow-up study of the Oregon Project*. Portland, OR: Portland State University, Regional Institute for Human Development.

Lamb, M. T. (1905). *The child and God.* Philadelphia, PA: American Baptist Public Society.

Lamphear, V. S. (1985). The impact of maltreatment on children's psychosocial adjustment: A review of the research. *Child Abuse and Neglect,* 9, 251–263.

Lawder, E. A. (1970). Postadoption counseling: A professional obligation. *Child Welfare,* 49, 435–442.

Lawder, E. A., Poulin, J. E., and Andrews, R. G. (1985). *185 foster children five years after placement.* Philadelphia, PA: Children's Aid Society of Pennsylvania.

Lazarus, R. S. and Folkman, S. (1984). *Stress, appraisal and coping.* NY: Springer Publishing Co.

Lee, R. E. and Hull, R. K. (1983). Legal, casework, and ethical issues in "risk adoption." *Child Welfare,* 62, 450–454.

Levitt, E. E. (1971). Research on psychotherapy with children. *In* A. E. Bergin and S. L. Garfield (Eds.), *Handbook of psychotherapy and behavior change* (pp. 474–494). NY: Wiley.

Livingstone, C. (1978). *Why was I adopted?* NY: Child Welfare League of America.

McCubbin, H. I. and Patterson, J. M. (1983). Family transitions: Adaptation to stress. *In* H. I. McCubbin and C. R. Figley (Eds.), *Stress and the family. Volume I: Coping with normative transitions.* NY: Brunner/ Mazel.

McDermott, V. A. (1987). Life planning services: Helping older placed children with their identity. *Child and Adolescent Social Work Journal,* 4, 245–263.

Macfarlane, J. W., Allen, L., and Honzik, M. P. (1954). *Developmental study of the behavior problems of normal children between twenty-one months and fourteen years.* Berkeley, CA: University of California Press.

McInturf, J. W. (1986). Preparing special needs children for adoption through the use of a life book. *Child Welfare,* 65, 373–386.

McRoy, R. G., Zurcher, L. A., Lauderdale, M. L., and Anderson, R. N. (1982). Self-esteem and racial identity in transracial and inracial adoptees. *Social Work,* 27, 522–526.

Maluccio, A. N. and Fein, E. (1983). Permanency planning: A redefinition. *Child Welfare,* 62, 195–201.

Maximus, Inc. (1984). *Child welfare statistical fact book. 1984: Substitute care and adoption.* Washington, D.C.: Office of Human Development Series.

Maza, P. L. (1983). *Characteristics of children free for adoption.* Child Welfare Research Notes #2. Washington, D.C.: Children's Bureau, Administration for Children, Youth and Families.

Maza, P. L. (1984). *Adoption trends: 1944–1975.* Child Welfare Research Notes #9. Washington, D.C.: Children's Bureau, Administration for Children, Youth and Families.

Meezan, W. (1980). *Adoption services in the states*. U.S. Department of Health and Human Services. Washington, D.C.: Author.

Meezan, W. and Shireman, J. F. (1982). Foster parent adoption. A literature review. *Child Welfare*, **61**, 525–535.

Meezan, W. and Shireman, J. F. (1985). *Care and commitment: Foster parent adoption decisions*. NY: State University of New York Press.

Meezan, W., Katz, S., and Russo, E. (1978). *Adoptions without agencies*. NY: The Child Welfare of America.

Menlove, F. L. (1985). Aggressive symptoms in emotionally disturbed adopted children. *Child Development*, **36**, 519–532.

Millar, T. P. (1985). What cherry tree? *Children Today*, **14**, 28–29.

Mississippi State Department of Public Welfare. (1986). *Annual report, FY 1985*. Jackson: Author.

National Association of Black Social Workers. (1972). *Position statement on trans-racial adoption*. NY: Author.

Nelson, K. A. (1985). *On adoption's frontier: A study of special needs adoptive families*. NY: Child Welfare League of America.

Nelson, K. E. (1986). Large boys and little women: The problem of family placement of older children in the nineteenth century. *Children and Youth Services Review*, **8**, 53–70.

Nerlove, E. (1985). *Who is David?* NY: Child Welfare League of America.

New York State Department of Social Services. (1986). *Annual report, 1984, statistical supplement*. New York: Author.

NIMH Staff. (1987). NIMH sponsors conference on psychosocial screening of school-age children in pediatric settings, February. *Focus*, **1**(2), 8.

North American Council on Post-Legal Adoption Committee. (1984). *Model statement on post-legal adoption services*. St. Paul, MN: Author.

Offord, D. R., Aponte, J. F., and Cross, L. A. (1969). Presenting symptomatology of adopted children. *Archives of General Psychiatry*, **20**, 110–116.

Olson, D. H., McCubbin, H. I., Barnes, H. L., Larsen, A. S., Muxen, M. J., and Wilson, M. A. (1983). *Families*. Beverly Hills, CA: Sage.

Organization for United Response, Inc. (1987). Brochure. Minneapolis, MN: Author.

Ostling, E. E. (1986). Loss of parental consortium: Why children should be compensated. *Pacific Law Journal*, **18**, 233–259.

Pannor, R. and Baran, A. (1984). Open adoption as standard practice. *Child Welfare*, **63**, 245–250.

Pardeck, J. T. (1983). *The forgotten children. A study of the stability and continuity of foster care*. Washington, D.C.: University Press of America.

Partridge, S., Hornby, H., and McDonald, T. (1986). *Legacies of loss-visions of gain. An inside look at adoption disruption*. Portland, OR: University of Southern Maine, Center for Research and Advanced Study.

Patterson, G. R. (1982.) *Coercive family process*. Eugene, OR: Castalia.

Patterson, G. R. and Reid, J. B. (1970). Reciprocity and coercion: Two facets of social systems. *In* J. Michaels and C. Nueringer (Eds.), *Behavior modification in clinical psychology* (pp. 133–117). NY: Appleton-Century-Crofts.

Pearlin, L. I. and Schooler, C. (1978). The structure of coping. *Journal of Health and Social Behavior.* **19,** 2–21.

Pecora, P. J., Fraser, M. W., Haapala, D., and Bartlome, J. A. (1987). Defining family preservation services: Three intensive home-based treatment programs (Research report #1). Salt Lake City: Social Research Institute. (Grant #90-CW-0731/01, Office of Human Development Services.)

Pennsylvania Children's Commission. (1925). *Report to the general assembly meeting in 1925.* Scranton, PA: Author.

Peterson, C. D., Peterson, J. L., and Seeto, D. (1983). Developmental changes in ideas about lying. *Child Development,* **54,** 1529–1535.

Policy Analysis for California Education (1986). The Condition of Education in California. Berkeley, CA: Author.

Post-Adoption Center for Education and Research. (1986). *Newsletter.* Walnut Creek, CA: Author.

Powers, D. (1983). Some adverse practices in the adoption of older children. *Residential Group Care and Treatment,* **2,** 137–146.

Proch, K. (1980). *The adopted child comes of age.* London: George, Allen and Unwin.

Proch, K. (1982). Differences between foster care and adoption: Perceptions of adopted foster children and adoptive foster parents. *Child Welfare,* **61,** 259–268.

Proch, K. and Taber, M. A. (1987). Alienated adolescents in foster care. *Social Work Research and Abstracts,* **23,** 9–13.

Raynor, L. (1980). *The adopted child comes of age.* London: George, Allen and Unwin.

Reid, W. J. and Hanrahan, P. (1982). Recent evaluations of social work: Grounds for optimism. *Social Work,* **27,** 328–340.

Reid, W. J., Kagan, R. M., Kaminsky, A., and Helmer, K. (1987). Adoption of older institutionalized youth. *Social Casework,* **68,** 140–149.

Reitnauer, P. D. and Grabe, P. V. (n.d.). *Focusing training for mental health professionals on issues of foster care and adoption.* Mercer, PA: Children's Aid Society of Mercer County.

Rindefleisch, N. and Rabb, J. (1984). How much of a problem is resident mistreatment in child welfare institutions? *Child Abuse and Neglect,* **8,** 33–40.

Rosenberg, E. B. (1980). Therapy with siblings in reorganizing families. *International Journal of Family Therapy,* **2,** 139–150.

Rosenthal, P. A. (1982). Triple jeopardy: Family stresses and subsequent divorce following the adoption of racially and ethnically mixed children. *Journal of Divorce,* **4,** 43–55.

Ruess, C. (1916). Personal correspondence to W. H. Slingerland, Oct. 1911. Quoted in Slingerland, W. H. *Child welfare work in California.* NY: Russell Sage Found.

Russell, A. B. and Trainor, C. M. (1984). *Trends in child abuse and neglect: A national perspective.* Denver, CO: American Humane Association.

Russo, E. M. and Shyne, A. W. (1980). *Coping with disruptive behavior in group care.* NY: Child Welfare League of America.

Rutter, M. (1980). *Changing youth in a changing society.* Cambridge, MA: Harvard University Press.

Ryan, P. (1978). *Training foster parents to handle lying and stealing.* Instructor's manual. (NIMH Grant #5721 MH 13742). Ypsilanti, MI: Eastern Michigan University.

Sack, W. H. and Dale, D. D. (1982). Abuse and deprivation in failed adoption. *Child Abuse and Neglect,* 6, 443–451.

Sandler, I. N. (1979). Social support resources, stress, and maladjustment of poor children. *American Journal of Community Psychology,* 7, 425–440.

Sandler, I.N. and Ramsay, T. B. (1980). Dimensional analysis of children's stressful life events. *American Journal of Community Psychology,* 8, 285–302.

Scarr, S. and Weinberg, R. A. (1976). IQ test performance of black children adopted by white families. *American Psychologist,* 31, 726–739.

Schneider, S. and Rimmer, E. (1984). Adoptive parent's hostility toward their adopted children. *Children and Youth Services Review,* 6, 345–352.

Segal, E. C. (1985). Adoption assistance and the law. *In* E. C. Segal (Ed.), *Adoption of children with special needs: Issues in law and policy* (pp. 127–168). Washington, D.C.: American Bar Association.

Shireman, J. F. and Johnson, P. R. (1986). A longitudinal study of black adoptions: Single parent, transracial, and traditional. *Social Work,* 31, 172–176.

Showell, W. H. (January–February, 1988). Adoptive families use FT well, according to Oregon findings. *Family Therapy News,* p. 4.

Shyne, A. W. and Schroeder, A. G. (1978). *National study of social services to children and their families.* Washington, D.C.: Dept. of Health, Education and Welfare.

Simon, R. J. and Alstein, H. (1987). *Transracial adoptees and their families.* NY: Praeger.

Simpson, E. (1987). *Orphans real and imaginary.* NY: Weidenfeld & Nicholson.

Skolnick, A. (1978). *The intimate environment.* Boston, MA: Little, Brown.

Slingerland, W. H. (1916). *Child welfare work in California.* NY: Russell Sage.

Smith, D. W. and Sherwen, L. N. (1983). *Mothers and their adopted children: The bonding process.* NY: Tiresias Press.

Sorich, L. J. and Siebert, R. (1982). Toward humanizing adoption. *Child Welfare,* 61, 207–216.

Sorosky, A. D., Baran, A., and Pannor, R. (1975). Identity conflict in adoptees. *American Journal of Orthopsychiatry,* 45, 18–27.

Sorosky, A. D., Baran, A., and Pannor, R. (1978). *The adoption triangle—The effects of sealed record on adoptees, birth parents and adoptive parents.* Garden City, NY: Anchor/Doubleday.

Spencer, M. (1985). Meeting the need for comprehensive post-legal adoption services. *Permanency Report*, 3(4), 5.

Spivack, G. and Marcus, J. (1987). Marks and classroom adjustment as early indicators of mental health at age 20. *American Journal of Community Psychology*, **15**, 35–55.

State of Alabama. (1985). *Alabama's vital events for 1983.* Montgomery, AL: Author.

State of Alaska. (1985). *Alaska vital statistics annual report, 1983.* Anchorage, AK: Author.

State of California Auditor General. (1983). *Adoption program needs improvement.* Sacramento, CA: Author.

State of California Department of Social Services. (1978). *Characteristics of relinquishment adoptions in California, July 1970–June 1975.* Sacramento, CA: Author.

State of California Department of Social Services. (1984a). *Characteristics of relinquishment adoptions in California, July 1980–June 1981.* Sacramento, CA: Author.

State of California Department of Social Services. (1984b). *Characteristics of relinquishment adoptions in California, July 1981–June 1982.* Sacramento, CA: Author.

State of California Health and Welfare Agency. (1977). *Aid for adoption of children—Relinquishment adoptions: Public agency placements in California January–December 1975.* Sacramento, CA: Author.

State of California Health and Welfare Agency. (1986). *Adoptions in California: Annual statistical report, July 1985–June 1986.* Sacramento, CA: Author.

State of California Legislative Analyst (1988). *Child welfare services: A review of the effect of the 1982 reforms on abused and neglected children and their families.* Sacramento, CA: Author.

State of California Statistical Services Branch. (1984). *Characteristics of relinquishment adoptions in California, July 1980–June 1981.* Sacramento, CA: Author.

State of California Statistical Services Branch. (1987). Unpublished data.

State of Colorado. (1985). *1982 annual report of vital statistics, Colorado.* Denver, CO: Author.

Stone, N. M. and Stone, S. F. (1983). The prediction of successful foster placement. *Social Casework*, **64**, 11–17.

Sudia, C. (1986). Preventing out-of-home placement of children: The first step to permanency planning. *Children Today*, **15**(6), 4–5.

TenBroeck, E. (1981). Protecting the family: A California act. *Children Today*, **19**(1), 7–11.

Thornberry, T., Moore, M., and Christian, R. L. (1985). The effect of dropping out of high school on subsequent criminal behavior. *Criminology*, **23**, 3–18.

Tizard, B. (1977). *Adoption: A second chance.* NY: Free Press.

Tremitiere, B. (1979). Adoption of children with special needs: The client-centered approach. *Child Welfare*, **58**, 681–685.

Tremitiere, B. T. (1984). *Disruption: A break in commitment.* (Available from Tressler-Lutheran Service Associations, 25 W. Springettsbury Ave., York, PA 17403.)

Unger, C., Dwarshuis, G., and Johnson, E. (1977). *Chaos, madness, and unpredictability . . . Placing the child with ears like Uncle Harry's.* Chelsea, MI: Spaulding for Children.

United States Bureau of the Census. (1984). *What's it worth? Educational background and economic status: Spring 1984.* (Current population reports, Household economic studies, Series P-70, No. 11.) Washington, D.C.: Author.

U.S. Department of Commerce, Bureau of the Census. (1982). *Current population reports.* Series P-20, No. 365, Marital Status and Living Arrangements, March 1980, Table 4.

U.S. Department of Commerce, Bureau of the Census. (1986). *State and metropolitan area data book.* Washington, D.C.: U.S. Government Printing Office.

United States Department of Agriculture. (1986). Updated estimates of cost of raising a child. *Family Economics Review*, pp. 30–31.

United States Department of Health and Human Services. (1980). *Broadening adoption opportunities.* Washington, D.C.: Author.

United States Department of Health and Human Services. (1984). *Report to Congress on Public Law 96–272—The Adoption Assistance and Child Welfare Act of 1980.* Washington, D.C.: Author.

Urban Systems Research and Engineering, Inc. (1985). *Evaluation of state activities with regard to adoption disruption.* Washington, D.C.: Author.

Veroff, J., Kulka, R. A., and Douvan, E. (1981). *Mental health in America: Patterns of help-seeking from 1957 to 1976.* NY: Basic Books.

Waldinger, G. (1982). Subsidized adoption: How paid parents view it. *Social Work*, **27**, 516–521.

Walton, J. (1985). Does the workplace work for waiting children? *Permanency Report*, **3**(4), 6.

Ward, M. (1978). Full house: Adoption of a large sibling group. *Child Welfare*, **57**, 233–241.

Ward, M. (1981). Parental bonding in older-child adoptions. *Child Welfare*, **60**, 24–34.

Waterman, R. H., Jr. (1987). *The renewal factor: How to best get and keep the competitive edge.* NY: Bantam Books.

Weeks, N. B. (1953). *Adoption for school-age children in institutions.* NY: Child Welfare League of America.

Wertlieb, D., Weigel, C., and Feldstein, M. (1987). Measuring children's coping. *American Journal of Orthopsychiatry*, **57**, 548–560.

Westat, Inc. (1986). *Independent living services for youth in substitute care.*
    Washington, D.C.: Department of Health and Human Services.
Witmer, H. L., Herzog, E., Weinstein, E. A., and Sullivan, M. E. (1963).
    Independent adoptions: A follow-up study. NY: Russell Sage Found.
Whitmore, W. H. (1876). *The law of adoption in the United States.* Albany,
    NY: J. Munsell.
Wisconsin General Laws. (1932). (Ter. ed). C210, Sec. 5A.
Wood, L. (1987). Some thoughts on surprise packages. *FAIR,* **17,** 7–8.
Young, D. W. and Allen, B. (1977). Benefit-cost analysis in the social
    services: The example of adoption reimbursement. *Social Service
    Review,* **51,** 249–264.
Youths without college education face earnings crunch. (1987, June). *CDF
    Reports,* pp. 1, 4.
Zelizer, V. A. (1985). *Pricing the priceless child.* NY: Basic Books, Inc.
Zimmerman, R. B. (1982). *Foster care in retrospect.* New Orleans, LA:
    Tulane University.
Zwimpfer, D. M. (1983). Indicators of adoption breakdown. *Social Case-
    work,* **64,** 169–177.

Author Index*

126 Congressional Record, 3, *221*
Achenbach, T. M., 132, 133, 141, 221, *225*
Adler, J., 198, *221*
Allen, B., 212, 214, *235*
Allen, L., 195, *229*
Alpert, G. P., 37, *221*
Alstein, H., 29, 31, 216, *232*
Amadio, C. M., 17, *226*
Andrews, R. G., 26, *229*
Aponte, J. F., 132, *230*
Ashman, A., 35, *221*

Bachrach, C. A., 29, *221*
Bain, A., 45, 61, *221*
Baran, A., 4, 29, 53, 77, 221, 230, *232*
Barnes, H. L., 57, 60, *230*
Barrett, C. L., 191, *221*
Barnett, W. S., 219, *222*
Barth, R. P., 18, 24, 26, 30, 70, 179, 186, 193, 194, 197, 215, *221, 222*
Bartlome, J. A., 210, *231*
Bass, C., 72, 103, 108, *222*
Bell, V., 103, *222*
Berns v. Pan Am., 35, *222*

Berrueta-Clement, J. R., 219, *222*
Berry, M., 18, 24, 70, 186, 215, *222*
Block, N. M., 26, *222*
Boas, F., 4, 5, *222*
Boersdorfer, R. K., 200, *222*
Bohannon, P., 56, *222*
Bohman, M., 30, *222*
Bolton, F. G., 25, *222*
Boneh, C., 25, 26, 34, 71, 72, 75, 94, 163, *223*
Borgatta, E. F., 132, *225*
Borgman, R., 53, 57, 73, 77, 132, 150, *223*
Boyne, J., 34, 70, 71, 72, 75, 163, *223*
Brace, C. L., 5, *223*
Braff, A. M., 28, *223*
Branham, E., 13, *223*
Brassard, J. A., 77, *224*
Breckenridge, S. P., 5, *223*
Brinich, E. B., 28, *223*
Brinich, P. M., 28, *223*
Brodzinsky, D. M., 21, 27, 28, 43, 44, 52, 132, *223*
Bronfenbrenner, U., 77, *223*

*Numbers in italics indicate the page where the complete reference is given.

237

Subject Index

243